BETRAYERS OF THE TRUTH

by
WILLIAM BROAD
and
NICHOLAS WADE

A TOUCHSTONE BOOK
Published by Simon & Schuster, Inc.
NEW YORK

Designed by Irving Perkins Associates

Manufactured in the United States of America

1 3 5 7 9 10 8 6 4 2
5 7 9 10 8 6 4   Pbk

Library of Congress Cataloging in Publication Data

Broad, William, [date].
Betrayers of the truth.

Includes bibliographical references and index.
1. Fraud in science. I. Wade, Nicholas. II. Title.
Q172.5.F7B76   1982   507'.24   82-10583

ISBN 0-671-44769-6
ISBN 0-671-49549-6 Pbk.

We acknowledge with thanks permission to reprint material from the following:

Nicholas Wade, "The Rise and Fall of a Scientific Superstar," *New Scientist,* 24 September 1981, pp. 35–36, © 1981, *New Scientist.*

Morton Hunt, "A Fraud That Shook the World of Science," *New York Times Magazine,* 1 November 1981, pp. 42–75, © 1981, The New York Times Company.

Nicholas Wade, "Discovery of Pulsars: A Graduate Student's Story," *Science* 189, 358–364, 1975; Nicholas Wade, "Thomas S. Kuhn: Revolutionary Theorist of Science," *Science* 197, 143–145, 1977; William J. Broad, "Imbroglio at Yale," *Science* 210, 38–41 and 171–173, 1980; Nicholas Wade, "A Diversion of the Quest for Truth," *Science* 211, 1022–1025, 1981; © 1975, 1977, 1980 and 1981, The American Association for the Advancement of Science.

CONTENTS

PREFACE

This is a book about how science really works. It is an attempt to understand better a system of knowledge that is regarded in Western societies as the ultimate arbiter of truth. We have written it in the belief that the real nature of science is widely misunderstood by both scientists and the public.

According to the conventional wisdom, science is a strictly logical process, objectivity is the essence of the scientist's attitude to his work, and scientific claims are rigorously checked by peer scrutiny and the replication of experiments. From this self-verifying system, error of all sorts is speedily and inexorably cast out.

We began to doubt this view in the course of reporting some of the recent cases in which scientists had been discovered publishing results that were fictitious. At first we examined these episodes of scientific fraud in terms of individual psychology: how could a researcher, committed to discovering the truth, betray the central principle of his profession by publishing false data? We were influenced by the spokesmen for the conventional ideology of science, who invariably stressed the individual nature of the crime. The falsification of data was the product of a deranged mind, they would say; it had been discovered, as was inevitable, by the self-policing mechanisms of science, and there was nothing more to worry about.

As more cases of fraud broke into public view, and whispers were heard of others more quietly disposed of, we wondered if fraud wasn't a quite regular minor feature of the scientific landscape. We noticed, upon closer examination, that the cases failed to conform to the model of science implied by the conventional wisdom. Logic, replication, peer review, objectivity—all had been successfully defied by the scientific forgers, often for extended periods of time. How had they managed to get so far for so long? And if fraud was as surely doomed to failure as the official spokesmen proclaimed, why did so many people try it?

Each case of fraud we studied was a fascinating vignette of human behavior, and often of human tragedy, but we soon came to perceive that a more serious and general issue lay beneath these individual incidents: fraud was a phenomenon which the conventional ideology of science could not properly account for; therefore the ideology itself must be flawed or seriously incomplete.

Since fraud had led us to doubt the conventional ideology, we believed it might also furnish a useful alternative perspective for looking at science. The conventional ideology, in our view, derived from the work of historians, philosophers, and sociologists who had looked at science not for its own sake but from the perspectives of their own disciplines. But, like travelers to a foreign land, these professional observers of science often learned more about themselves than the country they visited.

Fraud, we believe, offers another route to understanding science. Medicine, after all, has derived much useful knowledge about the normal functioning of the body from the study of its pathology. By studying science through its pathology rather than through some preconceived criterion, it is easier to see the process as it is, as distinct from how it ought to be. Cases of fraud provide telling evidence not just about how well the checking systems of science work in practice, but also about the fundamental nature of science—about the scientific method, about the relation of fact to theory, about the motives and attitudes of scientists. This book presents an analysis of what can be seen of science from the perspective of scientific fraud.

Our conclusion, in brief, is that science bears little resemblance to its conventional portrait. We believe that the logical structure discernible in scientific knowledge says nothing about the process by which the structure was built or the mentality of the builders. In the acquisition of new knowledge, scientists are not guided by logic and objectivity alone, but also by such nonrational factors as rhetoric, propaganda, and personal prejudice. Scientists do not depend solely on rational thought, and have no monopoly on it. Science should not be considered the guardian of rationality in society, but merely one major form of its cultural expression.

Parts of this book grew out of articles written by each of us for *Science*, a weekly scientific journal, and *New Scientist* of London. We were greatly assisted by the comments of those who read the book in draft—Karen Arms, Stephen G. Brush, Thomas Callan, Jonathan Cole, Robert C. Eckhardt, Colin Norman, and Leslie Roberts. We also thank those who gave us help and advice, including Philip Boffey, Rosemary Chalk, Eugene Cittadino, Linda Garmon, Jerry Gaston, Norriss Hetherington, A. C. Higgins, Gerald Holton, James Jensen, Peter Matson, Dennis Rawlins, Boyce Rensberger, Hal Sider, and Marcello Truzzi.

William Broad
Nicholas Wade

CHAPTER 1

THE
FLAWED
IDEAL

The young Congressman from Tennessee rapped his gavel, silencing the audience in the stately hearing room. "I cannot avoid the conclusion," he said, "that one reason for the persistence of this type of problem is the reluctance of people high in the science field to take these matters very seriously."

Fraud in scientific research was the problem of concern to Congressman Albert Gore, Jr. As a member of the House Committee on Science and Technology, Gore was troubled by the rash of serious cases that had recently come to light. As chairman of its investigations subcommittee, he was determined to do something about the problem. The hearings he held on March 31–April 1, 1981, marked the first time that Congress had inquired into the issue. Gore and his fellow Congressmen were moved to visible amazement and then anger at the attitudes of the senior scientists they had called as witnesses.

The first was Philip Handler, then president of the National Academy of Sciences and leading spokesman for the scientific community. Instead of opening with the ritual profession of thanks for being asked to appear before the committee, Handler at once announced that it gave him "little pleasure and satisfaction" to testify on the subject of scientific fraud. The problem had been "grossly exaggerated" by the press, he said—as plain a way as any of telling the committee it was wasting its time. Scientific fraud happens rarely, and when it does, Handler declared, "it occurs in a system that operates in an effective, democratic and self-correcting mode" that makes detection inevitable. His under-lying message came over loud and clear: fraud is a nonproblem, the existing mechanisms of science deal with it perfectly ade-quately, and Congress should mind its own business.

Handler's aggressive pitch might have succeeded at other times, but he had misjudged the occasion. Two of the most spectacular recent cases of fraud had occurred at elite institu-tions, Harvard and Yale, and could not be waved away as exag-geration by the press. On a more personal level, Congressmen themselves had been forced into the unpleasant business of self-policing by the recent Abscam bribery case, in which half a dozen members of Congress had been found willing to trade po-litical favors for cash. The scientists' disinclination to bite the bullet, even in their own self-interest as a profession, did not sit well with the members of the House Investigations and Oversight Subcommittee.[1]

The Congressmen also perceived a fact about scientific fraud that the scientists did not seem to have understood: no matter how small the percentage of scientists who might be fakers of data, it required only one case to surface every few months or so for the public credibility of science to be severely damaged. As witness after witness followed Handler's lead in saying that exist-ing scientific mechanisms were coping with the problem, the Con-gressmen became increasingly exasperated. "I was somewhat taken aback by the [witnesses'] chastisement of the committee for being presumptuous enough even to have the hearing at all," Bob Shamansky of Ohio dryly confessed. "What disturbs me in all of this," snapped Robert Walker of Pennsylvania, is that "there seems to be in a lot of the testimony we have heard here today a certain amount of arrogance within the scientific community about this, that we know best, and so therefore, we have asked the questions, and if we don't ask the questions, no one else should."

The Congressmen asked the questions anyway, but at every turn the scientists stonewalled them. Evident in the impasse was some fundamental disjunction of vision: the two sides were see-ing the same situation in totally different ways. The Congressmen saw a fellow group of professionals who apparently preferred to deny a problem existed rather than face up to it. The scientists, confident that their existing self-correction mechanisms made fraud a no-win venture, could not acknowledge it as a problem that might go beyond the mental imbalance of a few individuals.

The implication of the scientists' position was that anyone who tried to fake scientific data must be crazy. Yet their stance was undercut that day by the very rational testimony of John Long, a Harvard medical researcher who had confessed to inventing an experiment.[2] Long was contrite, but also articulate, urbane, and in evident control of himself. He was clearly not irrational. When Long's former boss, the research director of the Massachusetts General Hospital, later told the committee that Long had invented more than just the single experiment he had acknowledged faking, the Congressmen seemed more vexed at the scientists' failure to have resolved the situation than at Long himself. "In one short hour, the subcommittee went from the Olympian heights of a nonproblem to the depths of potential perjury," observed Chairman Albert Gore. "That kind of experience can produce scientific schizophrenia," he added. If any question of mental imbalance were involved, Gore seemed to be saying, it lay in what he called the scientific community's "double attitude" toward fraud.

It was barely a few weeks after Congressman Gore's hearings that yet another major instance of scientific fraud began to unravel, this time in the very heart of the American biomedical establishment, the Harvard Medical School.[3] The newest case seemed designed to exemplify the scientific schizophrenia remarked on by Congressman Gore. The Harvard authorities, confident in the self-policing mechanisms of science, could not see the dimensions of the problem unfolding before their eyes.

The crux of the Harvard case was that Eugene Braunwald, one of the country's leading cardiologists and physician-in-chief for two of Harvard's most prestigious hospitals, held nothing but the highest hopes for his brilliant young protégé, John Roland Darsee. Tall and affable, Darsee worked relentlessly at the cutting edge of cardiovascular research. In two years at Harvard, the young physician published nearly one hundred papers and abstracts, a phenomenal number by any standard, and many of them jointly authored with his mentor, Braunwald. Braunwald, who presided over two separate research laboratories and more than $3 million in funds from the National Institutes of Health (NIH), was considering setting up a separate lab for Darsee at Harvard's Beth Israel Hospital. In the competitive world of Boston biomedical research, a promotion of this kind, at Darsee's early age, would ensure a dazzling career.

Darsee was less highly regarded by the other young researchers in Braunwald's laboratory. Hard though Darsee worked, they could not understand how he did all the research on which his prodigious number of scientific articles was based. Secretly observing him one evening in May 1981, they saw him flagrantly forge the raw data for an experiment that was shortly to be published. Darsee confessed when confronted, but insisted that those were the only data he had ever faked. His colleagues were less inclined to agree. By comparing his actual experiments with what he later wrote up for publication, they decided that much of the work had been created out of whole cloth. "This thing did not come up overnight," one of Darsee's colleagues remarked later; "you suspect it for months." They told Braunwald they believed Darsee was systematically faking his work.

But Braunwald could not believe the troubling event was anything more than an isolated incident. "At the moment we had a brilliant person," he later remarked. "He clearly was one of the most outstanding, or the most outstanding, of the hundred and thirty research fellows I have been privileged to work with. Public disclosure would have ruined him for life." So Darsee was stripped of his Harvard appointment but was allowed to go on working in the laboratory. Other researchers were not told of the faked experiment, nor were any steps taken to inform scientists who might be depending on Darsee's numerous published results that a question mark hung over the whole corpus.

The actions of Harvard officials during the first five months of the affair seem to be predicated on the argument made by Handler at the congressional hearing. Scientific fraud happens rarely, and when it does, "it occurs in a system that operates in an effective, democratic and self-correcting mode" that makes detection inevitable; anyone who tries to fake scientific data, goes this argument, must be crazy. Since Darsee was clearly a rational person with a bright future, Harvard officials could see his admitted fabrication only as an isolated aberration, not as part of a general pattern. The chance of Darsee's cheating after he'd already been caught once, Braunwald said later, was "vanishingly low."

Darsee stayed on in the laboratory, doing research and publishing papers as if everything were just fine. Among the experiments he worked on was a $724,154 project funded by the NIH. For five months everything continued as before. But in October 1981 the Harvard authorities were told by an official at NIH that there were problems with the data which Darsee had submitted. Only then did they begin to realize that a researcher who had forged one experiment might possibly be tempted to fabricate others.

A blue-ribbon committee appointed by the dean of the Harvard Medical School confirmed three months later that the study done for NIH contained "unusual results which are highly suspect." Furthermore, a study undertaken by Darsee with another researcher appeared "to have been manipulated." Darsee denied any improprieties except for the original fakery in May. The blue-ribbon committee, made up largely of senior medical officials, could see little wrong with the way their colleagues at Harvard had handled the affair, although a senior NIH official chided Harvard on national television for the delay in reporting the incident of fraud.[4] As this book goes to press, one year after Darsee had been caught red-handed in fabricating data, the extent of fraud in his published work had still not been assessed and publicly pronounced upon by the Harvard Medical School authorities.

What is the conception of science in which scientists such as those who testified before the Gore committee put so much faith that they sometimes choose to believe it over even the starkest evidence to the contrary? The conventional conception of science exerts a powerful fascination because it is based on a highly attractive set of ideals about how science should work. It can accurately be described as an ideology, and it would not be so universally subscribed to by scientists did it not, in fact, contain much that is true about science.

The conventional ideology of science can be summarized under three headings: the cognitive structure of science; the verifiability of scientific claims; and the peer review process.

(i) THE COGNITIVE STRUCTURE OF SCIENCE

Scientific knowledge is organized in a hierarchical system, referred to by philosophers as the "cognitive structure" of science. First there are facts, such as a botanist may collect in observing the offspring of plant-breeding experiments, or a physicist in measuring the properties of subatomic particles. From the facts, a scientist will try to formulate a guess, or hypothesis, that explains some particular feature of the facts. The hypothesis must be tested by experiment, and preferably by one that will give a clear-cut corroboration or disproof. The back-and-forth procedure between hypothesis and experiment—getting an idea and testing it out—is a major part of what is known as the scientific method.

When a hypothesis has been confirmed a sufficient number of times, it may take on the character of a law, such as the law of gravity or the laws of Mendelian genetics. Laws are valued principles in science because they predict and account for large bodies of facts. They describe important regularities in nature. But they don't necessarily explain the facts they describe. The law that chemicals combine with each other in fixed proportions doesn't explain why this is the case but simply states the regularity. For explanations, it is necessary to go to the deeper-level structures called theories.

A theory in science has a much more solemn meaning than in everyday language. A theory makes sense of and explains a vast body of scientific knowledge, including both laws and the facts dependent on the laws. The theory is of course supported by the facts and laws it explains, but at the same time it often contains elements for which there is no immediate proof. These elements, or inferred entities, are usually a critical working part of the theory, despite their unverified status. The atomic theory of matter explains Dalton's law of fixed proportions, but at the time the theory was formulated and for long afterward, there was no direct evidence for the existence of atoms. Genes were first posited in theories about genetics long before their physical nature was discovered. The theory of evolution is another example of a theory highly valued by scientists because of its enormous explanatory power, but which lies in a sense too deep to be directly proved or disproved.

The cognitive structure of science extends from the plethora of observable facts, to the underlying laws which account for them, to the theories which explain the laws. An important feature of the structure is its flexibility. The laws can be changed or modified in the light of new facts, and the theories are liable to be toppled by revolutions in thought that replace them with better and usually more comprehensive theories. The structure of scientific knowledge is constantly expanding. It grows by generating new hypotheses, or predictions from theory, and exploring for new facts to bring into the domain of its explanatory systems.

(ii) THE VERIFIABILITY OF SCIENTIFIC CLAIMS

Science is a public activity, conducted by a community of scholars who probe and verify each other's work. A scientist must pass a series of tests which begin when he applies through the "peer review system" (described below) for funds to conduct a research program. He must publish the results of his research in a scientific journal, but before publication his article is sent out by the journal editor to scientific reviewers, known as referees. The referees advise the editor as to whether the work is new, whether it properly acknowledges the other researchers on whose results it depends, and most importantly, whether the right methods have been used in conducting the experiment and the right arguments in discussing the results.

A scientific claim has thus passed through two checks for reliability before it is published. Once in the open scientific literature, it is subject to a third and more exacting test, that of replication. A scientist who claims a new discovery must do so in such a way that others can verify the claim. Thus in describing an experiment a researcher will list the type of equipment used and the procedure followed, much like a chef's recipe. The more important the new discovery, the sooner will other researchers try to replicate it in their own laboratories.

Scientific knowledge thus differs from other forms of knowledge because it is verifiable. It is produced by a community of scholars who constantly check each other's work, weeding out the unreliable, building on the corroborated results. Science is a community of scholars engaged in the production of certifiable knowledge.

(iii) THE PEER REVIEW PROCESS

Most university science is funded by the federal government, the dominant patron of basic research. The government sets the overall amount of funds to spend in each area, but it is committees of scientists who decide which of their colleagues should receive the money. The committees, which are advisory to government agencies, constitute the "peer review system." Consisting of fellow experts in the field, they judge the merit of detailed grant applications submitted by their colleagues. By the decisions of the peer review committees, funds are channeled to those with the best ideas and the clearest evidence of ability to carry them out.

This is the complex of ideas and values that constitutes the prevailing ideology of science. It is the way science should, and does in part, work. Scientists are by and large so powerfully wedded to this ideology that they find it hard to see significance in any deviations from it. Yet the ideology is an imperfect description of how science works in practice. It derives from the studies of science undertaken particularly by philosophers, but also by historians and sociologists. These specialists have seen reflected in science the features and ideals of special interest to their own disciplines and have quite studiously ignored all others. Simply put, the philosophers have written solely about the logic of science, the sociologists have been interested only in the "norms" of scientific behavior, and the historians for the most part have been concerned to demonstrate the progress of science and the heartening triumph of rationality over superstition.

The conventional ideology of science is a composite picture

drawn from the findings of all three disciplines. But since each has described science from its own special perspective and ideals, the composite picture is, not surprisingly, a somewhat incomplete and idealistic representation. That is why there is no room in the picture for scientific fraud, or indeed for many other important aspects of the scientific process.

Where the conventional ideology goes most seriously astray is in its focusing on the process of science instead of on the motives and needs of scientists. Scientists are not different from other people. In donning the white coat at the laboratory door, they do not step aside from the passions, ambitions, and failings that animate those in other walks of life. Modern science is a career. Its stepping-stones are published articles in the scientific literature. To be successful, a researcher must get as many articles published as possible, secure government grants, build up a laboratory and the resources to hire graduate students, increase the production of published papers, strive to be awarded a tenured post at a university, write articles that may come to the notice of committees that award scientific prizes, gain election to the National Academy of Sciences, and hope one day to win an invitation to Stockholm.

Not only do careerist pressures exist in contemporary science, but the system rewards the appearance of success as well as genuine achievement. Universities may award tenure simply on the quantity of a researcher's publications, without considering their quality. A laboratory chief who has skillful younger scientists working for him will be rewarded for their efforts as if they were his own. Such misallocations of credit may not be common, but they are common enough to encourage a certain evident cynicism.

It is in the climate of cynicism that a scientist's mind may first turn to considering the previously unthinkable: that of embellishing the research results he reports. Fraud in science is of course the abnegation of a researcher's fundamental purpose, the search for truth. It is thus an act of considerable moment, and one that is unlikely to be taken without careful consideration of the prevailing attitudes and mores in the laboratory, as well as of the chances of getting caught.

The term "scientific fraud" is often assumed to mean the wholesale invention of data. But this is almost certainly the rarest kind of fabrication. Those who falsify scientific data probably start and succeed with the much lesser crime of improving upon existing results. Minor and seemingly trivial instances of data manipulation—such as making results appear just a little crisper or more definitive than they really are, or selecting just the "best" data for publication and ignoring those that don't fit the case—are probably far from unusual in science. But there is only a difference in degree between "cooking" the data and inventing a whole experiment out of thin air.

A continuous spectrum can be drawn from the major and minor acts of fabrication to self-deception, a phenomenon of considerable importance in all branches of science. Fraud, of course, is deliberate and self-deception unwitting, but there is probably a class of behavior in between where the subject's motives are ambiguous even to himself. Cases of self-deception are included in this book because they pose exactly the same test to the self-policing mechanisms of science as errors committed deliberately.

Science is considered here as a unity, in other words with no formal distinction made between its different disciplines. We doubt that there are serious differences among the ways that physicists, biologists, or sociologists go about their work. All are following the scientific method and share the same goals; only the substance of their concerns is different. The study of fraud sheds light on how all scientists behave; nevertheless, its incidence appears to be somewhat less in the "hard" sciences, i.e., those such as physics, which have a high mathematical content. The tight logical structure of mathematics virtually precludes falsification, so that highly mathematized sciences possess a certain built-in protection against fraud. In the spectrum that runs from hard sciences to soft sciences, from physics to sociology, the center is probably occupied by biology, a discipline in which fraud is by no means rare. Biology and medicine are also the disciplines in which fraud is likely to affect the public welfare most directly.

What is it about the structure of science that makes fraud possible? What features in the sociology of science make fraud tempting and often profitable? How can a person who has under-gone the lengthy training to become a scientist even consider faking data? The answers to questions such as these suggest a picture of science considerably different from that of the conventional ideology.

CHAPTER 2

DECEIT
IN
HISTORY

"Through experimental science we have been able to learn all these facts about the natural world, triumphing over darkness and ignorance to classify the stars and to estimate their masses, composition, distances, and velocities; to classify living species and to unravel their genetic relations. . . . These great accomplishments of experimental science were achieved by men . . . [who] had in common only a few things: they were honest and actually made the observations they recorded, and they published the results of their work in a form permitting others to duplicate the experiment or observation."

So says *The Berkeley Physics Course,* an influential text that has been used across the United States to impress college students with both the substance and the tradition of modern physics.[1] As with nonscientific systems of belief, however, the elements insisted on most strongly are often those with the least factual reliability. The great scientists of the past were not all so honest and they did not always obtain the experimental results they reported.

• Claudius Ptolemy, known as "the greatest astronomer of antiquity," did most of his observing not at night on the coast of Egypt but during the day, in the great library at Alexandria, where he appropriated the work of a Greek astronomer and proceeded to call it his own.

- Galileo Galilei is often hailed as the founder of modern scientific method because of his insistence that experiment, not the works of Aristotle, should be the arbiter of truth. But colleagues of the seventeenth-century Italian physicist had difficulty reproducing his results and doubted he did certain experiments.
- Isaac Newton, the boy genius who formulated the laws of gravitation, relied in his magnum opus on an unseemly fudge factor in order to make the predictive power of his work seem much greater than it was.
- John Dalton, the great nineteenth-century chemist who discovered the laws of chemical combination and proved the existence of different types of atoms, published elegant results that no present-day chemist has been able to repeat.
- Gregor Mendel, the Austrian monk who founded the science of genetics, published papers on his work with peas in which the statistics are too good to be true.
- The American physicist Robert Millikan won the Nobel prize for being the first to measure the electric charge of an electron. But Millikan extensively misrepresented his work in order to make his experimental results seem more convincing than was in fact the case.

Experimental science is founded on a paradox. It purports to make objectively ascertainable fact the criterion of truth. But what gives science its intellectual delight is not dull facts but the ideas and theories that make sense of the facts. When textbooks appeal to the primacy of fact, there is an element of rhetoric in the argument. Finding facts in actuality is less rewarded than developing a theory or law that explains the facts, and herein lies an enticement. In making sense out of the unruly substance of nature, and in trying to get there first, a scientist is sometimes tempted to play fast and loose with the facts in order to make a theory look more compelling than it really is.

It is difficult for a nonscientist to appreciate the overriding importance to the researcher of priority of discovery. Credit in science goes only for originality, for being the first to discover something. With rare exceptions, there are no rewards for being second. Discovery without priority is a bitter fruit. In the clash of rival claims and competing theories, a scientist often takes active measures to ensure that his ideas are noticed, and that it is under his name that a new finding is recognized.

The desire to win credit, to gain the respect of one's peers, is a powerful motive for almost all scientists. From the earliest days of science, the thirst for recognition has brought with it the temptation to "improve" a little on the truth, or even to invent data out of whole cloth, in order to make a theory prevail.

Claudius Ptolemy, who lived during the second century A.D. in Alexandria, Egypt, was one of the most influential scientists in history. His synthesis of early astronomical ideas resulted in a system for predicting the positions of the planets. The central assumption of the Ptolemaic system was that the earth was at rest and that the sun and other planets revolved around it in essentially circular orbits.

For nearly 1,500 years, far longer than Newton or Einstein have held sway, Ptolemy's ideas shaped man's view of the structure of the universe. The Ptolemaic system prevailed without challenge throughout the Dark Ages, from the early years of the Roman empire until the late Renaissance. Arab philosophers, the guardians of Greek science during the Middle Ages, dubbed Ptolemy's writing the *Almagest,* from the Greek word for "greatest." He came to be regarded as the preeminent astronomer of the ancient world. It was not until Copernicus in 1543 put the sun instead of the earth at the center of the planetary system that Ptolemy's 1,500-year reign as the king of astronomers began to come to an end. Yet this titan of the heavens had feet of clay.

In the nineteenth century, astronomers re-examining Ptolemy's original data began to notice some curious features. Back calculations from the present-day position of the planets showed that many of Ptolemy's observations were wrong. The errors were gross even by the standards of ancient astronomy. Dennis Rawlins, an astronomer at the University of California, San Diego, believes from internal evidence that Ptolemy did not make the observations himself, as he claims to have done, but lifted them wholesale from the work of an earlier astronomer, Hipparchus of Rhodes, who compiled one of the best star catalogs of ancient times.

The island of Rhodes, where Hipparchus made his observations, is five degrees of latitude north of Alexandria. Naturally there is a five-degree band of southern stars that can be seen from Alexandria but not from Rhodes. Not one of the 1,025 stars listed in Ptolemy's catalog comes from this five-degree band. Also, every example given in the *Almagest* of how to work out spherical astronomy problems is given for a latitude the same as that of Rhodes. "If one didn't know better," says Rawlins in an ironic comment, "one might suspect (as did even Theon of Alexandria, Ptolemy's most placid, tireless admirer in the 4th century) that Ptolemy took the examples from Hipparchus."[2]

Not only questions of theft hang over the head of antiquity's great astronomer. Ptolemy is also accused of a more modern scientific crime—that of having derived the data that he cites to support his theory from the theory itself instead of from nature. His chief accuser is Robert Newton, a member of the applied physics laboratory at Johns Hopkins University. In his book, *The Crime of Claudius Ptolemy*, Newton has assiduously collected scores of instances in which Ptolemy's reported result is almost identical with what the Alexandrian sage wanted to prove and greatly different from what he should have observed.[3] A striking example is that Ptolemy claimed he had observed an autumnal equinox at 2 P.M. on September 25, A.D. 132. He stressed that he had measured the phenomenon "with the greatest care." But, says Newton, back calculation from modern tables shows that an observer in Alexandria should have seen the equinox at 9:54 A.M. on September 24, more than a day earlier.

In giving his date for the equinox, Ptolemy was trying to show the accuracy of the length of the year as determined by Hipparchus. Hipparchus too had measured an autumnal equinox, 278 years earlier, on September 27, 146 B.C. Newton shows that if 278 times Hipparchus' estimate of a year (which is excellent but not quite right) is added to the Hipparchus equinox, then the time arrived at is within minutes of the time reported by Ptolemy. In other words, Ptolemy must have worked backward from the result he was trying to prove instead of making an independent observation.

Defenders of Ptolemy, such as historian Owen Gingerich, claim that modern scholars are being unfair in applying contemporary standards of scientific procedure to Ptolemy. Yet even Gingerich, who calls Ptolemy "the greatest astronomer of antiquity," concedes that the *Almagest* contains "some remarkably fishy numbers."[4] But he insists that Ptolemy chose merely to publish the data that best supported his theories and was innocent of any intent to deceive. Whatever Ptolemy's intent, his borrowing of Hipparchus' work won him nearly two millennia of glory before being detected.

The feature that supposedly distinguishes science from other kinds of knowledge is its reliance on empirical evidence, on testing ideas against the facts in nature. But Ptolemy was not the only scientist to neglect an observer's duties; even Galileo, a founding father of modern empiricism, is suspected of reporting experiments that could not have been performed with the results he claims.

Galileo Galilei is perhaps best remembered as the patient investigator who dropped stones from the Leaning Tower of Pisa. The story is probably apocryphal but it captures the quality that allegedly set Galileo apart from his medieval contemporaries—his inclination to search for answers in nature, not in the works of Aristotle. Galileo was persecuted by the Church for his defense of the Copernican theory and his trial is held up by today's scientific textbooks as a heroic object lesson in the battle of reason against superstition. Such textbooks naturally tend to stress Galileo's empiricism, in contrast to his opponents' dogmatism. "After Galileo," says one, "the ultimate proof of a theory would be the evidence of the real world."[5] The textbook approvingly cites how Galileo painstakingly tested his theory of falling bodies by measuring the time it took for a brass ball to roll down a groove in a long board: in "experiments near a hundred times repeated," Galileo found that the times agreed with his law, with no differences "worth mentioning."

According to historian I. Bernard Cohen, however, Galileo's conclusion "only shows how firmly he had made up his mind beforehand, for the rough conditions of the experiment would never have yielded an exact law. Actually the discrepancies were so great that a contemporary worker, Père Mersenne, could not reproduce the results described by Galileo, and even doubted that he had ever made the experiment."[6] In all likelihood, Galileo was relying not merely on his experimental skill but on his exquisite talents as a propagandist.[7]

Galileo liked to perform "thought experiments," imagining an outcome rather than observing it. In his *Dialogue on the Two Great Systems of the World,* in which Galileo describes the motion of a ball dropped from the mast of a moving ship, the Aristotelian, Simplicio, asks whether Galileo made the experiment himself. "No," Galileo replied, "and I do not need it, as without any experience I can affirm that it is so, because it cannot be otherwise."

The textbooks' portrayal of Galileo as a meticulous experimentalist has been reinforced by scholars. According to one translation of his works, Galileo reportedly said: "There is in nature perhaps nothing older than motion, concerning which the books written by philosophers are neither few nor small. Nevertheless, I have discovered *by experiment* some properties of it which are worth knowing and which have not hitherto been observed or demonstrated."[8] The words "by experiment" do not appear in the original Italian; they have been added by the translator, who evidently had strong feelings on how Galileo should have proceeded.

Unlike the textbook writers, some historians, such as Alexandre Koyré, have seen Galileo as an idealist rather than an experimental physicist; as a man who used argument and rhetoric to persuade others of the truth of his theories.[9] With Galileo, the desire to make his ideas prevail apparently led him to report experiments that could not have been performed exactly as described. Thus an ambiguous attitude toward data was present from the very beginning of Western experimental science. On the one hand, experimental data was upheld as the ultimate arbiter of truth; on the other hand, fact was subordinated to theory when necessary and even, if it didn't fit, distorted. The Renaissance saw the flowering of Western experimental science, but in Galileo, the propensity to manipulate fact was the worm in the bud.

Both sides of this ambiguous attitude to data reached full expression in the work of Isaac Newton. The founder of physics and perhaps the greatest scientist in history, Newton in his *Principia* of 1687 established the goals, methods, and boundaries of modern science. Yet this exemplar of the scientific method was not above bolstering his case with false data when the real results failed to win acceptance for his theories. The *Principia* met with a certain resistance on the Continent, especially in Germany where opposition was fomented by Newton's rival Leibniz, whose system of philosophy was at odds with Newton's theory of universal gravitation. To make the *Principia* more persuasive, Newton in later editions of his work improved the accuracy of certain supporting measurements. According to historian Richard S. Westfall, Newton "adjusted" his calculations on the velocity of sound and on the precession of the equinoxes, and altered the correlation of a variable in his theory of gravitation so that it would agree precisely with theory. In the final edition of his opus, Newton pointed to a precision of better than 1 part in 1,000, boldly claiming accuracies that previously had been observed only in the field of astronomy. The fudge factor, says Westfall, was "manipulated with unparalleled skill by the unsmiling Newton."

The hiatus between lofty principle and low practice could not be more striking. As amazing as it is that a figure of Newton's stature should stoop to falsification, even more surprising is that none of his contemporaries realized the full extent of his fraud. Using his contrived data as a spectacular rhetorical weapon, Newton overwhelmed even the skeptics with the rightness of his ideas. More than 250 years passed before the manipulation was completely revealed. As Westfall comments, "Having proposed exact correlation as the criterion of truth, [Newton] took care to see that exact correlation was presented, whether or not it was properly achieved. Not the least part of the *Principia*'s persuasiveness was its deliberate pretense to a degree of precision quite beyond its legitimate claim. If the *Principia* established the quantitative pattern of modern science, it equally suggested a less sublime truth—that no one can manipulate the fudge factor so effectively as the master mathematician himself."[10]

Newton's willingness to resort to sleight of hand is evident in more than just falsification of data. He used his position as president of the Royal Society, England's premier scientific club, to wage his battle with Leibniz over who first invented calculus. What was shameful about Newton's behavior was the hypocrisy with which he paid lip service to fair procedure but followed the very opposite course.[11] It would be an iniquitous judge "who would admit anyone as a witness in his own cause," announced the preface of a Royal Society report of 1712 which examined the question of priority in calculus. Ostensibly the work of a committee of impartial scientists, the report was a complete vindication of Newton's claims and even accused Leibniz of plagiary. In fact the whole report, sanctimonious preface included, had been written by Newton himself. Historians now believe that Leibniz' invention of calculus was made independently of Newton.

Newton having set the standards, it is perhaps not so surprising to find other scientists using the truth to support their own theories in ways that make a mockery of the scientific method. Historians have raised substantial questions about the experiments of John Dalton, a towering figure in early ninetenth-century chemistry and a founder of the atomic theory of matter. From his belief that each element is composed of its own kind of atoms, Dalton developed his law of simple multiple proportions. The law holds that when two elements form a chemical compound they do so in fixed proportions because the atoms of one element combine with a precise whole number—one, two, or more—of the atoms of the other element. Dalton supplied major evidence for this law from his study of the oxides of nitrogen, stating that oxygen would combine with a given amount of nitrogen only in certain fixed ratios.

Modern inquiry raises considerable doubts about Dalton's data. For one thing, historians are now sure that Dalton first speculated on the law and then made experiments in order to prove it.[12] For another, he seems to have selected his data, publishing only the "best" results, in other words those that supported his theory. His best results are distinctly hard to duplicate. "From my own experiments I am convinced that it is almost impossible to get these simple ratios in mixing nitric oxide and air over water," says historian J. R. Partington.[13]

Scientists' cavalier attitude toward data in the nineteenth century was sufficiently widespread that in 1830 the phenomenon was described in a treatise by Charles Babbage, inventor of a calculating machine that was the forerunner of the computer. In his book *Reflections on the Decline of Science in England,* Babbage even categorized the different types of fraud that were prevalent.[14] "Trimming," he wrote, "consists of clipping off little bits here and there from those observations which differ most in excess from the mean, and in sticking them on to those which are too small." Though not approving of the practice, Babbage found that at times it might be less reprehensible than other types of fraud. "The reason of this is, that the average given by the observations of the trimmer is the same, whether they are trimmed or untrimmed. His object is to gain a reputation for extreme accuracy in making observations; but from respect for truth, or from prudent foresight, he does not distort the position of the fact he gets from nature."

Worse than trimming, in Babbage's view, was what he described as "cooking," a practice known today as selective reporting. "Cooking is an art of various forms," wrote Babbage, "the object of which is to give ordinary observations the appearance and character of those of the highest degree of accuracy. One of its numerous processes is to make multitudes of observations, and out of these to select those only which agree, or very nearly agree. If a hundred observations are made, the cook must be very unlucky if he cannot pick out fifteen or twenty which will do for serving up."

Most pernicious of all, wrote Babbage, is the scientist who pulls numbers out of thin air. "The forger is one who, wishing to acquire a reputation for science, records observations which he has never made. . . . Fortunately instances of the occurrence of forging are rare."

As the number of scientists increased throughout the nineteenth century, new varieties of deception came into being. Out of competitive zeal and the battle for scientific glory grew an altogether novel scientific sin, that of omitting to mention similar work that had preceded the unveiling of a new theory. Because of the importance of originality in science, tradition requires that a scientist acknowledge in his publications those whose work in the field preceded his. The mere absence of such acknowledgment constitutes a claim for originality. But even Charles Darwin, author of the theory of evolution, was accused of failing to give adequate acknowledgment to previous researchers.

According to anthropologist Loren Eiseley, Darwin appropriated the work of Edward Blyth, a little-known British zoologist who wrote on natural selection and evolution in two papers published in 1835 and 1837. Eiseley points to similarities in phrasing, the use of rare words, and the choice of examples. While Darwin in his opus quotes Blyth on a few points, notes Eiseley, he does not cite the papers that deal directly with natural selection, even though it is clear he read them.[15] The thesis has been disputed by paleontologist Stephen J. Gould.[16] But Eiseley is not the only critic of Darwin's acknowledgment practices. He was accused by a contemporary, the acerbic man of letters Samuel Butler, of passing over in silence those who had developed similar ideas. Indeed, when Darwin's *On the Origin of Species* first appeared in 1859, he made little mention of predecessors. Later, in an 1861 "historical sketch" added to the third edition of the *Origin*, he delineated some of the previous work, but still gave few details. Under continued attack, he added to the historical sketch in three subsequent editions. It was still not enough to satisfy all his critics. In 1879, Butler published a book entitled *Evolution Old and New* in which he accused Darwin of slighting the evolutionary speculations of Buffon, Lamarck, and Darwin's own grandfather Erasmus. Remarked Darwin's son Francis: "The affair gave my father much pain, but the warm sympathy of those whose opinions he respected soon helped him to let it pass into well-merited oblivion."[17]

A champion of Darwin's evolutionary cause during the late nineteenth century, Thomas Henry Huxley, made a remark in a letter to a friend that well sums up the complexities in the struggle for recognition.[18] "You have no idea of the intrigues that go on in this blessed world of science. Science is, I fear, no purer than any other region of human activity, though it should be. Merit alone is very little good; it must be backed by tact and knowledge of the world to do very much." Moreover, as Darwin himself admitted, the sheer approbation of his peers was not an irrelevant factor.[19] "I wish I could set less value on the bauble fame, either present or posthumous, than I do, but not, I think, to any extreme degree." Though Eiseley's charges of theft are undoubtedly overstated, it is clear that Darwin was laggard in giving credit to earlier authors of theories of evolution.

More serious than a mere breach of scientific etiquette is the charge raised against that other pillar of modern biology, the Abbé Gregor Mendel. By breeding plants and noting that certain traits were inherited in a discrete fashion, Mendel discovered the existence of what are now called genes. His analysis of inheritance in peas allowed him to identify what he called dominant and recessive characters, and the proportions in which these would be expected to appear in the offspring. The elegance of his insights, culled after many years of tedious experiment, earned Mendel a reputation in the twentieth century as the founder of the science of genetics.

The extreme precision of his data, however, led the eminent statistician Ronald A. Fisher in 1936 to closely examine Mendel's methods.[20] The results were too good. Fisher concluded that something other than hard work must have been involved. "The data of most, if not all, of the experiments have been falsified so as to agree closely with Mendel's expectations," wrote Fisher. He politely concluded that Mendel could not have "adjusted" the outcome himself but must have been "deceived by some assistant who knew too well what was expected." Geneticists who later looked at the problem were not so kind, deciding that Mendel must have selected data in order to make the best case. "The impression that one gets from Mendel's paper itself and from Fisher's study of it," wrote one historian of genetics, "is that Mendel had the theory in mind when he made the experiments. He may even have deduced the rules from a particulate view of heredity which he had reached before beginning work with peas."[21] In 1966 geneticist Sewall Wright, in a brief but often quoted analysis, suggested that Mendel's only fault was an innocent tendency to err in favor of the expected results when making his tallies of peas with different traits: "I am afraid that it must be concluded that he made occasional subconscious errors in favor of expectation," concludes Wright.[22]

Wright's exculpation of the father of modern genetics did not win universal conviction. "Another explanation would be that Mendel performed one or two more experiments and reported only those results that agreed with his expectation," wrote B. L. van der Waerden in 1968. "Such a selection would, of course, produce a bias toward the expected values." But van der Waerden apparently saw nothing wrong with such methods: "I feel many perfectly honest scientists would tend to follow such a procedure. As soon as one has a number of results clearly confirming a new theory, one would publish these results, leaving aside doubtful cases."[23]

Academics may debate the precise nature of Mendel's misdeeds, but horticulturists have long since arrived at a verdict, if the following anonymous comment is anything to go by.[24] Entitled "Peas on Earth," it appeared in a professional journal: "In the beginning there was Mendel, thinking his lonely thoughts alone. And he said: 'Let there be peas,' and there were peas and it was good. And he put the peas in the garden saying unto them 'Increase and multiply, segregate and assort yourselves independently,' and they did and it was good. And now it came to pass that when Mendel gathered up his peas, he divided them into round and wrinkled, and called the round dominant and the wrinkled recessive, and it was good. But now Mendel saw that there were 450 round peas and 102 wrinkled ones; this was not good. For the law stateth that there should be only 3 round for every wrinkled. And Mendel said unto himself 'Gott in Himmel, an enemy has done this, he has sown bad peas in my garden under the cover of night.' And Mendel smote the table in righteous wrath, saying 'Depart from me, you cursed and evil peas, into the outer darkness where thou shalt be devoured by the rats and mice,' and lo it was done and there remained 300 round peas and 100 wrinkled peas, and it was good. It was very, very good. And Mendel published."

The debate over whether Mendel consciously or unwittingly improved upon his results cannot be resolved with certainty because many of his raw data do not exist. With twentieth-century scientists, it is more often possible to compare their published work with the raw material on which it was based. The comparison is necessary because it often reveals serious discrepancies between appearance and reality in the laboratory. As biologist Peter Medawar observes: "It is no use looking to scientific 'papers,' for they not merely conceal but actively misrepresent the reasoning that goes into the work they describe. . . . Only unstudied evidence will do—and that means listening at a keyhole."[25]

Consider the case of Robert A. Millikan, a U.S. physicist who won the Nobel prize in 1923 for determining the electric charge on the electron. He became the most famous American scientist of his day, winning sixteen prizes and twenty honorary degrees before his death in 1953. In addition he was an adviser to Presidents Hoover and Franklin D. Roosevelt, and president of the American Association for the Advancement of Science. A careful study of Millikan's notebooks has brought to light some bizarre procedures in the methods by which Millikan climbed to scientific fame and glory.

As an unknown professor at the University of Chicago, Millikan published his first measurements of e, the electronic charge, in 1910. The measurements, which depended on introducing droplets of liquid into an electric field and noting the strength of field necessary to keep them suspended, were difficult to make and subject to considerable variation. In strict accordance with the ethos that demands full disclosure of data, Millikan used stars to grade the quality of his thirty-eight measurements from "best" to "fair," and noted that he had discarded seven entirely.

The candor did not continue for long. Millikan's rival in measuring electric charge, Felix Ehrenhaft of the University of Vienna, Austria, immediately showed how the variability in Millikan's published measurements in fact supported Ehrenhaft's belief in the existence of subelectrons carrying fractional electronic charges. Battle was joined between Millikan and Ehrenhaft, and the question of subelectrons was discussed around the scientific world by leading physicists such as Max Planck, Albert Einstein, Max Born, and Erwin Schrödinger.

To rebut Ehrenhaft, Millikan published an article in 1913 full of new and more accurate results favoring a single charge for the electron. He emphasized, in italics, that "this is not a selected group of drops but represents all of the drops experimented upon during 60 consecutive days."

On the face of it, Millikan had achieved a brilliant rejoinder to Ehrenhaft and had proved beyond a doubt the correctness of his measure of the electron charge—all through the sheer power of scientific precision. However, a look through Medawar's keyhole shows a quite different situation. Harvard historian Gerald Holton went back to the original notebooks on which Millikan based his 1913 paper and found major gaps in the reporting of data.[26] Despite his specific assurance to the contrary, Millikan had selected only his best data for publication. The raw observations in his notebooks are individually annotated with private comments such as "beauty. publish this surely, beautiful!" and "very low, something wrong." The 58 observations presented in his 1913 article were in fact selected from a total of 140. Even if observations are counted only after February 13, 1912, the date that the first published observation was taken, there are still 49 drops that have been excluded.[27]

Millikan had no need to worry that his deceit would be exposed, for, as Holton notes, the "notebooks belonged to the realm of private science. . . . Therefore he evaluated his data . . . guided both by a theory about the nature of electric charge and by a sense of the quality or weight of the particular run. It is exactly what he had done in his first major paper, before he had learned not to assign stars to data in public."

Across the Atlantic, meanwhile, Ehrenhaft and his colleagues assiduously published readings, good, bad, and indifferent. The picture that emerged from their work did not support the notion of a single, indivisible electronic charge. This view was contrary to prevailing theory at the time and, as Holton notes, "from Ehrenhaft's point of view it was, for just this reason, to be regarded as an exciting opportunity and challenge. In Millikan's terms, on the contrary, such an interpretation of the raw readings would force one to turn one's back on a basic fact of nature—the integral character of e—which clearly beckoned."

For Millikan, the battle ended in a Nobel prize (which also cited his work on the photoelectric effect); for Ehrenhaft, in disillusionment and eventually a broken spirit. But Ehrenhaft, who had the more accurate equipment and made better measurements than Millikan, may yet be vindicated. Physicists at Stanford University using a similar methodology have recently found evidence of a kind of subelectronic charge.[28]

The example of Millikan and the other adepts of science who cut corners in order to make their theories prevail contains some alarming implications. Scientific history by its nature tends to record only the deeds of those few who have successfully contributed to knowledge and to ignore the many failures. If even history's most successful scientists resort to misrepresenting their findings in various ways, how extensive may have been the deceits of those whose work is now rightly forgotten?

History shows that deceit in the annals of science is more common than is often assumed. Those who improved upon their data to make them more persuasive to others doubtless persuaded themselves that they were lying only in order to make the truth prevail. But almost invariably the real motive for the various misrepresentations in the history of research seems to arise less from a concern for truth than from personal ambition and the pursuit, as Darwin put it, of "the bauble fame." Newton wanted to persuade the skeptics of his ideas in France and Germany. Millikan misreported data in order to defeat a rival, not to make his work mirror more perfectly an ideal of scientific precision.

The twentieth century has seen the development of science from a hobby to a career become almost complete. Galileo was supported in grand style by the Duke of Tuscany. Charles Darwin, born into the well-to-do Darwin and Wedgwood clans, never had to worry about making money from his scientific speculations. Gregor Mendel entered the Augustinian monastery in Brno where he was able to pursue his studies in complete freedom from financial worries. In the twentieth century, the cost of buying instruments and hiring technicians has put science almost entirely out of the amateur's reach. The tradition that kept curiosity about nature divorced from the generation of personal income has been left far behind. Almost all scientists nowadays pursue science as a career. Their vocation is also the source of their salary. Whether supported by government or industry, they work within a career structure that offers rewards for tangible, often short-term, success. Few scientists today can leave it to posterity to judge their work; their universities may deny them tenure, and the flow of grants and contracts from the federal government is likely to dry up quite quickly, unless evidence of immediate and continuing success is forthcoming.

If the luminaries of scientific history would on occasion misrepresent their data for the personal vindication of seeing their ideas prevail, the temptations must be all the greater for contemporary scientists. Not only personal justification but also professional rewards depend on winning acceptance for an idea or theory or technique. Often an extra measure of acceptance can be won by minor misrepresentations. "Tidying up" data, making results seem just a little more clear-cut, selecting only the "best" data for publication—all these seemingly excusable adjustments may help toward getting an article published, making a name for oneself, being asked to join a journal's editorial board, securing the next government grant, or winning a prestigious prize.

In short, careerist pressures are intense and unremitting. Many scientists, no doubt, refuse to let their work be distorted by them. Yet for those who do, the rewards for even deceitfully gained success are considerable and the chances of apprehension negligible. The temptations of careerism, and the almost total absence of credible deterrents to those who would cheat the system, are graphically demonstrated in the meteoric career of that uniquely twentieth-century scientist Elias Alsabti.

CHAPTER 3

RISE
OF THE
CAREERISTS

Elias A. K. Alsabti operated at the extreme edge of the U.S. research establishment, publishing stolen work with impunity in seldom-read journals. His goal, like that of many scientists, was to further his career by compiling a long list of published papers, the scientific article being the basic coin of career advancement. In the end, after three years of plagiary, it was his brash manner, his cavalier theft of whole papers word for word, that brought his downfall.[1] An operation more subtle might never have been detected.

The Alsabti affair sheds light not only on the careerist tendencies that pervade the research enterprise but also on many of the basic internal mechanisms of contemporary science. The exploits of Alsabti could never have occurred in a community of scientists where rigorous self-policing was the rule and instant expulsion was the automatic penalty for any form of dishonesty. Even when his methods eventually came to light, fellow researchers were reluctant to make a public issue of his cheating. Alsabti would be allowed to leave quietly, and would find a job in another laboratory where the same process would start over again. It was only after Alsabti's methods were described in a handful of international journals that the career of this Middle Eastern plagiarist came to a halt.

At first glance it appeared that Elias Alsabti, M.B., Ch.B.

(Bachelor of Medicine and Bachelor of Surgery), had everything he wanted out of life except a scientific career. He had money, power, and a quick mind. He claimed he was a blood relation of the Jordanian royal family. To those who worked with him, it seemed Allah had smiled on this twenty-three-year-old physician who had come to the United States in 1977 for a postgraduate medical education, an education paid for by His Royal Highness Crown Prince Hassan, brother of King Hussein of Jordan. In addition to his good fortune, Alsabti worked hard at whatever he did and rose rapidly into the higher reaches of academia. While gaining a Ph.D. in cancer immunology and membership in eleven scientific societies, Alsabti worked at one U.S. institution after another, including the world-renowned M. D. Anderson Hospital and Tumor Institute in Houston, Texas. He published sixty papers. The address listed on many of these papers was the Royal Scientific Society in Amman, Jordan, and Alsabti intimated to a few colleagues in America that on return to Jordan he would be named director of a prestigious cancer institute. In the meantime, he drove to and from work in a yellow Cadillac.

Why did Alsabti choose his unique path of career advancement? "Three things about Alsabti are important to keep in mind," says Giora Mavligit, a Houston professor of medicine with whom Alsabti worked for five months. "He is very smart, very ambitious, and rich as hell. He does not need any money. When you've got all these things together, all you want to do is become famous."

Alsabti was born in Basra, Iraq, a port town about seventy-five miles from the Persian Gulf. At the age of seventeen, in 1971, he entered the Basra Medical College. The Iraqi program in socialized medical education at the time called for six years of schooling, a year of mandatory service in the armed forces, and six years of work in the government health service. By the age of thirty Alsabti would be free to practice medicine on his own in some small Iraqi town. However, the backwater status of the Basra school and the vision of small-time socialized medicine were apparently at odds with Alsabti's search for greater things. In 1975 he approached the government with news that he had invented new tests for detecting certain types of cancer. With little or no investigation of the claims, the Iraqi government, controlled by the

Baath Party, swept Alsabti off to Baghdad, the capital, enrolled him as a fifth-year student in the medical school there, and gave him money to set up a lab and perform further research on his miracle methods of detection. In a politic bow to the party in power, Alsabti named his laboratory the Al-Baath Specific Protein Reference Unit. The government also advertised Alsabti as a conspicuous success of the country's new revolutionary "Baathist" order.

But neither the work in his laboratory nor that on his medical education made much headway. By his sixth year, Alsabti had put aside his studies for a moneymaking scheme that relied on the power of an institution funded by and named after the ruling party. To acquire cancer patients for treatment and to test methods of cancer detection, Alsabti in his role as director of the Al-Baath lab would go around to various factories outside Baghdad and screen workers for cancer. He charged a fee. Alsabti called the alleged test the Bakr Method, after the then president of Iraq, Ahmed Hassan Al-Bakr. However, according to a former Iraqi official familiar with the case, he merely pocketed the money and never did a stroke of clinical or scientific work with the blood samples he had drawn.

It was most unusual in a country with socialized medicine for a government-financed laboratory to be charging for medical tests, and complaints concerning Alsabti soon started to reach the Ministry of Health. Upon inquiry, however, it turned out that his whereabouts were unknown. Finally, the police were called in, but it was too late. By February 1977, Alsabti had fled the country.

On something of a medical odyssey, Alsabti worked his way through the desert in Saudi Arabia and finally ended up in Jordan. The authorities in Amman are quite circumspect about the details of how Alsabti gained their confidence, but it is clear that he made headway very quickly, in part by telling of his "political persecution" in Iraq, which at the time was at odds with Jordan. On the strength of Alsabti's claim to a cancer breakthrough of some sort, the office of His Royal Highness Crown Prince Hassan sent Alsabti to international conferences, gave him access to high officials in Jordan, and allowed him to work in the country's premier medical facility, King Hussein's Medical Center in Amman, the capital. Claiming a degree from the Medical College at Basra, Alsabti worked on a residency and treated cancer patients. But even this coup was not enough. Alsabti wanted to go to the Mecca of cancer research, the United States, and he persuaded the Jordanian government to send him.

"I met Alsabti at an international meeting in Brussels," says microbiologist Herman Friedman, who in 1977 taught at the medical school of Temple University in Philadelphia. "He was a tall guy in a white suit. He came out of the audience, introduced himself as an M.D. from Baghdad and said the Jordanian government was going to give him money to come to America to study for a Ph.D., and he would like to work for me."

Back in the United States, Friedman forgot about Alsabti until the would-be physician, equipped with a tourist visa, unexpectedly showed up in September of 1977, ready to go to work. Alsabti had used Friedman's name while corresponding directly with administrators at Temple. Despite the unexpected arrival, Alsabti was given a job as an unpaid volunteer in Friedman's lab and took graduate courses as a nondegree student pending the submission of his medical credentials. Not that Alsabti's life totally revolved around work. He rented what Friedman calls a "swingers" apartment and started dating one of his lab assistants. Alsabti lasted a month. "One day he came into my office and showed me a paper he was working on—a new vaccine for leukemia in Jordan. He had a hundred and fifty patients he had vaccinated and prevented from dying. The vaccine was a secret, however, and he only followed the patients for six months, whereas leukemia, of course, takes longer than six months to kill. I asked him about the method. He said the technicians did it. When I asked him some serious questions about science, it was clear that he knew nothing at all." Alsabti was soon asked to leave the lab. The chairman of Temple's microbiology department also asked Alsabti to drop his classes after repeated attempts to obtain copies of his medical credentials were unsuccessful. The chairman also wrote to two Jordanian ministries—both of whom had contacted Temple on Alsabti's behalf in the late summer and fall of 1977—and told them of Alsabti's failure. They apologized.

In the meantime, Alsabti moved across town to the laboratory of E. Frederick Wheelock, a microbiologist at the Jefferson Medical College in Philadelphia. Wheelock felt sorry for Alsabti. Here, after all, was a young, bright student of royal Jordanian blood who was having difficulty adjusting to a new country. Wheelock felt Alsabti had not been given a fair chance at Temple. "I tried to befriend him and even got him into a clinical oncology program here," says Wheelock. Alsabti also worked in Wheelock's lab, a kindness for which the authorities in Jordan were glad to pay. On January 31, 1978, Wheelock wrote to the office of the Crown Prince, outlining Alsabti's progress and saying, "I have, at Dr. Alsabti's request, made an estimate of the cost of the research that he will be doing in the forthcoming year. This cost is $10,000, mostly for the purchase and maintenance of mice which serve as the main host system for cancer cells in his experiments."

While at Jefferson, Alsabti got serious about weaving together the strands of his academic illusion. He received membership in several scientific societies. On his application to the American College of Physicians, based in Philadelphia, Alsabti wrote that his goals and interests included advanced "training in the field of oncology" so that he could eventually return to the Middle East and "direct the Jordanian Cancer Society." On the application he also said that he was currently on a postdoctoral fellowship at Jefferson, which was not the case. He had applied to a Ph.D. program at Jefferson, but officials there decided that Alsabti was not a "suitable" candidate. And evidence of his unsuitability was growing. "We found that basically he couldn't do anything at all in the lab," says Russell W. Schaedler, chairman of microbiology at Jefferson. "He didn't know how to inject mice, or how to work the scintillation counter," one researcher noted.

The end came in April 1978, some five months after Alsabti had arrived at Jefferson. Two young researchers said they had proof that Alsabti was making up data. Wheelock called Alsabti into his office, and all four of them talked over the situation. "The evidence was very strong," says Wheelock, "and I told him after the meeting that it was his last day in the lab."

Wheelock did not know it, but when Alsabti left, he took a copy of a completed grant application and the drafts of some manuscripts.

About two years later, long after Alsabti had moved on to other academic pastures, an observant graduate student in Wheelock's lab came across an article by Alsabti in a Czechoslovakian journal that was virtually identical to another Alsabti article published in an obscure U.S. journal. The student also noted that the articles were word-for-word digests of the papers Alsabti had snatched from Wheelock.[2] In a rage, Wheelock fired off a letter to Alsabti, demanding that he publish a letter acknowledging the source of the materials. Otherwise, Wheelock said, he would write prestigious journals and reveal the plagiarism.

Alsabti's reply? "You have made certain allegations," he wrote in a February 8, 1980, handwritten letter, "which are an insult to my integrity. First and foremost, let me take this opportunity to make it clear that I greatly appreciated the time and effort you showed me during my fellowship at your laboratory. This great misunderstanding confuses me as I in no way intended to plagiarize your work. References were made throughout the article crediting you, amongst others, for your individual achievements. Let me remind you that the article in question was a review, which gives the writer the opportunity to collaborate materials from various sources as long as credit is given. There can be no doubt that in this instance, when and if similarity did exist, credit was specifically designated. Certainly if you attempt upon [sic] writing your own letter for publication in a journal, I will be coerced into taking all legal steps to protect my interest." Among the sixty-six references at the end of the plagiarized papers, Wheelock is cited twice.

Events in the following months reveal the hesitancy on the part of many scientists to impugn the behavior or motives of a questionable colleague. Yet the ethos of science is unambiguous on this point: any result known to be false or dishonest in any respect must be retracted, lest other researchers who may be relying on the result be misled and waste time in following a false path. Researchers are sometimes reluctant to publish retractions through fear of looking foolish or damaging their reputations. Remarkable in the Alsabti case was the extraordinary reluctance of the principal gatekeepers of science, the editors of scientific journals, to live up to their clear and binding obligations.

Wheelock wrote to four journals of eminent repute, explaining the plagiarism and warning researchers that the same could happen to them. Letters were sent to *Nature, Science, The Lancet,* and the *Journal of the American Medical Association.* All the journals considered the letter for publication, some after high-level deliberations, but in the end it was almost universally decided that the affair was a personal one between Wheelock and Alsabti. The exception was *The Lancet,* which published the letter on April 12, 1980. "There is a simple way to avoid such episodes in the future," Wheelock noted in the published letter. "Editors of journals, on receiving review articles from individuals who have never published research papers on the subject of the review, should verify the credentials of that individual. This can be done by authenticating personal communications and acknowledgments cited in the article and by requesting reviews of such articles by individuals who are prominently referenced."

Despite the threat of legal action conveyed in Alsabti's handwritten reply, Wheelock never heard from his lawyers.

At the time, there was further evidence of reluctance on the part of editors to take note of unseemly events. Wheelock wrote Ekkehard Grundmann, a cancer researcher on the editorial board of one of the journals in which Alsabti had published, and asked for a retraction to be printed. Wheelock wrote in March 1980 and again in May 1980, but got no reply. When a reporter called Grundmann in West Germany, Grundmann said, "We never print a retraction. It's just not done." Only after the news sections of several journals started an international debate over the Alsabti affair did Grundmann publish a retraction.

But all this is getting ahead of the story. Back in 1978, after Wheelock told Alsabti to leave the lab in Philadelphia, the itinerant academician headed for the institutions of higher education in Texas. But not without a few preparations. Alsabti married the woman from Friedman's lab whom he had dated in Philadelphia, a move that brought not only domestic responsibilities but also the possibility of easier treatment from U.S. immigration officials.

How did Alsabti, with a long trail of deceit behind him, manage to climb into ever higher reaches of the academic establishment? The hesitancy on the part of those in the know to make public their knowledge of Alsabti's deceit was certainly a factor. But there is also Alsabti's flair for the art of persuasion, and his subtle knowledge of things human. "The guy knows the system well," says Giora Mavligit, a professor of medicine at the M. D. Anderson Hospital in Houston who for five months was Alsabti's boss. "He went right to the top—right to the president." In this case, the president was Lee Clark, head of M. D. Anderson. Alsabti showed Clark letters of introduction from Major General David Hanania, the Surgeon General of the Jordanian Armed Forces, letters saying Alsabti was in the United States for post-graduate medical education. In September 1978, Alsabti was assigned to work as a nonpaid volunteer in the lab of Mavligit.

By this time Alsabti was a veritable factory for the production of papers. Each passing month saw another group of Alsabti articles appear in various journals around the world. His method was simplicity itself. He would retype an already published paper, remove the author's name, substitute his own, and send the manuscript off to an obscure journal for publication. His tactics deceived the editors of dozens of scientific journals around the world. Alsabti papers were published in the *Journal of Cancer Research and Clinical Oncology* (U.S.), *Japanese Journal of Experimental Medicine, Neoplasma* (Czechoslovakia), *European Surgical Research* (Switzerland), *Oncology* (Switzerland), *Urologia Internationalis* (Switzerland), *Journal of Clinical Hematology and Oncology* (U.S.), *Tumor Research* (Japan), *Journal of Surgical Oncology* (U.S.), *Gynecologic Oncology* (U.S.), *British Journal of Urology*, and *Japanese Journal of Medical Science and Biology*.

The obscurity of most of the journals ensured that the cases of plagiarism would not be tracked down. The authors whose work was stolen would never read the pirated Alsabti version, and there the matter would rest. However, at M. D. Anderson another demonstrable case of plagiarism took place, an observant author in a distant lab having deduced some of the steps in Alsabti's deceit. In this case, the incident involved a paper[3] that had been sent to a researcher at M. D. Anderson for review prior to publication. What the editor of the journal had not realized was that the researcher, Jeffrey Gottlieb, could not possibly review the paper because he had been dead since July 1975. The manuscript from the *European Journal of Cancer* lay in a mailbox until one day Alsabti picked it up, made a few cosmetic changes, added his name and the names of two fictitious coauthors, Omar Naser

Ghalib and Mohammed Hamid Salem, and then proceeded to mail it off to a small Japanese journal for publication. The *Japanese Journal of Medical Science and Biology* published Alsabti's article before the original article from which it was lifted got into print.

"When I first saw the Japanese paper I went into a depression for about a week," says Daniel Wierda, the actual author of the paper who at the time was a Ph.D. candidate at the University of Kansas. "I didn't know what to do." Since Alsabti's paper had appeared first, Wierda feared that colleagues would think he had pinched his paper from Alsabti. Wierda wrote to the Japanese journal, explaining the circumstances and asking for a retraction. Again, it was only after the Alsabti affair emerged in the international press that a retraction was forthcoming.

Details of this plagiarism show Alsabti's method, and why following his trail through the literature is difficult at best. The text in each paper is nearly identical. But Wierda had entitled his paper "Suppression of Spleen Lymphocyte Mitogenesis in Mice Injected with Platinum Compounds," whereas Alsabti had changed the title to "Effect of Platinum Compounds on Murine Lymphocyte Mitogenesis." It is clear that a computer search based on Alsabti's titles would not necessarily reveal the authors from whom he had lifted material.

Nevertheless, clues to the fraudulent nature of Alsabti's work could have been noted by an observant editor. A computer search of the literature, for instance, could tell a journal editor that Alsabti's numerous coauthors, such as K. A. Saleh and A. S. Talat, never published independent papers but only coauthored with Alsabti, suggesting that they were fictitious. Another clue was the shifting source of the papers. With articles published in 1979 alone, Alsabti's address for reprint requests flits back and forth between the Royal Scientific Society in Jordan, the Al-Baath Specific Protein Reference Unit in Iraq, two residential addresses in the United States and three in England. Alsabti became so cavalier and trusted so completely in the credulity of the editorial review process that at times he did not even bother to be consistent. In a single volume of *Tumor Research,* which is published in Sapporo, Japan, Alsabti had three articles.[4] In the first his affiliation was listed as the Royal Scientific Society, in the second and third, as the Al-Baath Specific Protein Reference Unit. Never used by Alsabti was the address of the institution where he was working, and upon whose letterhead the pirated articles were submitted.

These clues were not enough to alert the worldwide network of scientific journals and editors to the fraudulent nature of Alsabti's process of production. Again, as had been the case in Philadelphia, complete penetration of the façade came about only as the result of observations by a close associate. One day in Houston, Alsabti asked Mavligit to critically review a paper he was working on. Mavligit took the paper home that night, and while reading it, noticed that Alsabti had forgotten to take out some words that clearly indicated it was a grant proposal by Wheelock. Mavligit went to M. D. Anderson President Clark with final confirmation of what he had grown to suspect. In February 1979, Alsabti was asked to leave.

A copy of Alsabti's vita that circulated around Houston in the spring of 1979 is quite impressive. The twenty-four-year-old polymath claimed to have authored forty-three scientific papers, to have graduated with M.B. and Ch.B. degrees from Basra Medical College in 1976, to have received membership in eleven scientific societies, and to have done postdoctoral work in England, Jordan, and the United States. He listed himself as married, and under "citizenship" put "permanent residence USA." On some of his papers published during this period there appeared the magical letters Ph.D.

Where could all this take Alsabti? Armed with a curriculum vitae that now boasted scores of publications, he applied at the Baylor College of Medicine in Houston for several residency programs. He was on the verge of being accepted into the neurosurgery program, but one careful administrator decided to call Mavligit at M. D. Anderson to check up on what seemed to be a wondrous record. "Alsabti knows the system," says Mavligit. "He knows nobody wants to be the first to say, hey, this guy is a fake."

But the record of misrepresentation was starting to catch up with Alsabti. Turned down by Baylor, Alsabti also ran into trouble with the Jordanians. The details of Alsabti's exploits had finally started to trickle into Amman, and Crown Prince Hassan cut off his funds. Alsabti's claims to royal blood were made in conversations and could be brushed aside as mildly eccentric. More annoying to the Jordanians was the fact that Alsabti had published a paper, possibly a pirated paper, in which he claimed as one of his coauthors Major General David Hanania, director of the Jordanian Royal Medical Services and Surgeon General of the Jordanian Armed Forces. The Jordanians say Hanania never worked with Alsabti on any paper.

At this point, in February 1979, Alsabti decided to lay low in Houston and pursue a more mundane path. Still without any kind of diploma, he applied for admission to the American University of the Caribbean (AUC), a last resort for would-be doctors who have been rejected by U.S. medical schools. The school is run by Paul S. Tien, an electrical engineer. Alsabti, rather than going to the school on the Caribbean isle of Montserrat, got a job at a Houston hospital and sent records of his clinical rotations to the administrators of AUC. At Houston's South West Memorial Hospital, Alsabti functioned like any other senior medical student. The hospital employs a number of medical students and has a family practice residency program affiliated with the University of Texas. Officials at the hospital said Alsabti had excellent recommendations and a convincing explanation of his situation. Alsabti told Harold Pruessner, director of medical education, that he had received his medical education in Iraq but had been forced to leave the country as a political refugee before completing the required social service. "We got taken in," Pruessner told a reporter. "But if other people think they wouldn't have, they're wrong."

After about nine months of clinical work, Alsabti in May 1980 flew off to Montserrat to take part in graduation ceremonies at AUC, where he finally received a medical degree.

Little by little, the scope of Alsabti's activity in the art of purloining other people's articles began to dawn on those who had worked with him. In Houston, Mavligit got an irate letter from the editor of a Japanese journal. "I was shocked," the editor wrote, "by the appearance of Dr. Alsabti's article which seems a copy of that by Yoshida et al. . . ." Alsabti had lifted the 1977 article and sent it halfway around the world to the Swiss journal Oncology, where it was published in 1979.[5]

Undaunted by letters he had not seen and unaware that his

reputation was slowly catching up with him, Alsabti kept forging ahead. In June 1980, armed with his AUC diploma and a vita that now boasted close to sixty papers, he was accepted into a medical residency program in Roanoke, Virginia, that was affiliated with the University of Virginia.

But time was running out for the "Jordanian" plagiarist who had worked with such impunity at medical centers all across the United States. A tempest had been brewing among the researchers whose work had been lifted by Alsabti, and the storm was now ready to break. Letters were starting to race back and forth between journals around the world. Wierda, the Ph.D. candidate whose paper had been pirated, wrote to the news sections of several scientific journals, and a slew of articles describing Alsabti's exploits began to appear in print.[6] John C. Bailar III, who was editor of the *Journal of the National Cancer Institute* when Alsabti's activities were reported, described the impact of one of the news articles in this manner: "I read about Alsabti in *Science* on a Sunday night, and I can assure you that I was in the office checking our files at the crack of dawn on Monday. Luckily, we'd rejected the three papers he'd sent us." Despite the media blitz, none of the aggrieved parties was able to track down Alsabti.

Meanwhile, at the University of Virginia in late June, administrators were taken aback by the article in *Science* that outlined the charges leveled by Wierda and Wheelock. This was their star student. Officials suspended Alsabti's clinical duties and confronted him with the charges. Alsabti denied them all. But he had difficulty explaining away some of his accomplishments. Officials later said he could not account for the article with his name on it that was so similar to the paper by Wierda. "He denied having written the article," William Reefe, codirector of the residency program, told a reporter, "and said it was not listed on his curriculum vitae—but it was." On July 2, Alsabti resigned from the program.

According to Hugh Davis, director of the hospital where Alsabti worked, at the time of his application he presented glowing letters of recommendation from South West Memorial in Houston. Davis said neither the University of Virginia nor the hospital called any of Alsabti's former employers to check his record. "We probably should have made those calls," Davis says ruefully. The only clue in what Alsabti presented that should not have been overlooked, according to university officials, was the astounding output of published papers for someone so young, especially since most of the articles appeared during a two-year period.

While in Virginia, Alsabti granted a short telephone interview to a reporter who called him at home. He alleged that other researchers had in fact pirated his papers. He would not, however, speculate on how or why this occurred. "I just want to find a good lawyer who will represent me, to sue the magazine, to sue all the people involved in this writing. And then I will show up in court to prove point by point, and then I will leave it up to the court to judge if I have plagiarized anybody's work or if somebody else is plagiarizing me." He also denied that he had told any researcher that he was a blood relation of the Jordanian royal family. "They thought that a crown on a letter meant the royal family. They were dumbling and bumbling about it, stupid idiots, when in fact they didn't know anything." He also noted that one of the articles describing his exploits was incorrect on the color of his automobile. "I have a white Cadillac, not a yellow one. The yellow one was sold." Soon after the interview, Alsabti put his $70,000 house in Roanoke up for sale. He hired no lawyers, and he left no forwarding address at the university. "He definitely knows medicine," said Davis. "I'm sure he will get another residency. There's just no way in the U.S. system to keep track of him."

New charges of plagiarism were now starting to emerge in the worldwide scientific press. In July 1980, the *British Medical Journal* recounted two additional cases where the published articles of reputable researchers had been appropriated by Alsabti.[7] Under the title "Must Plagiarism Thrive?" the article speculated on the possibility of preventing such theft. "There are at least 8,000 medical journals in the world, and many of these receive thousands of papers a year. Checking credentials of authors would be a vast and embarrassing business. And checking to see if a paper has been published before (under a different name and probably with a different title) would be nigh on impossible. Editors would seem to have little choice but to trust to the integrity of their contributors and the astuteness of their referees." Also in July, the British journal *Nature* reported an additional case of plagiarism that had been pulled off by the roving academician.[8]

Unrelenting in his quest for medical credentials and the trappings of a scientific career, Alsabti at this point turned northward to the hub of biomedical research in the United States: Boston. By the second week of July 1980, a mere ten days after he left Virginia, he was hard at work in a residency program in a hospital affiliated with Boston University. It was not long, however, before the news of his activities caught up with him. An article in the September issue of the magazine *Forum on Medicine* described the Alsabti affair in detail, and officials at the hospital read it in wonder.[9] They immediately had a meeting with Alsabti, and soon afterward asked him to leave. According to administrators at Carney Hospital in Dorchester, when Alsabti applied he said he had experienced "personal" problems in Virginia, but had mentioned nothing about charges of piracy. "He did not tell us that there were any allegations or accusations or anything that would raise questions regarding his character or competence or ethics," says John Logue, Carney's executive vice president. "If we hire an employee for a dishwashing job and they lie on the application, we consider that grounds for dismissal."

Alsabti left Carney, never to be heard from again. Whether he changed his name and continued in the tradition of grand plagiary is not known, but given his record, such a development seems not at all unlikely. Most significantly, his legacy lives on. Many of the demonstrable plagiaries were eventually retracted, but his name still stands atop dozens of papers in the computer files of the huge scientific indexing services, the overlords and compilers of scientific track records. Spokesmen for *Index Medicus* and the *Science Citation Index* say there is no precedent for retractions from their files, and that they would probably hesitate to set one, as it might force them in the future to pass judgment on disputes that sometimes arise over authorship.

Considering that the papers now have a life of their own, Alsabti may still claim his record, and today, somewhere, wield the power that comes with what many administrators would consider an impeccable set of scientific credentials.

An irony of the Alsabti story is that not only his credentials as a rising star in the world of medical research were stolen but the whole concept of his scientific rise back in Iraq had been borrowed from another Middle Eastern "genius" who had persuaded the Iraqi government to bankroll him. While Alsabti was still a medical student in Basra, his role model, Abdul Fatah Al-Sayyab, had risen to a position of power within the government in Baghdad. With two wonder drugs to his credit, the Basra-born researcher enjoyed a life of government-financed ease, including a lavish house. The drugs, which among other things allegedly cured certain types of cancer, were named Bakrin, after then president Ahmed Hassan Al-Bakr, and Saddamin, after Saddam Hussein, then vice president and later president of Iraq. Unfortunately, the drugs had no effect on cancer, and Al-Sayyab, by the time Alsabti fled Iraq in order to pursue his ambitious career goals, was under close surveillance and not allowed to leave the country.

Alsabti, in the course of constructing his academic illusion, had forged a medical degree, had duped the Jordanian government into giving him tens of thousands of dollars, had fabricated his relation to the royal family, had lied his way into U.S. universities, had bestowed a Ph.D. upon himself, and, while allegedly doing research in a handful of prestigious U.S. labs, had pirated many, perhaps all, of his sixty published papers. His tactics deceived the editors of dozens of scientific journals around the world. In addition, his lies and legerdemain took in the governments of two Middle Eastern countries, the review committees of eleven scientific societies, and the administrators from six U.S. institutions of higher education.

In Iraq, where Alsabti started his scientific career, he is still wanted by the police for misrepresentation and theft. In Jordan, he is a *persona non grata*. Says Shaher Bak, former deputy ambassador to the United States for Jordan: "If anyone can bring a legal case against him, we will be more than happy."

The case of Alsabti shows in pure form how contemporary science can be compromised by the ethos of the professional researcher. In his goals, if not his methods, Alsabti was no different from millions of other researchers. Most scientists, no doubt, still keep truth as their primary goal. For many, however, a more immediate objective often intrudes into vision, that of establish-

ing credit. The basic currency of credit in the scientific world is
the article published in a learned journal. A long list of publications to one's credit, commonly called a bibliography, helps in
the continual struggle to secure government grants and helps
with academic promotion. Since few scientists, much less administrators, have time to read these articles, the quantity of scientific
papers listed on a curriculum vitae can often be more important
than their quality.

The game of acquiring a long list of publications is a relatively
new development, as evidenced by the fact that just two decades
ago the current problems with paper inflation were unthinkable.
In 1958, when James D. Watson (who later won a Nobel prize)
had worked his way up to the rank of associate professor at Harvard, the young biochemist had on his curriculum vitae eighteen
papers. One of them, coauthored with Francis H. Crick, described
the structure of DNA, the master molecule of living things. Today, the bibliography of a candidate facing a similar climb often
lists fifty or even one hundred papers.

The preoccupation with publication has resulted in a veritable
ocean of journals and papers. As the *British Medical Journal*
noted, today there are at least 8,000 journals in medicine alone.
An additional reason for the number of journals is the tremendous
increase in the ranks of scientists themselves. It has been estimated that 90 percent of all scientists who ever lived are alive
today. A large part of the journal explosion, however, is due to
changes in the nature of publishing, changes that too often stress
quantity rather than quality. A safe generalization is that many
of the scientists and much of what they publish today are mediocre at best. The epitome of mindless publication is seen in the
case of Alsabti. According to Stephen M. Lawani,[10] a graduate
of the school of library science at Florida State University, not
one of Alsabti's articles had been cited by another scientist prior
to his exposure as a grand purloiner. Alsabti stole insignificant
research and thereby avoided detection. But the list of papers he
compiled still gave him instant entrée into the higher reaches of
U.S. academia.

An outsider to the scientific process might suppose that, in view
of the importance of scientific articles, the editorial boards of
scientific journals would carefully separate the wheat from the

chaff, ensuring that bad or fraudulent papers are never published. Again, Alsabti shows that this is clearly not the case. Bad papers are almost always published sooner or later. They may be turned down by the better journals, but, if their authors persist, they will find an outlet elsewhere. When Alsabti first worked in the United States, at Temple, he showed microbiologist Friedman a paper he was working on. "I made some suggestions," says Friedman, "but I told him that by any standards the paper was unacceptable." Despite this evaluation, the work was soon in print. Even the sheer volume of insignificant research put forth by Alsabti was not enough to slow his acceptance rate. The editor of *Journal of Clinical Hematology and Oncology,* Amanullah Khan, says that by the time Alsabti was exposed as a fraud, the would-be academician had submitted a total of nine articles to his journal. Seven were accepted, six were printed, and one that was slated for publication was pulled when the charges of plagiarism were leveled.

Alsabti is far from a lone figure in the arena of insignificant publication. Jonathan and Stephen Cole, sociologists who in 1972 published a trenchant analysis of scientific productivity entitled "The Ortega Hypothesis,"[11] have concluded that only a few scientists contribute to scientific progress. The majority publish work that has little or even zero impact on the forward march of knowledge. The Coles' survey was based on the fact that a scientist is obliged to acknowledge in his published work all the articles that have contributed to his own. The footnotes or references to other work, known as "citations," offer a powerful means of telling who influenced whom. From an analysis of citations, the Coles found that many scientific articles are never once cited in the scientific literature. "The data we have reported," they wrote, "lead to the tentative conclusion that reducing the number of scientists might not slow down the rate of scientific progress."

The world of science clearly could have survived without the work of Alsabti, and perhaps even without the journals in which he published. In his analysis of Alsabti's bibliography, Lawani concludes that none of the journals in which Alsabti published was "important for cancer research." None of them, for instance, was included in the *Yearbook of Cancer,* and none of them published any paper that was highly cited (fifty or more citations). Significantly, two of the journals did rank high compared to all cancer journals, but this was only because of the sheer volume of papers they printed.

Alsabti resorted to plagiarism in order to pad his bibliography with mediocre papers. Other researchers attain the same goal by a variety of other methods, most of them commonplace.[12] One example is the Least Publishable Unit, or LPU, a euphemism in some scientific circles for getting as many separate articles as possible out of a single piece of scientific work. Instead of publishing one comprehensive paper that ties work together, a researcher will publish four or five short ones. Sheer volume, he reasons, will help his career. "It's quite a problem," says Clifford A. Bachrach, editor of *Index Medicus*. "One case that I am familiar with concerned an epidemiological project that looked at the relationship of several variables to the incidence of disease. It ended up being printed as fairly brief papers in three journals instead of one slightly longer one." A few editors are fighting the trend. Arnold Relman, editor of the *New England Journal of Medicine,* says he handles the submission of LPU's "as tactfully as I can. There is a fine line between dictating how people should do their work and being a tough, rigorous editor. If it's clear that this is the first of many little pieces, then I try to tactfully inquire whether there might not be more."

Another example of getting more for less in the publishing game is revealed by the increase in coauthorships. Credit for a single piece of research will be shared among many researchers, complex webs of reciprocal obligation being formed among dozens of colleagues. Editors at the *New England Journal of Medicine* say coauthorships have risen exponentially since the journal's inception, today averaging about five authors per paper. The Philadelphia-based Institute for Scientific Information, which indexes 2,800 journals, says the average number of authors per paper rose from 1.76 to 2.58 between 1960 and 1980. And that is the average. It is not uncommon to see a paper with a dozen or more coauthors.

Some of this rise is related to the increasing mix of different subspecialists who will work on a single research problem. But much is strictly related to career advancement and the gratuitous addition of coauthors by a researcher trying to curry favor. An editor at one journal, *Blood,* received a call one day from an irate researcher who asked that his name be removed from a manuscript that he had just seen and with whose conclusions he did not agree. His sole contribution had been a few seconds of conversation with the lead author in an elevator.

The scientific paper at one time was a vehicle for the transmission of scientific truth and for speculation on the workings of nature, but today its importance has been diminished as it more and more has become a tool of the careerist. As might be expected, the growing dimensions of the publishing game have led to the development of a sort of reverse snobbery in some cases. Bachrach says editors of new journals who are lobbying for inclusion in *Index Medicus,* which contains some 2,600 journals, often send bibliographies of themselves or members of their editorial board in an attempt to show off. "We see things containing six or seven hundred papers," he says, "but I'm really much more impressed by thirty-five good ones."

One lesson that can be gleaned from the Alsabti affair is that the ocean of useless and unexamined research encourages the creation and concealment of frauds. As the *British Medical Journal* observed, in light of the thousands of existing journals, "checking to see if a paper has been published before (under a different name and probably with a different title) would be nigh on impossible."

The stakes are indeed high, but the journals appear to be here to stay. Why is this the case if so many of these journals and articles go unread? What are the economic mechanisms by which these journals are produced and financed? In fact, it is not the normal market forces of supply and demand that determine the price on the cover of many scientific journals. Since few copies are sold, publishers are wont to pass along production costs to researchers in the form of page charges. For most articles submitted, a check must also be enclosed for up to several hundred dollars. It might seem appropriate that the cost would come out of the researcher's pocket, since the published paper is sometimes nothing more than a status symbol. This, however, is not the case. Oftentimes page charges are written off against the researcher's government grant, so that the taxpayer is subsidizing the proliferation of papers that at least in some instances do little more than feather the nests of ambitious academicians.

The pile of papers, books, and articles that has mushroomed in the years following the Second World War has concealed dozens of plagiarists as well as Alsabti. Many of these cases of piracy would have gone unreported except that the principals later in their careers achieved positions of power and repute that resulted in widespread and detailed examination of their record. A case in point is that of James H. McCrocklin, who, when charges emerged in 1968, was president of Southwest Texas State College.[13] A magazine in Texas revealed that his Ph.D. and his wife's master's thesis were strikingly alike, and that both had borrowed heavily from an old, obscure Marine Corps report. What was at first merely a personal embarrassment quickly became a public controversy. McCrocklin denied any wrongdoing, and public opinion held that he might outlast the charges, especially since McCrocklin was a personal friend of then President Lyndon Johnson, and Southwest Texas State College was Johnson's alma mater. Nonetheless, McCrocklin resigned his post in April 1969.

Despite McCrocklin's setback, the academic world is far more indulgent than might be expected to those caught committing plagiary, provided that they occupy a sufficiently lofty position in the university or government hierarchy. Consider the case of William D. McElroy, a well-known biochemist distinguished for his work in the field of bioluminescence.[14] In 1964 McElroy wrote a review article in which verbatim quotations from another author appeared without complete attribution. McElroy had lifted more than 20 percent of his text from this author, the borrowed material being either verbatim or closely paraphrased. The incident went publicly unnoticed until McElroy was elevated to one of the top federal science posts in the country. In his defense, McElroy said he had inadvertently used the material through an oversight which he later corrected. He had taken the material in the summer of 1962, intending to rework it. However, the good intentions did not last into the fall, when the article was put into final form. "What happened, I don't know," McElroy told a reporter. "It's not like me not to rework it. But it's an area I'm not interested in. Maybe subconsciously I just wanted to get it over with." The author whose work had been borrowed later complained, and McElroy had the publisher send around an erratum to recipients of the article, stating that "credit for verbatim quotations" on nine different pages of McElroy's article should be given to the other author. The incident, and the subsequent controversy when McElroy was named director of the National Science Foundation, did not slow his career momentum, for he stayed on at the foundation. Critics at the time alleged that this was something of a double standard, and wondered what would have happened to a college student who tried to explain the appropriation of another's work by saying he had forgotten to rework the material.

Another instance in which high office furnished its occupant protection from charges of plagiary was the episode involving Morris E. Chafetz, who in 1971 was appointed the first director of the National Institute of Alcohol Abuse and Alcoholism.[15] This appointment occurred despite a controversy at the time over his having taken credit for other researchers' work. In 1965 Chafetz put out a book entitled *Liquor: The Servant of Man*. A quarter of a century earlier, Ferdinand Helwig and Walton Hall Smith also had written a book with the same title, which Chafetz explained the publisher had asked him to revise. But Chafetz in his 1965 book said he personally collected military hospital data. During the controversy he acknowledged that they were adapted from the earlier book because they corresponded to recollections of his own experiences. While conceding that he did something "silly," Chafetz vehemently denied that he did anything wrong. In an interview with a newspaper reporter, he noted that he had been exonerated by his Harvard colleagues.

Later, as the controversy rippled through the pages of science publications,[16] Harvard researcher Jack H. Mendelson noted that "the Executive Committee of the Department of Psychiatry did not press formal charges against Dr. Chafetz in 1969 because of their concern about possible entanglements. Dr. Chafetz hired an attorney who convinced the Executive Committee that he would bring suit if Dr. Chafetz were dismissed from the medical school, and the Committee, in a conservative vein, did not vote censure but anticipated that Dr. Chafetz would find employment elsewhere." In fact, Chafetz stayed on at Harvard until he became, in 1971, the government's top expert on alcoholism.

The hint of other, undetected plagiarists is reinforced because every time a new case breaks into print it always brings a slew of "if you think that is bad" letters to the editors of major journals. In a follow-up story on the piracy of Alsabti, the journal *Nature* detailed how another "Jordanian" researcher had plagiarized material.[17] In 1978 a journal received from the Jordanian a manuscript entitled "Influence of Electric Charges on the Corrosion of Metals." Close inspection revealed that the identical paper under the same title had been published by a group of Swedish authors a decade earlier. The plagiarized manuscript was not accepted for publication, and, upon complaint from the editor of the journal, the Jordanian was relieved of his visiting appointment to an unnamed university in the eastern United States and allowed to return to the University of Amman. One wonders what would have happened to the researcher had he been a citizen of the United States and, say, the chairman of a department.

The rewards in science are supposed to go strictly and exclusively for originality. That is why scientists strive so desperately to establish priority for their discoveries. It is also why, to judge from the frequency and bitterness of complaints, researchers sometimes fail to make fair acknowledgment of the work of their colleagues and competitors. The failure to make due acknowledgment of another researcher is, in a minor way, a theft of his work. Plagiary is an interesting phenomenon because it carries this common sin of scientific reporting to extremes. Plagiary, the wholesale theft of another's work, is so outrageous and obvious a crime that an outsider might predict scientists would never commit it. The evidence shows that, to the contrary, plagiary in the scientific community is not rare, that it probably often escapes detection, that it takes time for even the most blatant cases of plagiary to come to light, and that even those discovered committing plagiary are often able to continue their careers unaffected. If plagiary, the grossest offense against intellectual property, merits just knuckle-rap treatment from the scientific community, what degree of indulgence must be accorded to lesser crimes?

CHAPTER 4

THE LIMITS
OF
REPLICATION

Each time a new case of scientific fraud breaks into the headlines, the scientific establishment generally responds with one variant or another of the "bad apple" theory. The faker was a psychopath, or under great stress, or otherwise mentally disturbed, this theory goes. Its unspoken implication is that all blame should be put on the erring individual, not on the institutions of science.

The recent cases of fraud, says cancer researcher Lewis Thomas, "can be viewed as anomalies, the work of researchers with unhinged minds. . . ."[1] Philip Handler, then president of the National Academy of Sciences, told the Gore congressional hearing in March 1981: "One can only judge the rare such acts that have come to light as psychopathic behavior originating in minds that have made very bad judgments—ethics aside—minds which in at least this one regard may be considered deranged."[2]

If every smidgeon of fraud can be laid at the door of the poor unhinged, deranged psychopaths who nevertheless managed somehow to infiltrate the research community, clearly there is no need for any change in the institutional mechanisms whereby science is said to police itself. What are those mechanisms, and how efficiently do they work? The answer has an important bearing on the often asked question, How common is fraud in science?

The renowned German sociologist Max Weber saw science as a vocation. The individual scientist's devotion to the truth, in

Weber's view, is what keeps science honest. His French contemporary Émile Durkheim, on the other hand, considered that it is the community of science, not the individual, that guarantees scientific integrity. Weber's view that scientists are innately honest is still sometimes heard. "The scientists I have known . . . have been in certain respects just perceptibly more morally admirable than most other groups of intelligent men," said the scientist and novelist C. P. Snow.[3] But the opinion that scientists are somehow more honest than other people is not particularly fashionable. The prevailing view is that laid out by Robert Merton, the leading American sociologist of science, who like Durkheim attributes honesty in science to institutional mechanisms, not the personal virtue of scientists. The verifiability of results, the exacting scrutiny of fellow experts, the subjection of scientists' activities to "rigorous policing, to a degree perhaps unparalleled in any other field of activity"—these are the features, says Merton, that ensure "the virtual absence of fraud in the annals of science."[4]

Merton's description of the self-policing mechanisms has become a general article of faith among scientists. The self-policing nature of science is regularly cited as a reason why society at large has no need to interfere in scientific affairs. Science is a system "that operates in a highly effective, democratic, self-correcting mode," stated President Handler at the congressional hearings on scientific fraud. "There is no need for an extrinsic scientific criticism, because criticism is inherent in the process itself," says Snow. The "Keep Off" sign has perhaps been most graphically displayed by science writer June Goodfield. "Of all the professions," she opines in an account of the Summerlin fraud case, "science is the most critical. There are full-time critics of music, art, poetry and literature, but there are none of science, for scientists fulfil this role for themselves."[5]

There are three principal mechanisms that constitute the alleged self-policing system of science. These are (i) peer review, (ii) the referee system, and (iii) replication. Peer review is the name given to the committees of specialists who advise the government as to which scientists should be supported and which should be denied funds. Through its control over the distribution of research funds among individuals, the peer review system has a major influence on the conduct of science. Researchers applying for a government grant put considerable effort into the preparation of the very detailed paper work that goes before a peer review committee. The committee members are meant to read each application with great care, rating each according to its scientific merits. This process is the first stage at which any fraudulent research proposal might be caught.

The second safety net against fraud is the referee system, the practice whereby almost all scientific journals send out the manuscripts submitted to them to the appropriate expert authorities. Referees are expected to judge the merits and novelty of articles, and to spot any defects in argument or technique. Since this is the most rigorous test an article may undergo, it is a prime point at which fraud or self-deception should be caught.

The last and seemingly most formidable defense against fraud is replication. As philosophers who study the logical structure of science are at pains to point out, science differs from other branches of knowledge in that the assertions of one scientist can be objectively tested by another. In publishing his findings a scientist is supposed to describe exactly how he did his experiment, so that others can repeat it and either confirm or refute the result. Replication is the crucial test whereby theories and experiments in science are judged. Any fraudulent experiment, so established wisdom goes, is liable to be shown up when others try to replicate it. The more important the false claim, the more quickly will attempted replication by others bring it down. This chapter focuses on replication, the supposedly insurmountable barrier that no fraud can cross. Peer review and the referee system are discussed further in the next chapter.

The meteoric career of Alsabti, chronicled in Chapter 3, ran roughshod over all three barriers to fraud, but his might seem at first sight to be a special case. It was not Alsabti's practice to endure the tedium of doing experiments, so he never needed to apply through the peer review system for a grant. Since his articles were copied, not invented, there was nothing inherently false for referees or any would-be replicators to pick up. On top of which, Alsabti was operating on the periphery of the scientific mainstream, publishing in obscure journals on backwater subjects. A severer test of the replication system would be a fraudulent experiment at the cutting edge of a fast-moving frontier of science, one that made so important a claim as to attract the attention of all the leading researchers in the field.

Just such an example was afforded by the extraordinary episode of the kinase cascade. The case, an eighteen-month wonder, is remarkably revealing of how science works under stress, as opposed to the post hoc accounts given by historians and philosophers, and by scientists themselves. A single attempt at replication would have stopped the fraud dead in its tracks. But for a long time the basic human factors that often shape scientists' attitudes and motivations pushed out of mind the basic methodological safeguard of replication. During that period, the kinase cascade theory spread its web over the whole field of cancer research, tangling several leading scientists in its threads. Pride, ambition, excitement at a new theory, reluctance to listen to bad news, unwillingness to distrust a colleague, these are the ingredients that caused the kinase cascade theory to get so far. The point is not that these are dishonorable feelings—they are not—but that for a long time they prevented the institutional mechanism of replication from being put into effect. Replication was the *last* step in the episode, undertaken when everything else had failed and only after plain evidence of forgery had come to light.[6]

In the spring of 1981 a new superstar burst into cancer research and seemed to shed a marvelously illuminating light over the intractable field. Mark Spector, a twenty-four-year-old graduate student at Cornell University, and his professor Efraim Racker announced a remarkable new theory of cancer causation. The theory, for which Spector had provided all the prodigious experimental evidence, was of such strength and elegance that many were convinced it would win him and his professor the Nobel prize. Racker himself had no doubts about the beauty of the idea that he and his young protégé had conceived. At the head of the article announcing the discovery, he placed a quotation from G. K. Chesterton: "There are no rules of architecture for a castle in the clouds."[7]

The foundations of Racker's castle were laid in January 1980 when Mark Spector came to Cornell University from the University of Cincinnati with a glowing recommendation from his professor. Since his teens, Spector had been totally dedicated to science. As a graduate student in Racker's laboratory he was able to pick up new techniques with extraordinary rapidity. He could make tricky experiments work that no one else could get to go. Colleagues with Spector began to describe him as one of the most brilliant young people they had ever met. His success was inevitably resented by some of his fellow graduate students, but his senior colleagues regarded him as a prodigy with "golden hands."

Racker gave him the task of purifying an enzyme (known as sodium-potassium ATPase) that is part of the wall of living cells. Racker had long been interested in the enzyme because he had reason to believe that an inefficiency in its operation is one of the distinctive marks of certain cancer cells. Several people had tried and failed to purify the form of the enzyme found in cancer cells, but Spector did so in two months. Next, he found evidence to show that the ATPase operated inefficiently in cancer cells but efficiently in normal cells, a discovery that dramatically confirmed his professor's predictions.

Spector quickly ascertained the reason for the enzyme's inefficiency: in cancer cells, the enzyme undergoes a chemical modification known as phosphorylation. Each chemical change in a cell is mediated by a particular enzyme, so the next step in Spector's trail was to find the enzyme that causes the phosphorylation of the ATPase. The second enzyme, called a protein kinase, turned out to be present in all cells, Spector reported, but it assumed an active form only in cancer cells. The young genius capped this electrifying discovery by bringing to light a series of four different protein kinases. Like a row of dominoes, each kinase phosphorylated, and thereby activated, the next kinase in the cascade, with the last kinase phosphorylating the ATPase.

It is usually a year's work for a graduate student to purify a single enzyme, especially if it is a minor one. But by mid-1980, six months after his arrival in Racker's lab, Spector had purified the ATPase and the four kinases. The kinase cascade was a wonderfully interesting mechanism, suggestive to biochemists of all kinds of signal amplification and control systems, but better yet was to come. Spector managed to tie the cascade in with an extremely important new development that had just emerged from the study of viruses that cause tumors in animals.

The tumor-causing gene of these viruses, known as the *src*

("sarc") gene, is one that specifies a protein kinase enzyme. The viruses are thought to have pirated this gene, early in their evolution, from the cells of the species they infect. Cancer researchers had scrutinized animal cells for the present-day versions of these pirated genes, the so-called endogenous *src* genes, but no one had managed to isolate the genes' protein kinase products. Enter Mark Spector with the astonishing news that certain of his cascade kinases were the products of the elusive endogenous *src* genes.

Everything at last seemed to be dropping into place for a unified theory of cancer causation. A tumor virus infects a cell. Its *src* gene makes unmanageably large quantities of a kinase which trips off the cell's otherwise inactive cascade of kinases. The last kinase in the cascade phosphorylates the ATPase enzyme, making it inefficient and thereby setting off the further changes characteristic of malignant cells.

"Seductive" is a word biologists used to describe the compelling intellectual attraction of the Racker-Spector theory. The two of them had picked the most exciting new developments in cancer research and demonstrated, by a sequence of beautifully executed experiments, how each fitted into the overall theory. Before the details had even been published in the scientific literature, Racker started mentioning the theory in lectures given around the country.

A biochemist with a background in psychiatry, the sixty-eight-year-old Racker was an eminent figure in his field, a winner of the U.S. National Medal of Science, and his authority lent to the then unpublished theory a credence it would not otherwise have had. Soon, under Racker's aegis, Spector was collaborating with leading researchers in cancer biology, such as David Baltimore of MIT, and George Todaro and Robert Gallo of the National Cancer Institute.

When Racker gave a lecture about the theory on the campus of the National Institutes of Health in the spring of 1981, some 2,000 people attended. National Cancer Institute director Vincent De-Vita, then in trouble with Congress for not cracking down on cases of scientific fraud, was urged to spread the good news. DeVita held off, but within the biomedical research community enthusiasm was running high. "We have witnessed in this field a merger of biochemistry and molecular biology which was long overdue,"

Racker and Spector declared in a portentous and self-promoting paper published in the July 17, 1981, issue of *Science*.[8]

Leading researchers began to move into the field, but rather than go through the laborious task of replicating Spector's work by purifying their own kinase systems, they would send their reagents to him for testing. "The striking thing was that when you went there there were samples from all over the world waiting to be tested by this kid. If you looked at the labels on the shelves it was almost a Who's Who of cancer research," noted Todaro. Some researchers invited the young graduate student to their labs. One by one they became aware of a pattern familiar to Spector's colleagues at Cornell, that often the experiments would work only in Spector's hands and could not be repeated without him. But like Spector's colleagues, they found a simple explanation: Mark was just so good at making experiments go. "He is technically very gifted," says Todaro. "When he came to NIH, people would ask him for practical suggestions in doing their experiments and would get intelligent advice. People didn't talk to him the way one talks to a graduate student, but as to a colleague."

Among those intrigued by Spector's theory was Volker Vogt, a tumor virologist who worked in the department of biochemistry at Cornell on the floor above Racker's laboratory. In April 1980 Spector performed some experiments on his ATPase enzyme with a student of Vogt's, Blake Pepinsky. "These results were so clean and beautiful and convincing that I was seduced into putting my time in on this project," says Vogt.

There was one problem. Sometimes the experiments worked and sometimes they didn't. Vogt was worried that results so beautiful should also be so erratic. He devoted the summer of 1980 to trying to understand why the negative experiments didn't work. Whatever the reason, whether the wrong phase of the moon or having impurities in the distilled water, it was too elusive for Vogt to put his finger on. Eventually he gave up. He also decided he could not publish the experiments, however exciting they might be.

Pepinsky continued to help Spector, however, the two of them often working seventeen-hour days and sometimes through the night. "The work had nothing to do with my thesis but I would come and do the precipitations when Mark wanted to do it. They only worked when he was around to do them," notes Pepinsky. A year later, in early 1981, Vogt too was drawn back into the maelstrom when Spector started to find his kinases in cells infected with tumor-causing viruses. The particular experiment that caught Vogt's interest was one that showed that an antiserum to one of Spector's kinases also had an affinity for an important but so far undetected protein, the product of the *src* gene of a widely studied mouse tumor virus.

Pepinsky repeated the experiment twice but it didn't work. Vogt despaired that it seemed to be the same frustrating story as with the ATPase the year before. But this time, he told himself, he was really going to get to the bottom of things and find out why Spector's work was hard to reproduce. In an intensive two-day effort, Pepinsky and Spector redid the experiment.

It was another spectacular success. "There were fat radioactive bands of protein on the autoradiogram, everything looked as clean as could be," notes Vogt. "So I said, 'Here at least is something I can work with.'" He decided his first step would be to analyze the gels from which the autoradiogram was made. "Mark was very upset that I had got my hands on the gels. Previously he had done all these analyses himself," says Vogt. Pepinsky, also uneasy about the lack of reproducibility, had squirreled away the original gels.

The gels were the key pieces of data from Spector's experiments. Cell proteins picked out by antisera and tagged with radioactive phosphorus 32 would be placed on the gel and subjected to an electric field. Each protein would migrate through the gel a particular distance, determined by its size, and mark its presence by darkening a radiosensitive film placed next to the gel.

Hitherto only these films, called the autoradiograms, had been shown by Spector to his colleagues. When Vogt obtained an original gel, his first step was to run a hand Geiger counter over it to locate the radioactive protein bands. He realized instantly from the pattern of clicks that something was terribly wrong. The clicks were not saying phosphorus 32. Judging from the amount of darkening on the autoradiogram, they seemed to be saying iodine 125. A scintillation-counter measurement confirmed this diagnosis. But iodine had no business at all in the experiment.

It was forgery, very cunning but quite simple. The forger was evidently finding proteins of the right molecular weight to reach the desired point in the gel, tagging them with radioactive iodine, and mixing them into the antisera-tagged proteins just before they were put onto the gel.

Vogt was overwhelmed. The day was a Friday, July 24. "I was pretty shaken up by it. It was something of a nightmare. To begin with, I didn't tell anyone. I knew it was a big event in my career, in everyone's. I went home and brooded over it for one day. Then I went over to see Racker.

"He didn't doubt the actual facts but he was loath to believe that everything was wrong immediately. At that point we thought it might be a recent aberration. The next morning we confronted Mark. We thought he might say 'Mea culpa,' but he didn't. He didn't dispute the finding that it was iodine, but he said he didn't do it and that he didn't know how it happened."

With the discovery of the forged experiment, the castle in the clouds, which Racker had announced in *Science* just ten days earlier, began to evaporate.

Racker gave Spector four weeks in which to purify the ATPase enzyme and the four kinases from scratch and to put them in Racker's hands for testing. Spector agreed, saying the task would take him two weeks, not four. But progress was not so fast. It took three attempts before he could provide Racker with an ATPase that worked, but he did provide one. He also produced a kinase that appeared to phosphorylate the ATPase, but there was only enough material for Racker to do the experiment twice. The other kinases Spector supplied were not of the right molecular weight and did not work in the way they should have done. At the end of four weeks Racker told Spector not to come back to his laboratory anymore.

Spector's attempt to vindicate himself was on balance a failure, yet an ambiguous failure. He showed Racker that he could reproduce some, but not all, of his claimed results, thus creating uncertainty as to whether some or none of his previous work was reliable. But he declined to share whatever he knew with his colleagues. "Mark says that in five years he will be vindicated. But he won't help us find out what is good and what is not," commented Pepinsky, who in scientific terms knew Spector best.

Did Mark Spector fake all of his results, or none of them, or just some? There may never be a clear answer to the question. All that could be said with certainty was that data in some of his experiments had been deliberately and cunningly contrived by someone. "If it turns out that the whole thing was made up," remarked George Todaro, "it is an incredible tour de force, it really boggles the mind, and in any case something like this really might exist." "If we are talking about faking, it is very clever and careful and on a great scale—it's not like painting patches on a mouse," said another biologist familiar with the work.

As the kinase cascade theory started to fall apart, so did significant parts of Mark Spector's background. On September 9, 1981, he withdrew the thesis that was about to win him a Ph.D. degree earned in one and a half years instead of the usual five. Belated checks that should have been done when Spector entered the Cornell graduate school showed that he possessed neither an M.A. nor a B.A. degree from the University of Cincinnati, as he had claimed. "A check with law enforcement agencies in Cincinnati," reported the *Ithaca Journal*, "shows that Mark B. Spector pleaded guilty on June 12, 1980, to two forgery charges in connection with writing two checks for $4,843.49 to himself from his employer. . . . He was sentenced to prison and the sentence was suspended and he was put on three years' probation."[9]

"I treated him like the son I never had," Racker remarked to a colleague. The castle was built, brick upon miswrought brick, because of that relationship. Elderly, brusque, authoritarian, Racker was so impressed by his young protégé that he was arranging for Spector to take over part of his laboratory. The fatal flaw in their interaction was perhaps that Spector was emotionally unable to cope with authority. "Racker would come in and ask for the data," an observer of the affair commented later. Rather than saying he didn't have it, Spector would provide whatever he thought would please his professor. "The relationship was harmful to both of them. They fed each other for a while. Spector would provide the answers and please his 'father,' and at the same time he would be messing it up."

As in many scientific issues, subterranean human emotions were what guided the events above the surface. But the question of scientific methodology can still be asked: why wasn't the falsity of Spector's results discovered much earlier? Why did none of the many biologists caught up in his theory try first to replicate some of the basic results? The answer is: they did. Their failure to get the same answers as Spector should have stopped the theory dead in its tracks. It didn't.

The first clear danger signal from the outside came from Raymond Erikson, of the University of Colorado, a leading expert on the virus *src* gene problem. Racker asked him to test an antiserum Spector had prepared to one of the cascade kinases. As a favor, Erikson did so, and found the antiserum was not what Spector had represented it to be. It showed unmistakable signs of being identical to an antiserum that Erikson had himself sent to Racker sometime earlier, an antiserum with a chemical affinity for the protein product of a virus *src* gene. Had Erikson not spotted the clue that identified the antiserum, he would have drawn a significant but wholly erroneous conclusion from his tests: that Spector's kinase was closely related to the virus *src* gene product, which is exactly what Spector and Racker were hoping to hear.

Erikson informed Racker of his findings in November 1980, almost a year before the scandal finally broke. Racker evidently didn't believe a word Erikson was saying. He told Erikson that he got different results. He promised to send another batch of antiserum but never did. And in an article in *Cell*, later retracted, Racker criticized Erikson for failing to recognize the presence of the kinases.[10] Since Erikson didn't publish his discovery about having been sent the wrong antiserum, no one else knew.

Another clear warning signal came from Robert Gallo of the National Cancer Institute. He sent a monkey virus protein to Cornell in February 1981 and was told by Spector that it was related to one of the cascade kinases. After numerous attempts at trying to repeat the experiment in his own laboratory, Gallo finally sent one of his postdoctoral students to Cornell to perform a joint experiment. But he instructed the student to code the samples given to Spector, rather than to identify them by name. Why? "Because I'm a bad guy," chuckles Gallo: "I could not repeat the data here. Unless Spector was here, the experiments would not work."

Yet despite the coding, Spector twice picked the correct one out of nine samples in demonstrating a relationship between one of his cascade kinases and the gene product of Gallo's monkey virus. Gallo, however, had an independent reason, unknown to Spector, for doubting any such relationship. He asked Racker to send him the reagents so he could repeat the experiment in his own laboratory, but the reagents never arrived. "So I just quit the project. I thought there was something funny but I didn't know what, and I didn't want to get too speculative. I just told Racker we couldn't repeat it here," remarks Gallo. Asked why he didn't also mention to Racker his belief that something was funny, Gallo replies, "If you can't repeat something, if you don't have the reagents, what can you say? A lot of times people can't replicate things, and it's because they're doing it wrong."

The behavior of both Gallo and Erikson is typical of what almost all researchers would do in the circumstances, and yet it is the opposite of how the textbooks say scientists behave. The failure to replicate an experiment did not lead them to challenge either its validity, or that of the theory being based on it, let alone the good faith of the experimenter. Each had his own doubts, and each privately shared with Racker the basic reason for concern. But as Gallo observes, the failure to replicate an experiment is in no way sufficient basis for raising even the possibility of fraud.

The way in which the cascade kinase fraud was in fact detected is highly revealing of the way science actually works, as distinct from how the textbooks say it does. The first and most important check on a researcher's work—one so ordinary and basic that it is never mentioned by the philosophers of science—takes place inside the laboratory when his colleagues or professor looks at the raw data of the experiment. Only the insiders get the opportunity to see the recordings, the photographs, the instrument charts, and the other data on which the published account is based. Only they are in a position to judge whether or not the published facts accord with the raw data. Outsiders may doubt the published facts, but without some additional ground for suspicion, they cannot comfortably demand to see the raw data by which alone fraud could be proved, and would probably be refused if they did.

For most of his career, Spector managed to avoid a thorough check of his raw data by members of his own laboratory. According to a researcher who has looked through Spector's notebooks, "The original data are never there. Most people will staple an important print-out into their notebooks, but in Spector's case the figures are written in. Going back to his notebooks was something that was only done after the thing became unraveled."

The fraud was discovered for one critical reason: Volker Vogt decided to examine the original gel from which the autoradiogram was taken. No outsider would have had access to the gel. Moreover, Vogt's action, though it might seem an obvious logical step, was only so in retrospect. In fact it required a rare combination of intellectual clarity and persistence. Vogt blames himself for not having discovered the problem earlier, but others believe that he deserves considerable credit for uncovering the forged experiment when he did. Many researchers, maybe, would have been entirely enthralled by the elegance of the findings and would have tried only to extend them. Others, perhaps, would have just walked away from the baffling ambiguities. Vogt sailed straight through to the heart of the problem.

Had it not been for Vogt, the fraud would probably not have been detected until much later, and it might well have escaped attention altogether. Spector was about to leave Cornell and set up a laboratory of his own. In that circumstance, it is hardly likely that others would have gained access to any iodine-spiked gels. Spector's lack of B.A. and M.A. degrees would probably have come to light through bureaucratic mechanisms before he could receive his Ph.D., yet without the evidence of fraud he might well have stepped across this little obstacle.

As for Racker, what should have been the crown of a distinguished career ended up in fiasco. Considered by his peers to have long been a candidate for the Nobel prize, the kinase cascade was probably his last chance to win recognition in Stockholm. Should Racker have detected the problems earlier? "What this shows is that there is no defense against fraud. If we tried to run science so as to protect ourselves from fabrication, I think we would ruin the whole enterprise," remarks one molecular biologist.

On the other hand, Racker can be seen in retrospect to have ignored several warning signals. If he checked Spector's notebooks, he didn't see the indications of problems that later became visible. Although he made checks of parts of Spector's theory, no completely independent replication of Spector's work from start to finish was conducted in Racker's laboratory.

"I think Racker very much wanted to believe," suggested a researcher who had followed the case closely. "He is a very well respected scientist, but I think to some extent he might have suspended a little of his critical judgment. Because he had a lot of faith in Spector, things were not checked as carefully as they could have been."

"I think we did all reasonable checks," responded Racker. "It is unfortunate that this should happen to me because I am so well known for checking things." His point is a perfect illustration of the fact that even the most critical of scientists can let their critical faculties be lulled when more powerful motivations come into play. A brilliant kid with golden hands, who took one's most brilliant ideas and clothed them in the appearance of reality, who built a shimmering castle of dreams that mesmerized every cancer researcher in the country—few scientists could be sure of their immunity to such a siren call.

The affair of the kinase cascade theory is in one sense over, yet the full truth of what happened may never be known. Even the central character of the drama may not have all the answers. "If Spector had written [the kinase cascade] as just a hypothesis, he would have been recognized as a genius," says the chairman of the Cornell biochemistry department, Richard McCarty. A genius, if only he hadn't tried to prove it; a man without a bachelor's degree who came within apparent grasp of a Nobel prize; a brilliant kid, perhaps in search of paternal approval as much as of scientific kudos.

As the Spector case so clearly illustrates, it is not by public replication but by private verification that fraud is most often brought to light. A case that caused almost as much consternation as the Spector affair, but never became widely known, shook the world of biochemistry in 1961. As with the kinase cascade theory, the contrived experiments were uncovered by private means, by insiders from the same lab, not by outsiders who could not replicate the work from its published description.

The case involved two well-known biochemists, Fritz Lipmann of the Rockefeller Institute, who received the Nobel prize in

1953, and Melvin V. Simpson, then of the biochemistry department at Yale University.[11] With the assistance of an eager young student, Simpson in 1960 had shown that mitochondria, small particles found in cells, can synthesize the protein known as cytochrome c. The discovery was of considerable interest at the time because it confirmed the protein-synthesizing abilities of mitochondria and was also the first time that a protein had been synthesized in the test tube in such pure form.

Simpson's student, Thomas Traction,* duly received his Ph.D. from Yale and moved to Lipmann's laboratory at the Rockefeller Institute. Soon he and Lipmann published a provocative paper on a subject then of great interest to biochemists, the synthesis of a substance known as glutathione. Simpson, meanwhile, had gone to England to work for a few months with Francis Crick and Roy Markham, two leading English biologists. On his return, he unpacked his equipment and immediately started experiments to extend his findings on the synthesis of cytochrome c. To his vast chagrin, nothing worked.

"I had gone all round Europe giving seminars on our success. And now I couldn't repeat it. Imagine the agony," Simpson recalls. He spent almost a year trying to repeat the results. In despair he called Traction back from Lipmann's laboratory and had him redo the experiment.

Lipmann, as it happened, was also having doubts after meeting an English scientist at a conference in Holland who confided to having difficulties in repeating the Traction-Lipmann findings. Simpson remembers receiving a call from Lipmann after Traction's return to Yale:

"I understand Thomas Traction has been down with you," Lipmann said.

"Yes, we're having a little trouble in repeating experiments," Simpson replied cagily, not wishing to give too much away at that point.

"You put your cards on the table and I'll put mine on the table," Lipmann suggested. Simpson agreed. "We can't repeat anything Traction has done."

* Pseudonym.

"Neither can we," Simpson replied.

Simpson had had people watch Traction in shifts as he repeated the experiments. This time, none of them worked. As is now known, cytochrome c happens to be a protein that mitochondria do not produce. Simpson was desolated by what had happened. "The pain is all gone now," he says, "but it lasted a long time. I had to take a summer off from work, and I rebuilt a little sailboat I had. I couldn't go into the lab for about three months. It was so painful. Thomas was a confidence trickster. He'd do favors for everybody. If somebody wanted tickets to something, Thomas would get them. If you needed to borrow a car, Thomas would leave right on the spot. I don't know why he did it. Except that we felt he was really off his rocker. He was smart enough so that he didn't have to do it."

Traction's undergraduate college in Massachusetts has no record of his ever having received a degree. Traction left research and to this day denies any wrongdoing. "I have no explanation for why the cytochrome c experiment came out incorrectly," he explains. "All my life I've been thinking about it, and I don't understand it. If I had had the opportunity, I would have retracted those things myself, but they wouldn't let me."

Lipmann and Simpson announced their inability to repeat work performed with Traction in two brief articles that appeared in a leading journal of biochemistry. To biochemists who knew the story by word of mouth, that particular issue of the journal was known as the "reTraction issue," but the episode, as was typical of the time, received no press attention. Replication is meant to be a public procedure, a main beam of the open structure of science that allows a scientist in Australia to confirm or refute the claims of a researcher in Paris. But the replications performed by Simpson and Lipmann were based largely on private information and on private means. Most importantly, they had the equipment and knowledge to re-create the exact conditions of the experiment—something an outsider can never be sure he has succeeded in doing—and beyond that, they had Traction. By making Traction repeat the experiment under round-the-clock supervision, Simpson was able to conclude that the earlier result was definitely wrong. A scientist trying to repeat a colleague's work does not usually have such a satisfactory degree of control over not only the conditions of the experiment but the colleague as well.

The problems of exactly replicating an experiment begin to look increasingly formidable once the criterion of exactness is applied. The Simpson-Traction replication described above is probably one of the very few occasions in the history of science in which the philosopher's ideal of replicability has been attained. There are several reasons why in the real world exact replication is an impractical undertaking.

(*i*) *RECIPE INCOMPLETE.* The published descriptions of an experiment are often incomplete. The omissions lie not in the major conceptual elements but in the little details of practical technique. Just as cookbook recipes leave out the tiny points that every cook knows, so do scientists in describing their experiments. But these little points of technique are often crucial to a successful outcome. They also may be unknown, despite the author's assumptions to the contrary, to all but an intimate network of researchers. Quite often there may even be deliberate omissions of necessary minor details. A researcher who has made a new discovery will want to publish it so as to establish priority, but he may also wish to have the field to himself for a time while he explores the consequences of the discovery. Both objectives can be attained by publishing a slightly incomplete recipe.

(*ii*) *RESOURCES UNAVAILABLE.* Repeating an experiment often requires a major investment of time and money. Equipment has to be bought, a technique mastered, and often in biology, special cells or reagents have to be prepared or borrowed from the originator of the experiment. Replication is not like breathing; a scientist will try to replicate an experiment only if he believes the outcome will be significant.

(*iii*) *MOTIVATION LACKING.* What makes a replication significant? The short answer is that replications are not significant and therefore are rarely performed. The reasons for this at first surprising situation are rooted in the reward system of science. The prizes go for originality; being second wins nothing. A replica, by definition, is not original. There is no credit to be won in replicating and validating someone else's experiment except in unusual circumstances. Not being able to replicate an experiment is also of little practical consequence, so little, in fact, that scientists often don't bother to publish the fact. In sum, there is little chance of winning credit in any replication, whether the outcome is positive or negative, if the replication is done for the exclusive purpose of testing the validity of a colleague's work.

Experiments do, of course, get repeated in science, but not for any of the pure and sound methodological reasons so lovingly described by the philosophers. Scientists repeat the experiments of their rivals and colleagues, by and large, as ambitious cooks repeat recipes—for the purpose of *improving* on them. When a scientist announces an important new technique or experiment, his fellow researchers will repeat it with the idea of going one better, of taking it in a new direction, of trying to extend or develop or otherwise build upon what he has done. None of these endeavors will be exact replications of the original experiment, because their purpose is not to validate another scientist's discovery for him. All will be adaptations or improvements or extensions.

It is in this recipe-improvement process, of course, that an experiment is corroborated. If others find it works for them too, the recipe clearly has some relationship with the real world. It will be incorporated into the general cuisine of the specialty, and used to devise other and better recipes, for the greater glory of the chefs. Conversely, a recipe that doesn't work will simply not be used or cited by others. A chef cannot make a reputation for himself by demonstrating bad recipes. Almost all incorrect theories or experiments die from neglect.

It is only indirectly, in the course of trying to build upon another's work, that scientists confirm it. The notion of replication, in the sense of repeating an experiment in order to test its validity, is a myth, a theoretical construct dreamed up by the philosophers and sociologists of science. That this is so can be seen by considering the unusual difficulties that arise when a scientist attempts a replication for the specific purpose of testing its validity.

By its very nature, a replication test of this sort is seen as posing a direct challenge. The implication that there might be something amiss with a researcher's work arouses instant antagonism and defensiveness. When in March 1979 Helena Wachslicht-Rodbard asked merely for an investigation as to whether two Yale professors had done the experiment they said they'd done, she was pooh-poohed and rebuffed for a year and a half. Had it not been for a mere sixty words, which she showed the Yale researchers had lifted from an article of hers, she would never have had the hard evidence by which to insist upon her case. Yet once the investigation was undertaken, as is recounted in Chapter 9, a whole house of cards came tumbling down.

A critical assumption about the public nature of science is that a researcher will, within reason, make his raw data available to any colleague who might express a desire to see it. On the few occasions when this assumption has been put to scientific test, it was found to be sorely erroneous. Psychologist Leroy Wolins reported that a graduate student at Iowa State University wrote to thirty-seven authors of papers published in psychology journals asking for the raw data on which the papers were based.[12] Of the thirty-two authors who replied, Wolins noted, no fewer than twenty-one reported that unfortunately their data had been "misplaced, lost, or inadvertently destroyed." One might have supposed that something so precious as raw scientific data would have been kept in less accident-prone conditions. Two of the remaining eleven respondents "offered their data on the conditions that they be notified of our intended use of their data, and stated that they have control of anything that we would publish involving these data. . . . Thus raw data from nine authors were obtained. . . ."

The difficulty of laying hands on the twenty-eight sets of data that were "lost" or withheld was made somewhat more comprehensible by the horrors that emerged from the nine sets made available. Of the seven that arrived in time to be analyzed, three contained "gross errors" in their statistics. The implications of the Wolins study are almost too awesome to digest. Fewer than one in four scientists were willing to provide their raw data on request, without self-serving conditions, and nearly half of the studies analyzed had gross errors in their statistics alone. This is not the behavior of a rational, self-correcting, self-policing community of scholars.

The Wolins experiment was conducted in 1962. A similar inquiry undertaken in 1973 by J. R. Craig and S. C. Reese afforded much the same general picture, even if the details were less appalling.[13] Raw data were requested from fifty-three scientists who had published papers in psychology journals in a given month. Nine refused point-blank, saying that they were unavailable, lost, or destroyed; one apparently successful author even stated, "I have a firm policy of never releasing the original data." Eight didn't reply. Only half of the sample even offered to cooperate in some way—twenty sent data or a summary analysis, and seven offered the data on certain conditions.

"We deliberately have a very small police force because we know that poor currency will automatically be discovered and cast out," declared the then director of the National Institutes of Health, Donald Fredrickson, just prior to testifying before Congressman Gore's subcommittee investigating fraud in March 1981. Without doubt, Fredrickson believed exactly what he said, Scientists see their own profession in terms of the powerfully appealing ideal that the philosophers and sociologists have constructed. Like all believers, they tend to interpret what they see of the world in terms of what the faith says is there. The philosophers and sociologists say science is self-policing, and that replication is the automatic purifier of all defilement; scientists are taught this in their training as an article of faith; therefore so it must be.

But in fact it is seldom the case. About one-half of all scientific papers are never once cited in the year after they are published.[14] Since scientists are supposed to cite all papers on which their own work depends, for an article never to be cited means that it probably has had no influence on any other scientist's work, and hence no impact on the progress of science as a whole. This uncited half of the scientific community's gross national product is essentially unchecked, unreplicated, and maybe even unread. This is the milieu in which the Alsabtis of science thrive and flourish with no impediment to their activities. In this half of the scientific GNP at least, Fredrickson's notion that "poor currency will automatically be discovered and cast out" is probably close to fantasy.

A better test of the notion would be to take a finding that is heavily cited, that lies at the center of its discipline, and that is the focus of heated debate. If findings of this preeminence are not scrutinized, then the self-policing mechanism cannot be said to operate in even the most critical areas of the scientific enterprise. The case of Cyril Burt and the identical twins is an example of an important and highly influential finding that lay for years at the center of the scientific and public debates about the inheritability of intelligence, and that was never discovered or cast out by Burt's colleagues. As described further in Chapter 11, Burt's results were not tested or replicated or even seriously assessed by those who depended on them. Yet a few minutes' scrutiny by a skeptical observer some two decades later sufficed to show glaring implausibilities in Burt's statistics.

Another finding of central importance to the field of experimental psychology, which also escaped serious scrutiny for years, occurred in the case of Little Albert. Albert was an eleven-month-old child who gained undying fame in psychology textbooks. He was the one and only subject in a study described by J. B. Watson, founder of the Behaviorism school of psychology, which reigned supreme in the United States during the 1920's and '30's. Watson conditioned Little Albert to fear white rats and other furry objects in an experiment that became enshrined as the paradigm for human conditioning.

Later psychologists were unable to repeat the study, but that did not prevent the appealing tale of Little Albert from being related to psychology students for some sixty years. In 1980 Franz Samelson of Kansas State University raised grave doubts about the experiment. Little Albert existed, but a study of Watson's letters and records strongly suggests that the conditioning could not have occurred as Watson described.

How could the flawed experiments of both J. B. Watson and Cyril Burt have been accepted as valid by psychologists for so long? Samelson raises the bad-apple theory only to conclude that the real problem lies with the barrel: "Both of them may have, in their own ways, so convinced themselves of the truth of their theoretical ideas that the limitations of their actual data did not matter all that much. . . . But ultimately, the focus on these men's intentions is an evasion. It took more than two isolated individuals to give their data, for considerable time, an evidentiary status they did not deserve. The real, though painful, question turns out to be, Why did we not notice earlier (or say so in print if we had)?"[15]

One reason, of course, for the tolerance of error was that most of the psychologists who used Burt's or Watson's results did not try to replicate them. Besides the failure of internal criticism of the data, Samelson points to "the clear neglect of a cardinal rule of scientific method, that is, replication. Why did nobody helping to raise generations of undergraduates on Watson and Little Albert replicate the study? . . . At the technical level we have to admit, and face up to, some instances of failure of two major mechanisms that supposedly safeguard the integrity of scientific knowledge: (public) critical analysis and replication." Samelson remarks upon the high irony that both Burt and Watson "were very insistent on the objectivity and solidity of their science, as against the muddleheadedness of some of their opponents."

It is evident that replication is not an essential ingredient in the cookbook of academic science. Certainly, it is added for flavoring every now and then, but that is about all. How much erroneous or fraudulent science might be turned up if replication were regularly practiced, if self-policing were a more than imaginary mechanism? The question can be answered indirectly by looking at an area of science in which a small measure of *external* policing exists. The external police force, it so happens, turns up bad science, outright error, and deliberate fraud by the bucketful.

This unhappy corner of the scientific arena is biological testing. Each year thousands of test results on the safety of new foods, drugs, and pesticides are submitted by industry to the Food and Drug Administration (FDA) or the Environmental Protection Agency (EPA). Government officials review the data and, if they find cause to doubt their validity, can send an inspector to the physician or laboratory that provided the data. It might be imagined that only the grossest or most careless errors would be noticed in such a review. Nevertheless, an unending stream of falsified results is regularly detected by even what limited police powers the FDA and EPA possess. Following is a sampling of cases over the last decade.

RABBIT EBENEZER. A scientific investigations group set up within the FDA discovered that sixteen out of fifty physicians audited between 1967 and 1973 had submitted false data on drugs to the sponsoring companies and the government. One physician had submitted slides of liver sections from the animals in his study: the sections turned out to be all from a single liver. Similar economy was attained by a researcher who had performed all his animal trials in a single rabbit, who went by the name of Ebenezer.[16]

THE ANDREA DORIA *PHENOMENON.* FDA inspectors checking on suspicious cases find raw data are so accident-prone that they call it the *"Andrea Doria* phenomenon."[17] At hearings held before Senator Edward Kennedy in October 1979, FDA officials related the tale of "Dr. 31," who came to the agency's attention because he had furnished identical data to two companies on two different drugs. On being asked for his record, he explained to FDA inspectors that he was such a compulsive worker that he had taken all the original data with him on a picnic. They had been lost when the rowboat he was in capsized. He had tried to make the submitted data, which he conceded were invented, as close as possible to those that had been lost. The inspectors' appetite for this appealing story was diminished when they learned that he had tried to get a nurse to state that she had been in the rowboat when the accident occurred.[18]

MAGIC PENCIL RESEARCH. In 1975 an FDA official searching for something else pulled out by accident a file on Naprosyn, an anti-arthritic drug tested by a company called Industrial Bio-Test. Reading the file showed that an inspection was warranted. "What we found there is enough to make your hair stand up," said an FDA pathologist.[19] Among other horrors, rats were recorded on the data sheets as having died twice, and the weights of some animals continued to be logged in long after they had been listed as dead. Lab technicians jotted observations on their coat sleeves, and sometimes neglected to autopsy dead rats until decay rendered the task moot. Technicians nicknamed one experiment the "magic pencil study" because the final report contained analyses that had never been performed.[20]

The pulled file led six years later, in June 1981, to the indictment of the company's president and three other senior officials on charges of falsifying test results. The officials were accused of faking data on four animal studies between 1970 and 1977. An indictment alleged that they had concealed the fact that TCC, an agent in many deodorant soaps, caused the testes of mice to degenerate even at the lowest test doses. They were charged with fabricating blood and urine studies on Naprosyn, and inventing cancer-study data on an insecticide and an herbicide.[21]

THE IBT DISASTER. The four studies mentioned in the indictment represented only a fraction of the debacle. Industrial Bio-Test had been one of the country's largest independent testing labs. All together, it tested more than 600 chemicals, drugs, and food additives for both safety and effectiveness. Substances approved on the basis of IBT-conducted tests are found in consumer products ranging from garden pesticides to ice-cream dyes to jellies, fruit drinks, contact lenses, and household bleaches. Most of these tests were probably invalid. An audit by the EPA has showed that 100 percent of IBT's long-term rat studies and a majority of most other tests cannot be relied upon.[22]

RATS OUT OF A HAT. "We have encountered creative penmanship which causes test animals to appear and disappear throughout the course of a study, which makes us wonder who is running the show, a toxicologist or a magician," FDA official Ernest L. Bisson said in 1977.[23] These practices, he added, were "exceptions rather than characteristic of the data submitted to the Agency." But it is impossible to know how much fraud may exist besides these obvious lapses. "You have to rely on the integrity of the scientific community, but nothing is foolproof. When you have fraudulent data, data that have been falsified, it's never possible to always catch that," noted FDA spokesman Wayne Pines in the wake of the IBT scandal.[24] In response to the wide-scale fraud discovered at IBT and other laboratories, the FDA has drawn up regulations for good laboratory practice, and standards throughout the testing industry are being tightened. But cases of blatant fraud continue to come to light. Of the nation's estimated 12,000 clinical investigators, "perhaps as many as 10 percent do something less than (honest research)," FDA officials were saying in 1980.[25]

How common is fraud in science? The question of course does not admit of a precise answer. For one thing, the mechanisms that might detect fraud have been shown to work in a sporadic manner at best, and therefore the true dimensions of the problem can only be estimated. "Strangely enough, deliberate, conscious fraud is extremely rare in the world of academic science. . . . The only well-known case is 'Piltdown Man,' " the physicist and science watcher John Ziman stated in 1970.[26] Scientists in public forums will still often stress the rarity of fraud, despite the evidence to the contrary. Others believe that many cases go unreported, whether because fraud is difficult to detect, to prove, or in order to avoid public embarrassment. "I suspect," remarks a scientist in whose laboratory such a case occurred, "that there are many more attempts at deception than are publicized. Either they are too trivial to report, or it becomes too difficult to prove, or, more importantly, it is deemed too dangerous to make such accusations. The accuser is generally blackened with the accused. The more usual attitude toward such practices is 'Why rock the boat? Get rid of the man and say nothing.' "[27]

Some observers perceive a slight rise in the number of cases because of the increasing pressures on researchers and the quality control systems of science. Said University of Georgia ecologist Frank Golley at the 1981 meeting of the Council of Biology Editors: "We have reached the point where it is very expensive and very difficult to assure the quality of publication. An author who manufactures data or who plagiarizes another paper or a grant application is not likely to be detected. *Science* magazine reports the sensational cases of unethical performance but these cases are, I suspect, the tip of an iceberg."[28] The propensity to enhance the promise of data is particularly evident in "abstracts," a form of scientific publication that consists of the printed summary of a lecture. "There is a borderline falsification," says Robert H. Ebert, former dean of the Harvard Medical School, "that is more common than anybody knows, in which you are anticipating the results you are going to get when you put in an abstract for publication. That whole environment is bad. There should be such a great value put on accuracy that it would never occur to anybody to do that. It is kind of a moral issue of our times."[29]

The suspicion index suggested by observations such as these matches the tone of remarks that scientists will often make privately about their colleagues. Sometimes such imputations are not meant to be taken seriously, but often the listener may feel they are intended quite literally. Fraud, or at least the imputation of it, is so common that some scientific groups have their own vernacular terms—"dry-labbing it" is one expression for the activity of colleagues who prefer to derive their data from their imaginations rather than from the laboratory.

Much of course depends on what is meant by fraud in science. The complete fabrication of an experiment from start to finish is probably a rare event, not least because of the problems of verisimilitude. Minor cheating, on the other hand—tidying up data, fudging the statistics a little, finding reasons for reporting only favorable data—could well be just as common as scientific gossip assumes it to be. Respect for the canons of scientific research, remarks T. X. Barber in his study of experimental pitfalls, "is probably sufficient to prevent falsification of data on a 'grand scale' in behavioral research. It is open to question, however, whether these canons are also strong enough to prevent 'small scale' fudging in which the investigator alters his data or his statistics just enough to 'round off the edges,' to make his results more 'acceptable' (for journal publication or for his colleagues) or to more closely fit the theory to which he is committed."[30]

Beyond the conscious faking of data lies the probably vast underworld of self-deception. As is discussed further in Chapter 6, the human tendency for an observer to see what he wants to see is far from rare in science. More pernicious even than observer effects is unintentional bias in interpreting data, particularly when the scientist has some personal preference as to the outcome. "Unconscious or dimly perceived finagling is probably endemic in science, since scientists are human beings rooted in cultural contexts, not automatons directed toward external truth," writes paleontologist Stephen Gould.[31] There may appear to be a clear distinction between conscious and unconscious manipulation of data, but the two phenomena probably lie at opposite ends of a spectrum, with a murky region of semiaware legerdemain in between, rather than being totally separate behaviors.

Surveys of the problem of fraud are few and inadequate. The English magazine *New Scientist* asked its 70,000 readers in 1976 if they knew of or suspected any cases of "intentional bias."[32] Some 204 completed questionnaires were received, one purportedly from a laboratory rat. Perhaps not surprisingly, 92 percent of those who took the trouble to reply said they knew directly or indirectly of cases of cheating in science.[33] What this tells about the true frequency of cheating is probably not a great deal.

A more provocative survey was conducted in 1980 among

chemical engineers.[34] Each was asked what he would do if told by his boss to invent data and write a report saying that one catalyst was better than another, even though the real data pointed to the opposite conclusion. Somewhat amazingly, only 42 percent of the chemical engineers checked the option "Refuse to write the report, because to do so would be unethical." The rest opted for a variety of compromises, most of which involved going along to some extent with the boss's order to mispresent the situation.

Reliable data being unavailable, the frequency of fraud can only be estimated through general considerations. One view is that fraud in science should be expected to be no more and no less common than fraud in society at large. "Fraud, although it is contradictory to the aims of science as a cultural activity, is structurally endemic to institutionalized science in contemporary society," remarks sociologist Deena Weinstein.[35]

Our view is that the crime rate in science is influenced by three principal factors: the rewards, the perceived chances of getting caught, and the personal ethics of scientists. We assume the last to be generally similar to ethical standards in society at large, so we turn to the interplay of temptations and restraints in which a scientist's ethics are put to the test.

The chances of getting caught in committing a scientific fraud are probably quite small. Replication in science is a philosophical construct, not an everyday reality. It may be used to prove fraud when fraud is suspected on other grounds, but is almost never the prime cause of suspicion. Most of the cases described here are instances of whole-cloth fraud that came to light through egregious arrogance or carelessness on the part of the forger. The researcher who takes a modicum of care in committing a minor fraud is almost guaranteed immunity if the "self-policing mechanisms" of science are all he has to fear.

The rewards for cheating, on the other hand, may be quite substantial. Science works on results. A good result has a better chance than a mediocre result of being published, of helping to secure the next research grant, of winning promotion, tenure, prestige, and prizes. With high rewards, and low chances of apprehension, we would expect minor fraud to be quite commonplace.

Most of the cases described here involve major fraud, by which we mean the reporting of an experiment that did not take place. Minor fraud occurs when the experimenter selects or distorts the data from real experiments so as to make them appear smoother or more convincing. We would expect that for every case of major fraud that comes to light, a hundred or so go undetected. For each major fraud, perhaps a thousand minor fakeries are perpetrated. The reader can supply his own multiplication factors; ours would indicate that every major case of fraud that becomes public is the representative of some 100,000 others, major and minor combined, that lie concealed in the marshy wastes of the scientific literature.

The exact frequency of fraud in science is less important than the fact that it occurs, and at a far from negligible rate. The looseness of the self-policing systems of science, discussed in this and the following chapter, allows fraud to flourish. The reward system and career structure of contemporary science are among the factors that create the inducement to fraud. That is why the self-serving manipulation of data is endemic to modern science. The roots of fraud lie in the barrel, not in the bad apples that occasionally roll into public view.

CHAPTER 5

POWER
OF THE
ELITE

It is easy to envision how a community of scholars should be organized. Every idea would be taken on its merits, and every person judged on the worth of his ideas. The need for a social hierarchy would be strictly limited. Each member of the community would enjoy status that was determined by merit and that owed nothing to social standing or any other personal attribute. Elite groups might appear temporarily but would never outlast the original reason for their existence.

"The acceptance or rejection of truth claims entering the lists of science is not to depend on the personal or social attributes of their protagonists; his race, nationality, religion, class, and personal qualities are as such irrelevant," wrote the sociologist of science Robert Merton in the dark days of 1942.[1] Merton was describing "universalism," one of the four sets of institutional imperatives that in his view comprise the ethos of modern science.

Universalism is a principle noticeably absent from society at large, where stratification of all kinds is rife. Class structures of one kind or another are to be found in every country, and within them clannishness and clubbishness abound, and prestige and status are assiduously garnered for all the rewards they can bring. If Merton is right, the scientific community has insulated itself from such behavior, and it has done so not as a matter of choice but because universalism is an essential precondition if new ideas are to be efficiently assessed and added to the stock of certified knowledge.

How far is universalism realized in practice within the scientific community? We examine this question in conjunction with two mechanisms that depend critically upon universalism for the essence of their function. The first is peer review, the elaborate process by which government money is channeled to researchers. In the United States and most other countries, the government decides how much money to spend on research in cancer, defense, and so forth, but within these broad categories, the essential decisions as to which researchers should receive the money are made not by government officials but by committees of scientists expert in the field. These committees of colleagues constitute the peer review system; they wield great power within the scientific community because their verdicts on the grant applications submitted to them determine who gets funded and who goes without.

The second mechanism is the referee system, the practice whereby editors of scientific journals send out the manuscripts submitted to them for review by experts in the field. Reviewers are meant to assess whether the scientific methodology of a paper is sound, whether the results represent a significant enough advance to be worth publishing, and whether the author has made due reference in his citations to previous work in the field. Together with replication (discussed in Chapter 4) these mechanisms constitute the triple safety net against error, the "self-policing" system of science.

Unlike replication, however, peer review and the referee system depend directly on the ideals of fairness, impartiality, and freedom from bias, which are embodied in the notion of universalism. If the principle of universalism is always adhered to in science, peer review and the referee system can work perfectly; any deviation from universalism will produce correspondingly serious defects in the two mechanisms. Personal bias is one factor that can vitiate the efficiency of peer review and referees. Another is randomness, a phenomenon that occurs when there is no consistency of judgment between different judges, and the verdict depends not on the merit of the case but the judge who examines it.

The case of John Long illustrates how prestige and status can enshroud a scientific project in so much glitter that reviewers and referees are blinded as to its substance.[2] Long worked at the Massachusetts General Hospital, one of the most prestigious research and teaching hospitals in the world. He was a rising young researcher, held in high regard by the hospital authorities. His subject was Hodgkin's disease, a cancerlike disorder of uncertain causation.

Long joined the hospital as a resident in 1970 and received his research training from Paul Zamecnik, a distinguished researcher and a member of the National Academy of Sciences. Zamecnik, believing that Hodgkin's disease might be caused by a virus, was then trying to make cells from Hodgkin's disease tumors grow in the test tube. Establishing a test-tube culture of cells was an important first step toward studying their biochemistry and probing the cause of the disease. Most cultures of Hodgkin's cells die out after a time, but Long managed the unusual feat of establishing several permanent cell lines.

These cell lines became the basis of a flourishing research career for Long. He and Zamecnick described them in articles published in the *Proceedings of the National Academy of Sciences* and other journals. Long received a three-year grant for $209,000 in 1976 from the National Institutes of Health, and a further grant of $550,000 in 1979. He acquired two research assistants. He built up the right connections in the prestige-laden medical world of the Harvard-Boston community. In July 1979 he was promoted to associate professor in the department of pathology at the Massachusetts General Hospital. He started a collaboration with the group of David Baltimore, a leading cancer researcher. His work was respectfully cited by Henry Kaplan in the 1980 edition of his standard textbook on Hodgkin's disease.

Two years earlier, in the spring of 1978, Long had been presented with a vexing but minor problem. Together with his research assistant Steven Quay and others, he had written an article about the immunology of his test-tube cultures of Hodgkin's cells. Quay had measured a certain feature of the cells and found it was considerably smaller than expected. The journal to which Long had submitted the paper for publication rejected it on the advice of a referee who said that Quay's unusual measurement should be better substantiated.

In May 1978 Quay returned from a two-week vacation to learn

that Long had repeated the measurement himself and had obtained an answer nearer to the expected value. The article was resubmitted and was accepted for publication.[3]

A meticulous experimentalist, Quay was a little surprised that he had gotten the answer wrong. He was also puzzled that Long had been able to perform the complicated measurement so quickly. But it was not until more than a year later, around mid-October 1979, that Quay began to suspect that Long had never performed the measurement. With considerable trepidation, Quay asked Long to show him the raw data on which the measurement had been based. But at each request, Long insisted that the data had been lost, and angrily inquired if Quay realized what kind of accusation his request implied.

Quay realized only too well the seriousness of what he was doing. A junior biochemist who dares to imply that his superior in the hospital hierarchy may have invented data had better be right. Would a medical researcher so well connected and solidly positioned as John Long ever stoop, or even need, to invent an experiment? For two months Quay was in anguish over whether to persist or to drop his request to see Long's original data.

A few days before Christmas 1979, his worst fears came true. In an abrupt volte-face, Long suddenly presented him with a notebook full of the raw data on which the published paper had been based. Quay took one glance at it and was appalled at ever having doubted his colleague's integrity. He sat down with Long, distraught at what he had done, and poured out his regrets. Long accepted the apology graciously.

Two weeks later, Quay had still been unable to bring himself to look at the notebook in detail, but realizing he would soon have to return it to Long, he took it home for study. Late one night, after his wife and daughter were in bed, he had the notebook open in his living room. "The light was hitting the pages at an angle which showed me something I had never seen before," says Quay. It was throwing into relief a ridge in the tape that held a photograph into the notebook. Removing the tape, Quay saw part of a second piece of tape underneath, as if someone had torn the photo out of some other notebook and taped it into that one, without even bothering to hide the traces. Further scrutiny of the notebook convinced him that the data Long had provided were probably invented. In January 1980, he presented his doubts to the chairman of the pathology department at the Massachusetts General Hospital, Robert McCluskey.

McCluskey confronted Long, but Long flatly denied the charge. He had performed the experiments as reported, he said, and to prove it he produced the logbook of the laboratory's ultracentrifuge, one of the instruments used to make the questioned measurement.

The ball was now back in Quay's court. It seemed to him that the entries in the logbook had been written over, but McCluskey said that was not sufficient evidence to prove that Long was lying.

But Quay had also become suspicious of the logbook's records of the rotor count of the machine. From the other details given in the logbook about the length of run and speed of rotation, he worked out the expected rotor count. In each case, the count in the logbook was a fraction of what it should have been. An innocent explanation might have been that the machine, as is the wont of ultracentrifuges, had shut itself down through overheating before the run was completed.

In McCluskey's presence, Quay first asked Long if the machine had been still running when he came back to it. Long said, yes, it was. Quay then explained to him and McCluskey why the inconsistency of the data in the logbook meant that the experiment could not have been undertaken as described.

"Long admitted that this was a mistake made under great pressure, and said it was made under pressure for a grant application," McCluskey later recounted. Long resigned from the Massachusetts General Hospital immediately. Then began a process of investigation that led to the unraveling of Long's whole research career. Long's other research assistant, pathologist Nancy Harris, discovered an escalatingly grievous series of problems with the four lines of Hodgkin's cells on which almost all Long's work had been based.

Each of the four lines had supposedly been derived from a different patient. Harris' first discovery was that three of the lines came not from different patients but from the same individual. Further probing established the bizarre fact that whoever that individual might have been, he or she or it was not a member of the human species. After more research, the owner of the cells was found to be a northern Colombian brown-footed owl monkey.[4]

Searching back through the notebooks of Zamecnik's laboratory, where Long had first established the cell lines, Harris found that Long had been working at the same time with cells derived from an owl monkey. Evidently the test tubes of Hodgkin's cells had become contaminated with owl monkey cells, which had taken over the culture while the Hodgkin's cells died out. Long denies that the contamination was deliberate.

As for the fourth cell line, it turned out to be of human origin, but it had possibly even worse problems. Long and his mentor, Zamecnik, referred to the cell line as being derived "from Hodgkin's disease tumors in spleens."[5] But an examination of the patient's records undertaken after Long's resignation showed that the patient had no spleen tumors.[6] Zamecnik, who established the particular line, explained that he had reason to suppose that the tumors were there but just were not observed, and that the absence of tumors had been noted in earlier papers. Be that as it may, it is wrong to state that a cell line was derived from a Hodgkin's disease tumor when the patient had no observable tumors. The fourth of Long's cell lines cannot properly be described as a line of Hodgkin's disease cells.

Of the $759,000 awarded to Long for the study of his Hodgkin's cell lines, some $305,000 had been spent at the time of his resignation. Since none of the cells were of Hodgkin's disease, the money spent was an almost total waste. But the more important issue is the question of how Long succeeded in getting his applications through the peer review system, and in publishing his research in prestigious, refereed journals, when it was so largely worthless.

There was no lack of warning signals. The basic problem with Long's cell lines was contamination by other cells, an ever-present danger that has been widely advertised in the biomedical research community. The circumstance that Long and Zamecnik were almost the only researchers to have succeeded in establishing permanent Hodgkin's cell lines should have made the possibility of cell contamination stick up like a red flag. But Long's grant applications sailed twice through the peer review system without the signal being received.

"The nature of the data he was presenting had a sufficient de-

gree of plausibility that the peer review system had little opportunity to make the kind of judgment which might have detected
this earlier," says William Raub, the head of extramural research
at the National Institutes of Health. But contamination of cell
cultures by foreign cells is a frequent occurrence, and the very
kind of problem that peer review committees are supposed to
spot. According to Stephen Schiaffino, of the office that adminis-
ters the NIH peer review system: "With the credentials of background and training that Long presented, the study section [peer
review committee] would expect that he would be aware of this
problem."

In other words, because of Long's credentials—his training
under Zamecnik, his position at the Massachusetts General Hospital—the peer review system took certain aspects of his work for
granted. Long benefited from the prestige and status of the
people and institutions with which he was associated. Just as
Alsabti based a research career on nothing but stolen papers,
Long built his out of little more than elitism. Alsabti came soon
to grief, but the power of the elite bore Long aloft for a decade,
and would doubtless have carried him much further but for his
single miscalculation of placing forged data under Quay's scrutiny.

The same immunity may have allowed his published papers to
slip through the referee system, and to pass without challenge
once published. The identical photograph of the chromosome set
of one of the cell lines was published in the *Proceedings of the
National Academy of Sciences*[7] and in the *Journal of Experimental Medicine.*[8] "It is immediately obvious that this is not a human
cell line," says Walter Nelson-Rees, a cell culture expert at the
Naval Biosciences Laboratory in Oakland. Nelson-Rees suggests
two reasons to explain why the episode continued for as long as
it did: "First of all, it was a very prestigious group—Paul Zamecnik was the director of the unit. Also there seems to have been a
wholesale swallowing without adequate checks." Human cells
kept for a long period in culture can develop unusual chromo-
somes, but this should not have prevented journal referees from
realizing there was something wrong with the cells. Says Nelson-
Rees: "It just does not make sense that anyone in their right mind
would have accepted [the photograph of the chromosome set] as
proof that it was a human cell line, even a highly altered one."

Even after the Long case had come to light, the authorities at the Massachusetts General Hospital were unable to recognize that the peer review and refereeing mechanisms had not operated as they are supposed to. Long passed through both these systems more than once without the slightest difficulty; he was caught by a circumstance that had nothing to do with the formal safety mechanisms of science—the fact that a suspicious and persistent junior colleague was able to compare Long's unpublished notebooks with the ultracentrifuge logbook, also an unpublished document. Despite these facts, the research director of the Massachusetts General Hospital, Ronald Lamont-Havers, told the congressional hearings on scientific fraud that peer review is the key process that prevents error in science. He even linked this observation specifically with the Long case: "I would like to confine my remarks to those incidents, as in the case of Dr. Long, in which the individual deliberately disseminated falsified scientific data. Inherent in the scientific process itself is the means by which such error is detected and rejected. . . . It is very difficult to fudge data so that it will be uncritically accepted by an interested and knowledgeable audience. The greatest protection in science is the critical review and analysis of the published data and procedures by the scientist's peers. . . . The key element is critical review of the scientist's peers."[9]

Lamont-Havers' testimony illustrates the unshakable strength with which scientists believe in the ability of the peer review system to detect error. Despite the completely contrary evidence of the very case he was talking about, he spoke as if the theory of peer review had in no way been contradicted by it. Peer review detects all fraud, Long was a fraud, therefore peer review must have detected Long—this is the syllogism that presumably underlay his thoughts.

Long's motives in inventing data may never be known, perhaps not even to himself. When he first admitted he had done so to his department chairman, he ascribed his behavior to the pressure of having to prepare a grant application. The nature of that pressure was succinctly described and deplored by none other than a former dean of the Harvard Medical School. Commenting on the Long case in a letter to *The New York Times*, Robert Ebert wrote of the "spirit of intense, often fierce competition, which begins during the premedical experience [to get into medical school] and is encouraged thereafter. Stories of cheating among premedical students are common. . . . Once training is completed and the long hard climb on the academic ladder has begun, there is intense pressure to publish, not only to obtain research grant renewals but in order to qualify for promotion. . . . In an environment which can ever permit success to become a more coveted commodity than ethical conduct, even the angels may fall," Ebert opined.[10]

David Baltimore, who collaborated with Long on a project, raises the same possibility: "There is no question that the pressure on research workers grows because of the limitation of funds and the increasing formalism of the academic world, with its demands to produce and appear successful, and I am sure that everyone has a cracking point. But whether any of this has to do with John Long or not, I have no idea."

By the time of the congressional hearings, however, at which he appeared as a witness, Long had changed his mind about competitive pressures. In a graceful admission of error, but one perhaps couched with an eye to not offending the medical world in which he still works, Long lifted all blame from the system and placed it on his own shoulders. "I do not believe that the environment in which I worked was responsible for what I have done," he told the congressional committee under oath. "An honest investigator should be able to deal effectively with the traditional 'publish or perish' pressures. Such pressures probably exert an important positive incentive in many institutions. The loss of my ability to be an objective scientist capable of working critically and honestly in the laboratory cannot, in my case, be linked to defects in the system in which I worked. Rather, it seems to me that the system has worked effectively to correct the misdeeds of an errant investigator."

Desire to belong to the elite of medical research was perhaps a motive that led Long to slip into fraud. An elite cannot be blamed if others want to join it. But it should indeed be taken to task if its mantle allows its members to escape the scrutiny that they are loudest in proclaiming is applied to all.

Take the remarkable case of Hideyo Noguchi, a researcher who achieved worldwide fame under the patronage of Simon Flexner, one of the founders of American medical research. Flexner's better-known brother, Abraham, transformed medical education in the United States with his famous report of 1910. Simon Flexner, the first to isolate the organism that causes dysentery, helped organize the Rockefeller Institute for Medical Research (now Rockefeller University) in New York. Under his leadership, it became a leading world center for research on virus diseases.

On a visit to Japan in 1899, Flexner met an ambitious young Japanese researcher with a burning desire to succeed in medical research. Hideyo Noguchi later turned up on Flexner's doorstep in the United States and was taken under Flexner's wing. Noguchi became a scientific superstar. Following in Flexner's footsteps, he proceeded to isolate the causative organisms of numerous diseases. He reported that he had cultivated the organisms of syphilis, yellow fever, polio, rabies, and trachoma. In the course of his career he published some 200 papers, an astounding output for his time.

When Noguchi died in 1928, his achievements had brought him international fame as a medical researcher. A colleague at the Rockefeller Institute, the eminent pathologist Theobald Smith, proclaimed: "He will stand out more and more clearly as one of the greatest, if not the greatest, figure in microbiology since Pasteur and Koch."

Noguchi's work did not stand the test of time quite as well as has that of Pasteur and Koch. As the years went by, his claims to have cultivated the organisms of various diseases were at first politely contested and then quietly relegated to the long, dark corridors of forgotten research. Perhaps Noguchi had felt under pressure to produce a steady stream of outstanding results for Flexner, a stern administrator whom Noguchi held in awe as a father figure. Whatever the reason for the spurious nature of much of Noguchi's work, it was for the most part unchallenged during his lifetime. As the protégé of Flexner, and a luminary of the most prestigious research institute of its kind, Noguchi was a member of the elite. That membership shielded his work from the scientific scrutiny that should have found it wanting.

When a comprehensive evaluation of Noguchi's work was undertaken some fifty years after his death, little of it was left standing.[11] "Perhaps the chief lesson to be learned from a study of

Noguchi's career," commented a reviewer of the extraordinary episode, "is that the eminence of an investigator should not preclude a thorough testing of his scientific reports."[12]

Elitism in science has a legitimate basis, but its ubiquitous excesses affront the principle of universalism. Bad ideas get accepted because their proponents are members of the elite. More seriously, good ideas may be ignored because their advocates may have poor standing in the social structure of science.

Elitism can remain legitimate only if the elite is continually tested by the winnowing mechanisms of peer review and the referee system. As is demonstrated by the cases of Hideyo Noguchi and John Long, if you belong to the elite, your articles are less carefully reviewed, your grant proposals may be less carefully scrutinized, and you will find it easier to pick up more prizes, editorships, lectureships, and the other honorifics with which science is laden.

However legitimate may be the origins of an elite, the plain fact is that no one likes to lose his membership in it, or to give up the powers and perquisites he once enjoyed. There is an inevitable human tendency for all elites to try to render themselves immune from the very selective mechanisms that separate them from the crowd. To what extent does this happen in science? To what extent is the elite illegitimate, in the sense of accepting or retaining unworthy individuals and excluding those who deserve to belong? The issue is important because members of the elite wield enormous power and influence in the distribution of funds and promotions.

"Most scientists are aware that science is a highly stratified institution. Power and resources are concentrated in the hands of a relatively small minority," say the sociologists of science Jonathan and Stephen Cole. The Coles inquired whether the reason for the elite was because "the scientists who publish the most significant work receive the ample recognition they deserve" or whether the existing elite had firm enough control over the social institutions of science to perpetuate their own ideas and promote their own supporters and students.

As mentioned earlier, one relatively easy and effective way of measuring the importance of a scientific article is to count the number of times it is cited as a reference in other articles in the scientific literature. Since scientists are supposed to acknowledge all important work that has preceded theirs, the number of citations to a particular article is, generally speaking, a significant measure of the article's influence or lack of it. By extension, the number of citations to the lifetime work of a scientist can also be an indication of his influence in the field.

Using citations as a yardstick, the Coles conclude that for the most part, a relatively small number of physicists produce a disproportionately large share of the most important papers in physics.[13] Conversely, a large number of physicists produce work that apparently makes no contribution to the advance of science, because it is rarely or never cited. Even in *Physical Review,* one of the leading physics journals in the world, 80 percent of the articles appearing in 1963 were cited only four times or less in the whole physics literature in 1966, and 47 percent of the articles were cited once or never in that year. In other words, the bulk of articles in even the best physics journals have been virtually forgotten by physicists three years later.

The picture given by the Coles' study is of a small number of highly cited physicists working in a crowd of less productive researchers. The highly cited physicists seem to be members of the social elite of physics in that they tend to be concentrated at the nine best physics departments in the country, and to be members of the National Academy of Sciences. Thus at least some members of the power elite of the physics community are there by merit, and probably to a large extent the elite is intellectually legitimate. But there may be a "halo effect"—the mere fact of belonging to an elite physics department would make a scientist's work more visible and therefore more highly cited.

What the Coles allude to as the halo effect is called the "Matthew effect" by sociologist Robert Merton. He has described "a complex pattern of the misallocation of credit for scientific work," whereby already eminent scientists tend to get credit for an idea at the expense of young or unknown scientists.[14] The phenomenon is particularly evident in joint projects; if a paper is signed by an unknown scientist and his Nobel laureate professor, the world will tend to credit the laureate for the discovery, regardless of his actual contribution. "For unto every one that hath shall be given, and he shall have abundance: but from him that hath not shall be taken away even that which he hath," says the text in St. Matthew's gospel from which Merton names the effect.

Merton believes that the Matthew effect is generally beneficial in the communications system of science because, amid the increasing clutter of scientific papers, it helps draw attention to those likely to be particularly significant. But he recognizes the less benign aspect of the effect, that it obscures the work of unknown scientists: "The history of science abounds in instances of basic papers having been written by comparatively unknown scientists, only to be neglected for years." Ohm's discovery of the law of electrical resistance, which now bears his name, was at first ignored by scientists at German universities; they thought little attention could be worth paying to the work of a math teacher at the Jesuit Gymnasium in Cologne. Mendel's writings on the basic laws of genetics were widely distributed in the scientific community of his time, but as an obscure abbé with no scientific standing, his work was ignored throughout his lifetime.

"When the Matthew effect is thus transformed into an idol of authority," Merton concedes, "it violates the norm of universalism embodied in the institution of science and curbs the advancement of knowledge. But next to nothing is known about the frequency with which these practices are adopted by the editors and referees of scientific journals and by other gatekeepers of science."

Since this observation was made, there have been several attempts to assess how fairly and efficiently the gatekeepers of science perform their function. The scientists who sit on the peer review committees are among the most important gatekeepers of science, since without their nod of approval a researcher generally cannot raise the money to support his work. To what extent is peer review a fair and efficient system?

The peer review system is sometimes accused of operating like an old-boy network because its members are drawn from the same elite groups and institutions that end up receiving the bulk of the grants. According to one critic, former Representative John B. Conlan of Arizona, the peer review system operated by the National Science Foundation "is an 'old boys system' where program managers rely on trusted friends in the academic community to review their proposals. These friends recommend their friends as reviewers. . . . It is an incestuous 'buddy system' that frequently stifles new ideas and scientific breakthroughs, while carving up the multimillion-dollar Federal research-and-education pie in a monopoly game of grantsmanship."

The best test of the efficiency of the peer review system would be to conduct a follow-up study to measure the productivity of the scientists funded by the various U.S. government agencies. No such study has been done, so that no definitive verdict can be given. The next-best insight into peer review comes from a study by the Coles of the system operated by the National Science Foundation. The results surprised both critics and defenders of the peer review system.

The Coles found the system fair in the sense that they observed no tendency for reviewers at elite institutions to favor proposals from elite institutions over those from places outside the elite. The system is "exceedingly equitable," they concluded; in other words, they could find no evidence for an old-boy network or buddy system.[15] But the Coles came up with an unexpected and far more fundamental criticism: that there is a large element of chance in the verdicts handed down by the peer review system.

The more rational the review process, the greater measure of agreement there should be among two groups of reviewers assessing the same proposals. The Coles took grant applications that had already been reviewed by the NSF and submitted them to a second group of equally competent reviewers. The proposals were drawn, fifty each, from the three fields of solid-state physics, chemical dynamics, and economics. In fact, there was wide disagreement in the ratings given to the same proposal by the two review groups. Many proposals that the NSF had decided to fund would have been rejected by the Coles' reviewers and vice versa. The Coles calculate that the fate of a particular grant application depends only half on its merits and half on "apparently random elements which might be characterized as the 'luck of the reviewer draw.' "[16]

The reviewers disagree among themselves so much, the Coles believe, because they disagree as to what good science in their fields is or should be. The conclusion is particularly interesting because two of the fields of science chosen, chemical dynamics and solid-state physics, are hard sciences in which a considerable measure of consensus would have been expected. The Coles conclude: "Contrary to a widely held belief that science is character-ized by wide agreement about what is good work, who is doing good work, and what are promising lines of inquiry, our research . . . indicates that concerning work currently in process there is substantial disagreement in all scientific fields."

The random element in the peer review system is probably present to at least the same extent in the referee system, which judges the quality of papers rather than grant applications. At least anecdotally, refereeing seems more susceptible to personal bias than peer review. For almost every scientist who has had an article rejected, the letter written by T. H. Huxley expresses a familiar thought: "Merit alone is very little good; it must be backed by tact and knowledge of the world to do very much. For instance, I know that the paper I have just sent in [to the Royal Society] is very original and of some importance, and I am equally sure that if it is referred to the judgment of my 'particular friend'——that it will not be published. He won't be able to say a word against it, but he will pooh-pooh it to a dead certainty. . . . So I must manoeuvre a little to get my poor memoir kept out of his hands."[17]

Personal bias in the referee system can work the other way too. The eminent English physicist Lord Rayleigh submitted a paper from which his name had been inadvertently omitted. According to his son and biographer, "The Committee 'turned it down' as the work of one of those curious persons called paradoxers. How-ever, when the authorship was discovered, the paper was found to have merits after all."[18] More systematic studies of bias in the referee system have produced mixed results.

A study of refereeing practices in the leading physics journal *Physical Review* detected no systematic bias. "For this journal at least, the relative status of referee and author had no perceptible influence on patterns of evaluation," state Robert Merton and Harriet Zuckerman.[19] Less comforting are the tests of consistency that have been applied to the system. When ten high-quality published articles in psychology were resubmitted, with the authors' names and affiliations changed, to the very same journals that had published them some two years earlier, only three of the pseudomanuscripts were detected as masquerades. The other seven went out for review before twenty-two editors and reviewers, only four of whom (18 percent) recommended publication. "A rather massive lack of reliability exists in the editorial practices," conclude the authors of the study.*[20]

A more elaborate investigation was designed to scrutinize referees' theoretical biases in assessing papers. Michael J. Mahoney had a journal send out fictitious manuscripts on a hotly debated aspect of child psychology to seventy-five referees whose personal positions on the problem were on record. The manuscripts all described the same experimental procedure but the purported results were different, some favoring the reviewer's perspective, some refuting it. The result: "Identical manuscripts suffered very different fates depending on the direction of their data. When they were positive (i.e., in accord with the referee's particular bias), the usual recommendation was to accept with moderate revisions. Negative results earned a significantly lower evaluation. . . ."[21]

By accident, a glaring error was introduced in the manuscripts sent out for review. The error was not spotted equally by all reviewers: in manuscripts with "positive" results, only 25 percent of the reviewers noted it; but the error was obvious to 71 percent of the reviewers when the results were "negative," i.e., inconsistent with the reviewer's theoretical perspective.

As a principal mechanism for the screening out of fraud and incompetence, the refereeing system seems sometimes to suffer from plain dysfunction. Take the notable case of the three scientists at the Indian Veterinary Research Institute in Uttar Pradesh who announced in an article in *Science*, a leading research magazine, that they had discovered cysts of a parasite known as toxoplasma in hens' eggs. The parasite had not been previously detected in eggs, and the new finding raised the specter of a public health hazard. The Indians did not neglect to point out this implication: "Our data support the hypothesis that raw eggs could serve as sources of infections for human beings," they concluded.[22] Just the kind of article that would undergo assiduous review be-

---

* The study was inspired by the experiment of a free-lance writer who submitted a retyped manuscript of *Steps*, a National Book Award winning novel by Jerzy Kosinski, to fourteen major publishing houses as if it were the work of an aspiring but unknown author. All fourteen publishers rejected the manuscript, including Random House, which had originally published it.

fore publication, one might suppose. Alas, not all turned out to be well with the photographs of the toxoplasma that accompanied the article. First, lurking in the background were the obvious shapes of mammalian red blood cells, curious entities to find in an egg. Second, one photograph with the article was on inspection clearly the same as the purportedly different second photograph, except that it was enlarged and turned on its side. Third, the photograph had been first published by another scientist five years earlier. "We apologize to our readers for this unfortunate event," said the members of the editorial board of *Science,* noting that the editors of the *Journal of Infectious Diseases* had similarly been taken by the three Indians.[23]

No one would expect the peer review and referee systems to be perfect, despite the exalted claims that are often made for them. But both seem to have a significant random element built into them. A semirandom system is, of course, far easier to manipulate than one that dispenses exact justice. It allows greater leeway for all the nonlogical factors that influence human decision-making. The fraudulent scientist who can make his results look plausible may have a better chance of slipping through the system than does a genius with a radically innovative idea. The looseness of the system allows the John Longs of science to penetrate it time after time without challenge.

A spectacular example of how a whole scientific enterprise can be corrupted by rampant elitism is afforded by the case of M. S. Swaminathan and the wheat strain known as Sharbati Sonora.[24] In this debacle, personal bias ran roughshod over the mechanisms of peer review and the referee system at every turn. In 1967 Swaminathan, one of India's most eminent agricultural scientists, announced that he and his team at the Indian Agricultural Research Institute had developed a new strain of high-yielding wheat. Called Sharbati Sonora, the strain was claimed to have more protein and more of the important amino acid lysine than does the Mexican dwarf wheat strain from which it was derived.

Since lysine is low in plant protein and vegetarians may not get enough lysine in their diets, the development of Sharbati Sonora was hailed as a triumph of Third World science that would help improve nutrition in developing countries. Unfortunately the claims of higher protein and lysine contents proved to be incor-

rect. An analysis published in 1969 by CIMMYT, Norman Bor-
laug's institute in Mexico where the dwarf wheat strains were
developed, shows that the lysine and protein contents of Sharbati
Sonora were no different from those of the parent strain.

Swaminathan published at least one paper repeating the higher
claims after they had been disproved by the CIMMYT report.
But how were the incorrect results arrived at in the first place?
In 1972 Swaminathan became director general of the Indian
Council of Agricultural Research. A few months later a senior
agronomist on his staff, Vinod H. Shah, committed suicide. A
note left by Shah and addressed to Swaminathan complained
of promotion practices but also alleged that "a lot of unscientific data are collected and passed on to you to fit your line of
thinking."

A committee was appointed by the Indian government to investigate the charges. The measured lysine content of the parent
wheat had been "deliberately changed" by a senior official in the
council in 1968 "so that Sharbati Sonora might appear in a more
favourable light," reported an advisory panel to the investigatory
committee. But the alteration was merely a symptom of more
widespread disease. "Many junior scientists in IARI [the Indian
Agricultural Research Institute], rightly or wrongly, feel that
they are not free to publish a scientific finding because it does
not suit somebody higher up or that in fact unscientific data are
being passed on to the higher authorities in return of favours
and promotions," said the panel.

The panel did not feel that it was dealing with an isolated
phenomenon. "Barring minor exceptions," continued the report,
"it pervades the entire scientific and academic community in this
country. At the root of it is the greed for bureaucratic power and
love of a comfortable life that afflicts this class."

Indian cultural traditions may differ widely from those of
Europe or America. But even allowing for a measure of over-
emphasis or spite that may be detectable in the panel's words,
its report suggests that elitism can become a severely corrupting
influence within a scientific community if not kept severely in
check. The bureaucratic power structure of the Indian research
system ran roughshod over the mechanisms that supposedly
guarantee the integrity of scientific results. The Sharbati Sonora

incident was not seen in India as any reflection on Swaminathan. In 1982 he was appointed by Prime Minister Indira Gandhi to lead a new national scientific council intended to coordinate India's hundreds of research institutes.[25]

Universalism is an ideal in science, but one with serious limitations in practice. The elites that pervade all branches of science may have a legitimate basis, but there is also a strong illegitimate component in scientific elitism that is the direct antagonist to universalism. Members of the elite are sheltered from the scrutiny that is supposedly applied without fear or favor to all scientists.

Immunity from scrutiny constitutes a severe blind spot in the peer review and referee systems. Moreover, the random element built into these two systems, deriving from a lack of consensus as to what constitutes good science, severely limits their ability to accept radical new ideas and to reject bad or fraudulent science. Peer review and refereeing are at best coarse screens, not the infallible, fine discrimination systems that scientists often portray them to be. They separate wheat from chaff on a better than random basis but still allow a considerable measure of chaff to enter along with the wheat. A system that has serious difficulty in consistently recognizing good science is unlikely to be invariably successful in detecting fraud, and in practice, frauds are almost never detected in this way.

The ultimate gatekeeper of science is neither peer review, nor referees, nor replication, nor the universalism implicit in all three mechanisms. It is time. In the end, bad theories don't work, fraudulent ideas don't explain the world so well as true ideas do. The ideal mechanisms by which science should work are applied to a large extent in retrospect. "The key element is critical review of the scientist's peers," a scientist can say of the Long case, even though peer review failed entirely. Time and the invisible boot that kicks out all useless science are the true gatekeepers of science. But these inexorable mechanisms take years, sometimes more than a millennium, to operate. During the interval, fraud may flourish, particularly if it can find shelter under the mantle of immunity that scientific elitism confers.

CHAPTER 6

SELF-DECEPTION
AND
GULLIBILITY

In 1669 the distinguished English physicist Robert Hooke made a wonderful discovery. He obtained the long-sought proof of Copernicus' heliocentric theory of the solar system by demonstrating stellar parallax—a perceived difference in position of a star due to the earth's motion around the sun. One of the first to use a telescope for this purpose, Hooke observed the star Gamma Draconis and soon reported to the Royal Society that he had found what he was looking for: the star had a parallax of almost thirty seconds of arc. Here at last was impeccable experimental proof of the Copernican theory.

This heartening triumph of empirical science was only momentarily dashed when the Frenchman Jean Picard announced he had observed the star Alpha Lyrae by the same method but had failed to find any parallax at all. A few years later England's first Astronomer Royal, the brilliant observer John Flamsteed, reported that the Pole Star had a parallax of at least forty seconds.

Hooke and Flamsteed, outstanding scientists of their day, are leading lights in the history of science. But they fell victim to an effect that to this day has continued to trap many lesser scientists in its treacherous coils. It is the phenomenon of experimenter expectancy, or seeing what you want to see. There is indeed a stellar parallax, but because of the vast distance of all stars from earth, the parallax is extremely small—about one second of arc.

It cannot be detected by the relatively crude telescopes used by Hooke and Flamsteed.[1]

Self-deception is a problem of pervasive importance in science. The most rigorous training in objective observation is often a feeble defense against the desire to obtain a particular result. Time and again, an experimenter's expectation of what he will see has shaped the data he recorded, to the detriment of the truth. This unconscious shaping of results can come about in numerous subtle ways. Nor is it a phenomenon that affects only individuals. Sometimes a whole community of researchers falls prey to a common delusion, as in the extraordinary case of the French physicists and N-rays, or—some would add—American psychologists and ape sign language.

Expectancy leads to self-deception, and self-deception leads to the propensity to be deceived by others. The great scientific hoaxes, such as the Beringer case and the Piltdown man discussed in this chapter, demonstrate the extremes of gullibility to which some scientists may be led by their desire to believe. Indeed, professional magicians claim that scientists, because of their confidence in their own objectivity, are easier to deceive than other people.

Self-deception and outright fraud differ in volition—one is unwitting, the other deliberate. Yet it is perhaps more accurate to think of them as two extremes of a spectrum, the center of which is occupied by a range of actions in which the experimenter's motives are ambiguous, even to himself. Many measurements that scientists take in the laboratory admit judgment factors to enter in. An experimenter may delay a little in pressing a stopwatch, perhaps to compensate for some extraneous factor. He can tell himself he is rejecting for technical reasons a result that gives the "wrong" answer; after a number of such rejections, the proportion of "right" answers in the acceptable experiments may acquire a statistical significance that previously was lacking. Naturally it is only the "acceptable" experiments that get published. In effect, the experimenter has selected his data to prove his point, in a way that is in part a deliberate manipulation but which also falls short of conscious fraud.

The "double-blind" experiment—in which neither doctor nor patients know who is receiving a test drug and who a placebo—

has become standard practice in clinical research because of the powerful effects of the doctor's expectancy, to say nothing of the patients'. But the habit of "blinding" the experimenter has not become as universal in science as perhaps it should. A dramatic demonstration of experimenter expectancy has been provided in a series of studies by Harvard psychologist Robert Rosenthal. In one of his experiments he gave psychology students two groups of rats to study. The "maze-bright" group of rats, the students were told, had been specially bred for its intelligence in running mazes. The "maze-dull" group were genetically stupid rats. The students were told to test the maze-running abilities of the two groups. Sure enough, they found that the maze-bright rats did significantly better than the maze-dull rats. In fact there was no difference between the maze-bright and maze-dull animals: all were the standard strain of laboratory rats. The difference lay only in the students' expectancies of each group. Yet the students translated this difference in their expectancies into the data they reported.[2]

Perhaps some of the students consciously invented data to accord with the results they thought they should be getting. With others, the manipulation was unconscious and much more subtle. Just how it was done is rather hard to explain. Perhaps the students handled more gently the rats they expected to perform better, and the treatment enhanced the rats' performance. Perhaps in timing the run through the maze the students would unconsciously press the button on the stopwatch a fraction too early for the maze-bright rats and a fraction too late for the maze-dull animals. Whatever the exact mechanism, the researchers' expectations had shaped the result of the experiment without their knowledge.

The phenomenon is not just a pitfall for laboratory scientists. Consider the situation of a teacher administering IQ tests to a class. If he has prior expectations about the children's intelligence, are these likely to shape the results he gets? The answer is yes, they do. In an experiment similar to that performed on the psychology students, Rosenthal told teachers at an elementary school that he had identified certain children with a test that predicted academic blooming. Unknown to the teachers, the test was just a standard IQ test, and the children identified as "bloomers" were chosen at random. At the end of the school year, the children were retested, by the teachers this time, with the same test. In the first grade, those who had been identified to the teachers as academic bloomers gained fifteen IQ points more than did the other children. The "bloomers" in the second grade gained ten points more than the controls. Teachers' expectancies made no or little difference in the upper grades. In the lower grades, comments Rosenthal, "the children have not yet acquired those reputations that become so difficult to change in the later grades and which give teachers in subsequent grades the expectancies for the pupil's performance. With every successive grade it would be more difficult to change the child's reputation."[3]

A particularly fertile ground for scientific self-deception lies in the field of animal-to-man communication. Time and again, the researcher's expectation has been projected onto the animal and reflected back to the researcher without his recognizing the source. The most famous case of this sort is that of Clever Hans, a remarkable horse that could apparently add and substract and even solve problems that were presented to it. He has acquired immortality because his equine spirit returns from time to time to haunt the laboratories of experimental psychologists, announcing its presence with ghostly laughter that its victims are almost always the last to hear.

Hans's trainer, a retired German schoolteacher named Wilhelm Von Osten, sincerely believed that he had taught Hans the ability to count. The horse would tap out numbers with his hoof, stopping when he had reached the right answer. He would count not just for his master but for others as well. The phenomenon was investigated by a psychologist, Oskar Pfungst, who discovered that Von Osten and others were unconsciously cuing the equine prodigy. As the horse reached the number of hoof taps corresponding to the correct answer, Von Osten would involuntarily jerk his head. Perceiving this unconscious cue, Hans would stop tapping. Pfungst found that the horse could detect head movements as slight as one-fifth of a millimeter. Pfungst himself played the part of the horse and found that twenty-three out of twenty-five questioners unwittingly cued him when to stop tapping.

Pfungst's celebrated investigation of the Clever Hans phenomenon was published in English in 1911, but his definitive account did not prevent others from falling into the same trap as Von Osten. Man's age-old desire to communicate with other species could not so easily be suppressed. By 1937 there were more than seventy "thinking" animals, including cats and dogs as well as horses. In the 1950's the fashion turned to dolphins. Then came an altogether new twist in the dialogue between man and animals. The early attempts to teach speech to chimpanzees had faltered because of the animals' extreme physical difficulty in forming human sounds. Much greater progress was made when Allen and Beatrice Gardner of the University of Nevada taught American Sign Language to their chimpanzee Washoe.

Washoe and her imitators readily acquired large vocabularies of the sign language and, even more significantly, would string the signs together in what appeared to be sentences. Particularly evocative was the apes' reported use of the signs in apposite novel combinations. Washoe was said to have spontaneously made the signs for "drink" and "fruit" on seeing a watermelon. Gorilla Koko reportedly described a zebra as a "white tiger." By the 1970's the signing apes had become a flourishing subfield of psychological research.

Then came a serious crisis in the form of an ape named Nim Chimpsky, in honor of the well-known linguist Noam Chomsky. Nim's trainer, psychologist Herbert Terrace, found he learned signs just like the other chimps, and started using them in strings. But were the strings of signs proper sentences or just a routine that the crafty ape had learned would induce some appropriate action in its human entourage? Certain features in Nim's linguistic development threw Terrace into a crisis of doubt. Unlike children of his age, Nim suddenly plateaued in his rate of acquisition of new vocabulary. Unlike children, he rarely initiated conversation. He would string signs together, but his sentences were lacking in syntactic rigor: Nim's longest recorded utterance was the sixteen-sign declarative pronouncement, "Give orange me give eat orange me eat orange give me eat orange give me you."

Terrace was eventually forced to decide that Chimpsky, and indeed the other pointing pongids, were not using the signs in a way characteristic of true language. Rather, they were probably making monkeys out of their teachers by imitating or Clever Hansing them. Nim's linguistic behavior was more like that of a highly intelligent, trained dog than of the human children he so much resembled in other ways.

The critics began to move in on the field. "We find the ape 'language' researchers replete with personalities who believe themselves to be acting according to the most exalted motivations and sophisticated manners, but in reality have involved themselves in the most rudimentary circus-like performances," wrote Jean Umiker-Sebeok and Thomas Sebeok.[4] At a conference in 1980, Sebeok was even more forthright: "In my opinion, the alleged language experiments with apes divide into three groups: one, outright fraud; two, self-deception; three, those conducted by Terrace. The largest class by far is the middle one."[5] The battle is not yet over, but the momentum at present lies with the critics. Should they prove correct, the whole field of ape language research will slide rapidly into disrepute, and the ghost of Clever Hans will once again enjoy the last laugh.

Researchers' propensity for self-delusion is particularly strong when other species enter the scene as vehicles for human imaginings and projections. But scientists are capable of deluding themselves without any help from other species. The most remarkable known case of a collective self-deception is one that affected the community of French physicists in the early 1900's. In 1903 the distinguished French physicist René Blondlot announced he had discovered a new kind of rays, which he named N-rays, after the University of Nancy, where he worked.

In the course of trying to polarize X rays, discovered by Röntgen eight years earlier, Blondlot found evidence of a new kind of emanation from the X-ray source. It made itself apparent by increasing the brightness of an electric spark jumping between a pair of pointed wires. The increase in brightness had to be judged by eye, a notoriously subjective method of detection. But that seemed to matter little in view of the fact that other physicists were soon able to repeat and extend Blondlot's findings.

A colleague at the University of Nancy discovered that N-rays were emitted not just by X-ray sources but also by the nervous system of the human body. A Sorbonne physicist noticed that N-rays emanated from Broca's area, the part of the brain that governs speech, while a person was talking. N-rays were discovered in gases, magnetic fields, and chemicals. Soon the pursuit of N-rays had become a minor industry among French scientists. Leading French physicists commended Blondlot for his discovery. The French Academy of Sciences bestowed its valuable Leconte prize on him in 1904. The effects of N-rays "were observed by at least forty people and analyzed in some 300 papers by 100 scientists and medical doctors between 1903 and 1906," notes an historian of the episode.[6]

N-rays do not exist. The researchers who reported seeing them were the victims of self-deception. What was the reason for this collective delusion? An important clue may be found in the reaction to an article written in 1904 by the American physicist R. W. Wood. During a visit to Blondlot's laboratory, Wood correctly divined that something peculiar was happening. At one point Blondlot darkened the laboratory to demonstrate an experiment in which N-rays were separated into different wavelengths after passing through a prism. Wood surreptitiously removed the prism before the experiment began, but even with the centerpiece of his apparatus sitting in his visitor's pocket, Blondlot obtained the expected results. Wood wrote a devastating account of his visit in an English scientific journal. Science is supposed to transcend national boundaries, but Wood's critique did not. Scientists outside France immediately lost interest in N-rays, but French scientists continued for several years to support Blondlot.

"The most astonishing facet of the episode," notes the French scientist Jean Rostand, "is the extraordinarily great number of people who were taken in. These people were not pseudo-scientists, charlatans, dreamers, or mystifiers; far from it, they were true men of science, disinterested, honorable, used to laboratory procedure, people with level heads and sound common sense. This is borne out by their subsequent achievements as Professors, Consultants and Lecturers. Jean Bacquerel, Gilbert Ballet, André Broca, Zimmern, Bordier—all of them have made their contribution to science."[7]

The reason why the best French physicists of their day continued to support Blondlot after Wood's critique was perhaps the same as the reason for which they uncritically accepted Blondlot's findings in the first place. It all had to do with a sentiment that is supposed to be wholly foreign to science: national pride. By 1900 the French had come to feel that their international reputation in science was on the decline, particularly with respect to the Germans. The discovery of N-rays came just at the right time to soothe the self-doubts of the rigid French scientific hierarchy. Hence the Academy of Sciences, faced after the Wood exposé with almost unanimous criticism from abroad and strong skepticism at home, chose nonetheless to rally round Blondlot rather than ascertain the truth. The members of the academy's Leconte prize committee, which included the Nancy-born Henri Poincaré, chose Blondlot over the other leading candidate, Pierre Curie, who had shared the Nobel prize the year before.

Most historians and scientists who have written about the N-ray affair describe it as pathological, irrational, or otherwise deviant. One historian who is not part of this consensus is Mary Jo Nye. To seek an understanding of the episode, she chose to examine "not the structure of Blondlot's psyche, but rather the structure of Blondlot's scientific community, its organization, aims and aspirations around 1900." Her conclusion, in brief, is that the episode arose from at most an exaggeration of the usual patterns of behavior among scientific communities. The N-ray affair, she says, "was not 'pathological,' much less 'irrational' or 'pseudoscientific.' The scientists involved in the investigations and debate were influenced in a normal, if sometimes exaggerated, way by traditional reductionist scientific aims, by personal competitive drives, and by institutional, regional, and national loyalties."[8]

That a whole community of scientists can be led astray by nonrational factors is a phenomenon that bears some pondering. To dismiss it as "pathological" is merely to affix a label. In fact the N-ray affair displays in extreme form several themes endemic to the scientific process. One is the unreliability of human observers. The fact is that all human observers, however well trained, have a strong tendency to see what they expect to see. Even when subjectively assessed qualities such as the brightness of a spark are replaced by instruments such as counters or print-outs, observer effects still enter in. Careful studies of how people read measuring devices has brought to light the "digit preference phenomenon" in which certain numbers are unconsciously preferred over others.[9]

Theoretical expectation is one factor that may distort a scientist's observation. The desire for fame and recognition may prevent such distortions from being corrected. In the case of N-rays, a nexus of personal, regional, and national ties combined to carry French physicists far away from the ideal modes of scientific inquiry, and not only that, but to persist in gross error for long after it had been publicly pointed out.

Do scientists take adequate steps to protect themselves from experimental pitfalls of this nature? "Blinded" studies, in which the researcher recording the data does not know what the answer is supposed to be, are a useful precaution but are not sufficient to rule out self-deception. So pervasive are the coils of self-deception in the biological sciences that a foolproof methodology is hard to devise. Theodore X. Barber compiled a manual of pitfalls in experimental research with human subjects, which he concluded with the following poignant postscript: "Before this text was mailed to the publisher, it was read critically by nine young researchers or graduate students. After completing the text, three of the readers felt that, since there were so many problems in experimental research, it may be wiser to forsake experimentation in general (and laboratory experiments in particular) and to limit our knowledge-seeking attempts to other methods, for example, to naturalistic field studies or to participant observation."[10]

The bedrock of science is observation and experiment, the empirical procedures that make it different from other kinds of knowledge. Yet observation turns out to be most fallible when it is most needed: when an experimenter's objectivity falters. Take the case of the eighteenth-century savant Johann Jacob Scheuchzer, who set out to find evidence that mankind at the time of Noah had been caught up in a terrible flood. Find it he did, and Scheuchzer hailed the skeletal remains of his flood man as *Homo diluvii testis.* Examination years later showed the fossil to be a giant amphibian, long ago extinct.

Twentieth-century science has not escaped the danger to which Scheuchzer fell victim. When the American astronomer Adriaan van Maanen announced in 1916 that he had observed rotations in spiral nebulae, the result was accepted because it confirmed a prevailing belief that the nebulae were nearby objects. Later work by Edwin Hubble, van Maanen's colleague at the Mount Wilson Observatory, showed that, to the contrary, the spiral nebulae are galaxies at an immense distance from our own, and that they do not rotate in the manner described by van Maanen. What made van Maanen's eyes deceive him?

The standard explanation, promulgated in such publications as the *Dictionary of Scientific Biography,* is that "the changes he was attempting to measure were at the very limits of precision of his equipment and techniques."[11] But random error of the sort suggested cannot explain the fact that van Maanen over the course of a decade reported many nebulae to be rotating in the same direction (unwinding rather than winding up). The subjectivity of scientific observers has prompted a historian of the van Maanen affair, Norriss Hetherington, to comment that "today science holds the position of queen of the intellectual disciplines. . . . The decline of the dominance of theology followed from historical studies that revealed the human nature and thus the human status of theology. Historical and sociological studies that begin to investigate a possible human element of science similarly threaten to topple the current queen."[12]

Self-deception is so potent a human capability that scientists, supposedly trained to be the most objective of observers, are in fact peculiarly vulnerable to deliberate deception by others. The reason may be that their training in the importance of objectivity leads them to ignore, belittle, or suppress in themselves the very nonrational factors that the hoaxster relies on. The triumph of preconceived ideas over common sense has seldom been more complete than in the case of Dr. Johann Bartholomew Adam Beringer.

A physician and learned dilettante of eighteenth-century Germany, Beringer taught at the University of Würzburg and was adviser and chief physician to the prince-bishop. Not content with his status as a mere healer and academician, he threw himself into the study of "things dug from the earth," and began a collection of natural rarities such as figured stones, as fossils were then called. The collection assumed a remarkable character in

1725, when three Würzburg youths brought him the first of a series of extraordinary stones they had dug up from nearby Mount Eivelstadt.[13]

This new series of figured stones was a treasure trove of insects, frogs, toads, birds, scorpions, snails, and other creatures. As the youths brought further objects of their excavations to the eager Beringer, the subject matter of the fossils became distinctly unusual. "Here were leaves, flowers, plants, and whole herbs, some with and some without roots and flowers," wrote Beringer in a book of 1726 describing the amazing discovery. "Here were clear depictions of the sun and moon, of stars, and of comets with their fiery tails. And lastly, as the supreme prodigy commanding the reverent admiration of myself and of my fellow examiners, were magnificent tablets engraved in Latin, Arabic, and Hebrew characters with the ineffable name of Jehovah."

Shortly after the publication of his book, historical accounts relate, Beringer discovered on Mount Eivelstadt the most unusual fossil of all, one that carried his own name.

An official inquiry was held, at Beringer's request, to discover who was responsible for perpetrating the hoax. One of the young diggers turned out to be in the employ of two of Beringer's rivals, J. Ignatz Roderick, professor of geography, algebra, and analysis at the University of Würzburg, and the Honorable Georg von Eckhart, privy councillor and librarian to the court and to the university. Their motive had been to make Beringer a laughingstock because "he was so arrogant."

What also emerged at the inquiry was that the hoaxsters, apparently fearful that things might go too far, had tried to open Beringer's eyes to the prank before the publication of his book. They started a rumor that the stones were fakes, and when that didn't work they had him told directly. Beringer could not be persuaded that the whole thing was a massive piece of fakery; he went ahead and published his book.

Even within Beringer's lifetime, the legend of the "lying stones" began to gain momentum. By 1804, James Parkinson in his book *Organic Remains of a Former World* mentioned the debacle and drew out a lesson: "It plainly demonstrates, that learning may not be sufficient to prevent an unsuspecting man, from becoming the dupe of excessive credulity. It is worthy of being mentioned, on another account: the quantity of censure and ridicule, to which its author was exposed, served, not only to render his contemporaries less liable to imposition; but also more cautious in indulging in unsupported hypotheses."[14]

Parkinson was not the only observer to comment on the salutary effect of hoaxes in promoting skepticism. In 1830, in his book *Reflections on the Decline of Science in England,* Charles Babbage remarked: "The only excuse which has been made for them is when they have been practised on scientific academies which had reached the period of dotage." By way of example he noted how the editors of a French encyclopedia had credulously copied the description of a fictitious animal that a certain Gioeni claimed to have discovered in Sicily and had named after himself, *Gioenia sicula.*[15]

When hoaxes go awry, it is often for want of occasion, not of gullibility on the part of the intended victims, as in the case of the Orgueil meteorite, a shower of stones that fell near the village of Orgueil, France, on the night of May 14, 1864. A few weeks earlier, Louis Pasteur had started a furious debate in France by delivering the famous lecture before the French Academy in which he derided the long-standing theory of spontaneous generation, which held that life-forms can develop from inanimate matter. Noticing that the material of the Orgueil meteorite became pasty when exposed to water, a hoaxster molded some seeds and particles of coal into a sample of the meteorite and waited for them to be discovered by Pasteur's opponents. The hoaxster's motive was presumably to let them adduce the seeds as evidence for life spontaneously generating in outer space, whereupon he would pull the rug out from under them by announcing the hoax.

What went wrong with the scheme was that the doctored fragment was never examined during the debate. Though other pieces of the meteorite were intensively studied at the time, the hoaxster's carefully prepared fragment lay unexamined in a glass display jar at the Musée d'Histoire at Montauban, France, for ninety-eight years. When its turn at last came, in 1964, the incentive for belief had disappeared, and the forgery was immediately recognized as such.[16]

Had the fragment been studied at the time, the hoax would doubtless have been successful. When the conditions are right, there is no limit to human gullibility, as was proved by the remarkable incident of the Piltdown man.

British national pride in the early years of the twentieth century suffered from a matter of serious disquiet. The Empire was at its height, the serenity of the Victorian era was still aglow, and to educated Englishmen it was almost self-evident that England had once been the cradle, as it was now the governess, of world civilization. How then to explain that striking evidence of early man—not just skeletal remains but Paleolithic cave paintings and tools as well—was coming to light in France and Germany but not in Britain? The dilemma was exacerbated in 1907 with the discovery near Heidelberg, Germany, of a massive, early human jawbone. It seemed depressing proof that the first man had been a German.

The discovery of the Piltdown man was made by Charles Dawson, a lawyer who maintained a quiet practice in the south of England and dabbled in geology. A tireless amateur collector of fossils, Dawson noticed a promising-looking gravel pit on Piltdown Common, near Lewes in Sussex. He asked a laborer digging there to bring him any flints he might find. Several years later, in 1908, the laborer brought him a fragment of bone that Dawson recognized as part of a thick human skull. Over the next three years further bits of the skull appeared.

In 1912 Dawson wrote to his old friend Arthur Smith Woodward, a world authority on fossil fishes at the geology department of the British Museum of Natural History, saying he had something that would top the German fossil found at Heidelberg. Woodward made several visits with Dawson to the Piltdown gravel pit. On one of these expeditions, Dawson's digging tool struck at the bottom of the pit and out flew part of a lower jaw. Close examination led Woodward and Dawson to believe that it belonged to the skull they had already reconstructed.

In great excitement, Smith Woodward took everything back to the British Museum, where he put the jaw and cranium together, filling in missing parts with modeling clay and his imagination. The result was truly remarkable. The assembled skull became the "dawn man" of Piltdown. Kept secret until December 1912, it was unveiled before a full house at the Geological Society in London, where it created a sensation. Some skeptics suggested that the human skull and apelike jaw did not belong together; others pointed out that two characteristically abraded molar teeth were not enough to prove the jaw was human. But these objections were ignored, and the find was accepted as a great and genuine discovery.[17]

The talk in clubs and pubs could note with satisfaction the new proof that the earliest man was indeed British. The Piltdown skull was also of scientific interest because it seemed to be the "missing link," the transitional form between ape and man that was postulated by Darwin's still controversial theory of evolution. Subsequent excavations at the gravel pit were not disappointing. A whole series of new fossils emerged. The clinching evidence came from a pit a few miles away—the discovery a few years later of a second Piltdown man.

Yet some were troubled by the Piltdown finds, among them a young zoologist at the British Museum, Martin A. C. Hinton. After a visit to the site in 1913, Hinton concluded that the whole thing was a hoax. He decided to smoke out the tricksters by planting clearly fraudulent fossils and watching the reactions. He took an ape tooth from the collection at the museum and filed it down to match the model canine tooth that Smith Woodward had fashioned out of clay. Hinton had the obvious forgery placed in the pit by an accomplice and sat back to wait for it to be discovered and the entire Piltdown collection to be exposed.

The tooth was discovered, but nothing else went right with Hinton's plan. All involved with the "discovery" seemed delighted and soon notified the nation about the new find. Hinton was astonished that his scientific colleagues could be taken in by so transparent a fake, and he suffered the additional mortification of seeing Charles Dawson, whom he suspected to be the culprit, acquiring kudos for his handiwork. He decided to try again, only this time with something so outrageous that the whole country would laugh the discoverers to scorn.

In a box in the British Museum he found a leg bone from an extinct species of elephant. He proceeded to carve it into an extremely appropriate tool for the earliest Englishman—a Pleistocene cricket bat. He took the bat to Piltdown, buried it, and waited for the laughter.

It was a long wait. When the bat was unearthed, Smith Woodward was delighted. He pronounced it a supremely important example of the work of Paleolithic man, for nothing like it had ever been found before. Smith Woodward and Dawson published a detailed, serious description of the artifact in a professional journal but stopped short of calling it an actual cricket bat.[18] Hinton was astonished that none of the scientists thought of trying to whittle a bit of bone, fossil or fresh, with a flint edge. If they had, they would have discovered it was impossible to imitate the cuts on the cricket bat. "The acceptance of this rubbish completely defeated the hoaxsters," notes a historian of the Piltdown episode.[19] "They just gave up, and abandoned all attempts to expose the whole business and get it demolished in laughter and ridicule." Perhaps Hinton and friends should have considered planting a bone on which the name Smith Woodward had been carved.

Piltdown man retained its scientific luster until the mid-1920's and the discovery of humanlike fossils in Africa. These indicated a very different pattern of human evolution to that suggested by the Piltdown skull. Instead of a human cranium with an apelike jaw, the African fossils were just the reverse—they had humanlike jaws with apelike skulls. Piltdown became first an anomaly, then an embarrassment. It slipped from sight until modern techniques of dating showed in the early 1950's that the skull and its famous jaw were fakes: an ape jaw, with filed-down molars, and a human skull had each been suitably stained to give the appearance of great age.

Circumstantial evidence pointed to the skull's discoverer, Dawson, as the culprit. But many have doubted that he could have been the instigator; although he was best placed to salt the gravel pit, he probably lacked access to the necessary fossil collections as well as the scientific expertise to assemble fossils of the right age for the Piltdown gravel. Indeed, the real mystery is not who did it but how a whole generation of scientists could have been taken in by so transparent a prank. The fakery was not expert. The tools were poorly carved and the teeth crudely filed. "The evidences of artificial abrasion immediately sprang to the eye. Indeed so obvious did they seem it may well be asked —how was it that they had escaped notice before," remarked anthropologist Le Gros Clark.[20]

The question is one that the victims always ask in retrospect yet seldom learn to anticipate. A group of scientists particularly plagued by tricksters and charlatans are parapsychologists, researchers who apply the scientific method to the study of telepathy, extrasensory perception, and other paranormal phenomena. Because parapsychology is widely regarded as a fringe subject not properly part of science, its practitioners have striven to be more than usually rigorous in following correct scientific methodology.

The founder of parapsychology, J. B. Rhine, made great strides in putting the discipline on a firm scientific footing. As a mark of its growing scientific acceptability, the Parapsychological Association in 1971 was admitted to the American Association for the Advancement of Science. The field seemed to be making solid headway toward the goal of scientific acceptability. Noting this progress with satisfaction, Rhine in 1974 commented on the decline of fraudulent investigators: "As time has passed our progress has aided us in avoiding the admission of such risky personnel even for a short term. As a result, the last twenty years have seen little of this cruder type of chicanery. Best of all, we have reached a stage at which we can actually look for and to a degree choose the people we want in the field." Rhine also warned against the danger of relying on automatic data recording as a means of avoiding the pitfalls of subjective measurement: "Apparatus can sometimes also be used as a screen to conceal the trickery it was intended to prevent," he noted.[21]

Less than three months after his article had appeared, Rhine's Institute for Parapsychology in Durham, North Carolina, was rocked by a scandal that involved Walter J. Levy, a brilliant young protégé whom Rhine had planned to designate his successor as director of the institute.

Levy had developed a highly successful experiment for demonstrating psychic ability in rats: through psychokinetic powers, the animals could apparently influence an electric generator to activate electrodes implanted in the pleasure centers of the brain. For more than a year the experiment had given positive results, and Rhine urged Levy to have it repeated in other labs. The work, however, quickly took a turn for the worse; results fell back to the chance level.

At this point one of the junior experimenters noticed that Levy was paying more than usual attention to the equipment. He and others decided to check out their suspicions by observing their senior colleague from a concealed position. They saw Levy manipulating the experimental apparatus so as to make it yield positive results. To Rhine's credit, he published an article recounting the whole episode.[22] "Right from the start the necessity of trusting the experimenter's personal accuracy or honesty must be avoided as far as possible," he concluded.

Most parapsychologists have training in a conventional scientific discipline, and they bring their scientific training to bear on the study of the paranormal. The competence with which the study is conducted is probably a measure of that training. But if so, scientists have not shown themselves to be highly successful in dealing with the unexpected problems of the occult world. Their subjects, those who claim occult powers, have invariably followed one of two patterns when put under systematic observation: either their powers "fade" or they are exposed as tricksters. That background might lead parapsychologists to approach new claimants with a certain degree of skepticism. But when the Israeli mentalist Uri Geller toured the United States demonstrating his psychic powers, the parapsychologists gave an enormous boost to his claims by confirming them in the laboratory.

Harold Puthoff and Russell Targ, two laser physicists at the Stanford Research Institute, wrote a scientific article corroborating Geller's ability to guess the number on a die concealed in a metal box. The article was accepted and published by *Nature*, a leading scientific journal.[23] Other scientists, such as the English physicist John Taylor of London University, endorsed Geller's psychic abilities. It fell to a professional magician, not a scientist or a parapsychologist, to explain to the public what was behind the Geller phenomenon. James Randi, of Rumson, New Jersey, showed audiences that he could duplicate all Geller's feats, but by simple conjury. "Any magician will tell you that scientists are the easiest persons in the world to fool," says mathematical columnist Martin Gardner.[24] Geller, note two students of deception, "prefers scientists as witnesses and will not perform before expert magicians, and for good reason. Scientists, by the very nature of their intellectual and social training, are among the easiest persons for a conjuror to deceive. . . ."[25]

For an extreme example of gullibility among some of America's best physicists and engineers, consider the remarkable case of the Shroud of Turin Research Project, a group of scientists devoted to studying a relic that believers say is the true burial cloth of Christ. Members of the group work at the Los Alamos National Laboratory, where America's nuclear weapons are designed, and at other military research centers. "The great majority of them are, or until recently were, engaged in the design, manufacture, or testing of weapons, from simple explosives to atomic bombs to high-energy 'killer' lasers," notes an admiring article.[26]

In their spare time the scientists study the Shroud of Turin with the most modern scientific instruments. Though careful not to say it is genuine, they say they cannot prove it is a fake, leaving the strong impression that it is the real thing. They add that there are features of the shroud that cannot be explained by modern technology; its image, of a full-length crucified man, was not painted, they say, because there is no sign of pigment. It is a reverse image, like a photographic negative, and encodes three-dimensional information. From what they tell reporters, they seem to favor a short intense burst of light, presumably from inside the body, as the cause of the image.

But consider some brief facts about the Shroud of Turin: (i) it first came to light in about 1350, at a time when medieval Europe was swamped with purported Holy Land relics of all kinds; (ii) the bishop of Troyes, France, in whose diocese it first appeared, "discovered the fraud and how the said cloth had been cunningly painted, the truth being attested by the artist who had painted it," according to a letter written to the Pope in 1389 by one of the bishop's successors; (iii) traces of two medieval pigments have been discovered in particles lifted off the shroud.[27] The negative image with its three-dimensional encoded information is simply the result of an artist trying to paint an image as it might be expected to register on a cloth covering a dead body. He put in shading to indicate the body's contours, and used so dilute a pigment that even modern tests mostly fail to reveal it. How did a group of the nation's elite bomb designers get so far along the road of persuading themselves (and numerous reporters) that they had a miracle on their hands?

"In entering upon any scientific pursuit," said the nineteenth-century astronomer John Herschel, "one of the student's first endeavours ought to be to prepare his mind for the reception of truth, by dismissing, or at least loosening, his hold on all such crude and hastily adopted notions respecting the objects and relations he is about to examine, as may tend to embarrass or mislead him." Good advice but hard to follow, as the long and continuing history of self-deception and gullibility in science repeatedly shows.

The frequency of scientific self-deception and hoaxes takes on special significance when it is remembered that the skeptical frame of mind is supposedly an essential part of the scientist's approach to the world. The scientific method is widely assumed to be a powerful and self-correcting device for understanding the world as it is and making sense of nature. What is the scientific method, and what are the flaws that make this adamantine armor so strangely vulnerable to the unexpected?

CHAPTER 7

THE MYTH
OF
LOGIC

Science is the distinctive enterprise of Western civilization in the twentieth century, and yet it is perhaps the least well understood. A major reason for this gap is that the philosophers of science, who have influenced the general conception of how science works, describe it as a purely logical process.

There is indeed a logical structure to the body of scientific knowledge, but the logic is often easier to see in retrospect, *after* the knowledge has been gathered. The way in which scientific knowledge is produced and disseminated is a wholly different matter. It is an activity in which nonrational elements such as creativity or personal ambition play conspicuous roles. Logical thought is of course a vital element in scientific discovery, maybe even more so than it is in poetry, art, or any other high exercise of intellect. But it is not the only element.

The myth of science as a purely logical process, constantly reaffirmed in every textbook, article, and lecture, has an overwhelming influence on scientists' perceptions of what they do. Even though scientists are aware of the nonlogical elements of their work, they tend to suppress or at least dismiss them as being of little consequence. A major element of the scientific process is thus denied existence or significance.

The prevalence of the myth of logic is due in large measure to an influential group of European philosophers. During the 1920's and 1930's the Logical Empiricists, also known as the Vienna Circle, constructed a powerfully attractive analysis of science. Scientific knowledge, in their view, is superior to all other kinds because it is empirically verifiable. Scientists propose hypotheses on the basis of inductive logic, and confirm or refute them by experimental test. From the hypotheses may be derived general principles about nature, known as scientific laws. The laws may be derived from or explained by the high-level cognitive structures known as theories. When old theories fail, new theories are proposed and adopted because of their greater explanatory power, and science thereby progresses another inexorable step toward the truth.

The Logical Empiricists deliberately ignored the historical context of science as well as psychological factors such as intuition, imagination, or receptivity to new ideas. Being more interested in science as a logical structure than in science as a process, they passed over the critically revealing subject of scientific change. Typical of the empiricist philosophers' abstractions is the doctrine of falsifiability propounded by Karl Popper of the University of London. A scientific theory, in Popper's view, can never be proved true, it can only be refuted, and once refuted in any serious way it is abandoned.

Popper's theory is at once profoundly true and profoundly absurd. No matter how well a theory is corroborated, it is always vulnerable to falsification at some time in the future, so maybe all scientific theories should be accepted only on the limited and pro tem basis that Popper prescribes. But that is not what happens in practice. Scientists will cling to a theory, no matter how damaging the counterevidence, at least until a better theory comes along and often for longer.

The Logical Empiricists' conception of science has impressed itself not just on the public but also on scientists as well. Researchers are imbued in their lengthy training with the notion that science is a realm of thought where logic and objectivity reign supreme. They are taught that science works just the way the philosophers say it should work. They learn the ideal as if it were reality. The myth has thoroughly pervaded even the central communications systems of science: it dictates with absolute authority the form in which all scientific articles and textbooks are written.

Considered as a literary form, a scientific paper is as stylized as a sonnet: if it fails to obey rigid rules of composition, it will simply not be published. In essence, the rules require that an experiment be reported *as if* every aspect of the procedure had been performed according to the philosophers' prescriptions. The conventions of scientific reporting require the writer to be totally impersonal, so as to give the appearance of objectivity.

Thus a scientist cannot describe the excitement of discovery, the false leads, the hopes and disappointments, or even the path of thinking that may have led him through the various steps of his experiment. Only in the most formalized way, usually by describing the current state of research in the field, may a scientist allude to his reasons for undertaking an investigation. Then comes a "materials and methods" section, where the ingredients and techniques are described in telegraphic form, supposedly so as to enable anyone in the world to repeat the experiment. The "results" section is a dry tabulation of the data produced by the given techniques. Last come the "conclusions," in which the researcher indicates how his data confirm, refute, or extend current theory, and what implications they may hold for future research.

The very nature of the scientific paper is profoundly antihistorical, because the guiding principle of scientific reporting demands that the historian's basic principles—who did what, why, and when—be jettisoned from the start. Because science aspires to be a universal truth, linked to neither time, place, or person, the iron dictates of scientific style demand that all reference to these particulars be omitted. In the name of objectivity, all purpose and motive must be suppressed. In the name of logic, the historical path to understanding must pass unmentioned. The literary framework of a scientific paper, in other words, is a fiction designed to perpetuate a myth.

Scientific textbooks are equally antihistorical, although in a different way. To the extent they refer to the past, they do so only to present it as reflecting the views or concerns of the present. All the false leads, fallible theories, and failed experiments which form so great a part of scientific endeavor are resolutely ignored:

the textbooks portray the history of science as a straight line pointing inexorably forward. "From such references," notes the historian Thomas Kuhn, "both students and professionals come to feel like participants in a long-standing historical tradition. Yet the textbook-derived tradition in which scientists come to sense their participation is one that, in fact, never existed. . . . Partly by selection and partly by distortion, the scientists of earlier ages are implicitly represented as having worked upon the same set of fixed problems and in accordance with the same set of fixed canons that the most recent revolution in scientific theory and method has made seem scientific." The depreciation of historical fact, Kuhn believes, "is deeply, and probably functionally, ingrained in the ideology of the scientific profession."[1]

That ideology is seldom discussed or examined, yet it is all the more potent for being implicit. Most scientists would probably declare if asked that science has no ideology, that science itself is the opposite of ideology. But scientists in fact hold strong and definite views about their profession, about how it should operate, about what is a proper or improper procedure in terms of scientific methodology. These views amount to an ideology, because they are not derived solely from the facts but are shaped by preconceived ideals.

The ideology of the scientific profession has emerged from the writings of three groups of professional observers, the philosophers, historians, and sociologists of science. Each of these three groups has imposed its own professional biases on its descriptions of how science works. All have looked to science to embody the ideals so lacking in the real world. They have read into science the virtues of justice, of fairness, of lack of prejudice, of desire for the truth, of taking a man and his ideas on their merits alone regardless of his prestige or qualifications or status. They have described the scientific scene through spectacles made in Utopia.

Thus philosophers such as the Vienna Circle have explained science as a logical and purely empirical process. Sociologists have posited "norms" of the scientific ethos, contending that science is characterized by "organized skepticism," the acceptance of ideas on their merits, and the disinterested pursuit of truth. Historians, animated by the idea of progress of which scientific knowledge seems so shining an exemplar, have sought to portray scientific history in terms of its success, its great men, and its moral object lessons that show reason triumphing over superstition.

What philosophers, sociologists, and historians have had to say about science has been read and noted by scientists and adopted as the general basis of how they see themselves. The philosophers have said they are objective, so scientists strictly forbid any reference to subjective experience in the scientific literature. The sociologists have said they are disinterested, so scientists disdain any overt manifestation of competition or credit-seeking. The historians have said that science is the defense against unreason, so scientists deny with a passion that human passions have any place whatsoever in their work.

Robert Merton's influential essay describing the principles of the scientific ethos was written in 1942, under the shadow of the Second World War. The Vienna Circle formulated their views of science while Europe was sliding into economic and political chaos. They perhaps saw in science a way of dealing with facts, a rationality, a fairness and justice, that were so conspicuously absent in the real world around them. Here at least was a small enclave of human activity where men could be said to act by the pure light of intellect, not by the dark brutish forces then engulfing humanity.

History, said Edward Gibbon, "is, indeed, little more than the register of the crimes, follies and misfortunes of mankind." With what relief have many historians turned to the history of science, the single arena of human endeavor where it could invariably be reported that right had vanquished wrong, that truth had cast out error, that reason had prevailed over superstition and ignorance.

The high place that science holds in today's world, particularly among the educated, probably owes little to its practical accomplishments. If science is worshiped in Western societies, it is not because of the technological toys or comforts it may produce. It is for the far more fundamental reason that science seems to represent an ideal, a set of values, an ethical example of how human affairs could and should be conducted were reason to be man's guide. In the secular world of the twentieth century, science performs part of the inspirational function that myths and religions play in less developed societies.

It is because of this inspirational role that it is so difficult to see science as it really is. Scientists take it for granted that their way of thinking about the world—the "scientific method"—is different from everyone else's. But does the scientific method really exist? And if it does, do scientists always follow it?

The conventional ideology of science still retains a firm hold on the imaginations of both scientists and the public, but its basis long ago began to crumble among its formulators. The Logical Empiricists, despite the intellectual attraction of their analysis, left themselves vulnerable to criticism because of their deliberate neglect of the psychological and historical context of science. Among the most serious challenges was Thomas Kuhn's brilliant essay of 1962, entitled *The Structure of Scientific Revolutions.*[2] Though written by a historian of science, the book has had a profound influence on the philosophy of science because by looking at science as a changing, not a static, process it uncovered important general insights hitherto neglected by the philosophers.

Kuhn wastes little time on demolishing the Logical Empiricist view of science as an objective progression toward the truth. Instead he erects from ground up a structure in which science is seen to be heavily influenced by nonrational procedures, and in which new theories are viewed as being more complex than those they replace but not as standing any closer to the truth. "Objectivity and progress, the pride of traditional interpretations of science, have both been abandoned," was one critic's dismayed verdict.

Science, in Kuhn's view, is not the steady, cumulative acquisition of knowledge that is portrayed in the textbooks. Rather, it is a series of peaceful interludes punctuated by intellectually violent revolutions. During the interludes, scientists are guided by a set of theories, standards, and methods which Kuhn refers to as a "paradigm."

The paradigm is the basis of the research tradition. It defines which problems are interesting and which are irrelevant. During the paradigm-governed interludes, called periods of "normal science" by Kuhn, scientists essentially solve puzzles generated by the new paradigm. Study of mechanics after Newton's *Principia* is one example of a period of normal science; astronomy after Copernicus is another.

Nature is too complex to be explored at random; the paradigm is an exploration plan which both points to puzzles and guarantees that they are soluble. That is the reason for the rapid progress of the paradigm-based natural sciences compared with those in a pre-paradigm stage, such as the social sciences.

But the tranquillity of normal science does not last. Sooner or later, scientists trying to extend the paradigm find that there are puzzles they cannot solve. Often such anomalies were there from the outset but could be ignored during the heady process of paradigm explication. In fact, during normal science, scientists try to suppress novelties. Yet against the background of the paradigm the anomalies stand out with increasing prominence. The time comes when they can be ignored no longer. Then the field enters into crisis, such as befell earth-centered astronomy before Copernicus, or the phlogiston theory of burning before the understanding of oxygen.

During crises, scientists turn from puzzle-solving to worried discussion of fundamentals. A new paradigm may be proposed, its underlying discoveries almost always being made, Kuhn states, by men who are "either very young or very new to the field whose paradigm they change." But defenders of the old paradigm patch it up with ad hoc fixes, and battle is joined as the supporters of each paradigm compete for the allegiance of the community.

The means by which this battle is waged is of central importance: in Kuhn's view, nonrational factors play an essential role in the contest. Logic and experiment, says Kuhn, are not sufficient: "The competition between paradigms is not the sort of battle that can be resolved by proofs." In fact, a scientist's transfer of allegiance from one paradigm to another "is a conversion experience that cannot be forced." The grounds for conversion may include arguments that appeal to the individual's sense of the appropriate or the aesthetic, as well as faith that the new paradigm will be better able to resolve the anomalies that precipitated the crisis.

Why is logic alone not enough to resolve the competition between two paradigms? Because paradigms are logically incommensurable. Two paradigms may seem to use the same words and concepts, but in fact these elements are logically different. Mass, for example, is conserved in Newtonian physics but is convertible with energy in Einsteinian physics. Earth in pre-Copernican theory denoted a point of fixity. Proponents of rival paradigms are not speaking exactly the same language; they are bound to talk past each other because their terms of reference are not comparable.

The incommensurability of competing paradigms has another important consequence in the Kuhnian thesis. A new paradigm cannot build on the one it succeeds; it can only supplant it. Science is not the cumulative process portrayed in the textbooks; it is a succession of revolutions, in each of which one conceptual world view is replaced by another. But Kuhn sees no ground for believing that the new paradigm gives a *better* understanding of the world than did the old. The idea of progress in science can be conceded only in the relative sense that new paradigms can be recognized as being more evolved or more complex than those they replace. We may, says Kuhn, "have to relinquish the notion, explicit or implicit, that changes of paradigm carry scientists and those who learn from them closer and closer to the truth."

Kuhn did not deny the importance of logic and experiment in science; but he argued compellingly that nonrational factors are also important, and that scientific belief, particularly when in the traumatic conversion from one paradigm to another, has certain elements in common with religious belief.

An even more radical critic of Logical Empiricism is the Vienna-born philosopher Paul Feyerabend of the University of California, Berkeley. Feyerabend not only admits nonrational elements into the scientific process but sees them as dominant. Science, he says, is an ideology, completely shaped at any moment in time by its historical and cultural context. Scientific disputes are resolved not on their merits but by the theatrical and oratorical skills of their advocates, much as are legal cases. There is no one scientific method, good for all times and places; in fact, there is no such thing as scientific method. Despite scientist's claims, the rule in science is that "anything goes."

Since there is no one scientific method, success in science depends not only on rational argument but on a mixture of subterfuge, rhetoric, and propaganda, Feyerabend holds. He believes that the distinction commonly made between science and other modes of thought is unjustified, an artificial barrier erected by scientists to set them above their fellow citizens. "Those who do not like to see the state meddling in scientific matters should re-member the sizeable chauvinism of science: for most scientists the slogan 'freedom for science' means the freedom to indoctrinate not only those who have joined them, but the rest of society as well. . . . Combining this observation with the insight that sci-ence has no special method, we arrive at the result that the sep-aration of science and non-science is not only artificial but also detrimental to the advancement of knowledge," states Feyerabend in his book *Against Method.*[3]

Is the scientific method merely an abstraction of philosophers? Do scientists deceive themselves in supposing logic alone to be their guide? Do rhetoric and propaganda play just as large a role in science as they do in politics, law, and religion? An interesting light on the problem comes from consideration of a quite regular phenomenon, the resistance of scientists to new ideas.

If science is a rational process, with logic its light and factual evidence its only guide, then scientists should quickly embrace new ideas and abandon old ones as soon as the evidence for the better idea has become reasonably convincing. But in fact scien-tists often cling to old ideas for long after they have been dis-credited. "The mere suggestion that scientists themselves some-times resist scientific discovery clashes, of course, with the stereo-type of the scientist as 'the open-minded man,' " notes sociologist Bernard Barber.[4] But history is replete with instances where open-mindedness and objectivity have failed. Tycho Brahe, the greatest observational astronomer of his time, resisted the theory of Co-pernicus to his dying day, and encouraged many other astrono-mers to do likewise. In the nineteenth century, Thomas Young's wave theory of light, Pasteur's discovery of the biological nature of fermentation, and Mendel's theory of genetics all met with dis-missal or resistance from the professional scientists of the special-ties concerned.

For any who might suppose that the twentieth century is im-mune to such foibles, consider the concept of continental drift, proposed by the German meteorologist Alfred Wegener in 1922. With one glance at the globe, a child can see the intuitive plausi-bility of Wegener's theory by noting how snugly the shoulder of South America tucks into the armpit of Africa. But it took geolo-gists and geophysicists almost forty years, from 1922 to about

1960, to accept that the continents are in motion. Sometimes the excuse is offered that geologists knew of no mechanism by which the continents could be moved, but this is not so; a well-known article written by geologist Arthur Holmes in 1928 correctly advocated convection currents as the force that moves the continents.

It was the leaders of their profession, Harold Jeffreys in England and Maurice Ewing in the United States, who spearheaded the opposition. When in the 1960's geologists finally conceded that the earth's continents had moved, it was because the dating of the sediments on the sea floor provided incontrovertible evidence of the sort that compelled even the blind to see.

The reasons for scientists' resistance to new ideas are quite varied, and they have much in common with the reasons for which people in general resist giving up ideas they rely on or have grown comfortable with. Because of their own religious beliefs, scientists in the nineteenth century resisted both Darwin's theory of evolution and the findings of geologists that pointed to the great age of the earth.

The old commonly resist the young, and it is no different in science. "That academies and learned societies—commonly dominated by the older foofoos of any profession—are slow to react to new ideas is in the nature of things. For, as Bacon says, *scientia inflat,* and the dignitaries who hold high honors for past accomplishments do not usually like to see the current of progress rush too rapidly out of their reach," remarks biologist Hans Zinsser.[5] The same thought was expressed even more forcefully by the German physicist Max Planck, the originator of quantum theory, who in a famous passage proclaimed that old ideas in science die only with those who hold them: "An important scientific innovation rarely makes its way by gradually winning over and converting its opponents: it rarely happens that Saul becomes Paul. What does happen is that its opponents gradually die out and that the growing generation is familiarized with the idea from the beginning."[6] Evidently the height of intellectual resistance has been reached when death is the persuader: but of all the realms of human thought, why should science provide the example?

Despite the claim of science to be universal, social or professional standing can often influence receptivity to new ideas. If the originator of a revolutionary new concept either has low standing in the elite system of his own discipline or if he comes from outside the discipline, his ideas are particularly likely not to receive serious consideration: they will be judged on his perceived merits, not on their own. But it is just such people—the outsiders and the neophytes, neither of whom have been indoctrinated in the established dogmas of the discipline—who so often contribute the original ideas by which a discipline advances. That is why resistance to new ideas is such a constant theme in the history of science.

George Ohm, the nineteenth-century German who discovered the law of electrical resistance, was a math teacher at the Jesuit Gymnasium in Cologne; his ideas were ignored by scientists at German universities. Mendel's genetic laws were ignored by professionals in his field for thirty-five years, in part because, as an abbé with an experimental plot in his backyard, he seemed to be a mere amateur. The specialists' contempt for the outsider is evident in the geologists' attitude to Wegener, who was a meteorologist by training. The medical profession in particular has a long history of resisting scientific innovations from both without and within. Louis Pasteur met with violent resistance from doctors when he advanced his germ theory of disease; they regarded him as a mere chemist poaching on their scientific preserves. Joseph Lister's discovery of antisepsis was initially ignored in both England and the United States, in part because Lister, a doctor working in Glasgow and Edinburgh, was regarded as a provincial.

Few episodes in the illustrious annals of scientific progress are more striking than that of the nineteenth-century Hungarian physician Ignaz Semmelweis. He discovered that puerperal, or childbed, fever, then causing typically 10 to 30 percent mortality in maternity hospitals throughout Europe, could be virtually abolished by the simple expedient of having doctors wash their hands in a chlorine solution before examining the mother. In his division of the obstetric clinic in Vienna where Semmelweis first tried out his idea, the mortality rate dropped from 18 percent to 1 percent. By 1848 Semmelweis was losing not a single woman to childbed fever. But this experimental evidence failed to convince his superiors at the hospital.

Eighteen forty-eight was the year that a liberal political revolution swept Europe, and Semmelweis took part in the events in

Vienna. His political activities only increased the resistance to his ideas. Dismissed from the clinic, he returned to Hungary and from his own obstetrical experience over the next ten years amassed copious evidence that antiseptic technique would prevent death from childbed fever. His findings were summarized in a book, published in 1861, copies of which he sent to medical societies and to the major obstetricians of Germany, France, and England.

The book was almost universally ignored by the medical profession, even though throughout Europe puerperal fever continued to ravage maternity hospitals. In Prague, 4 percent of the mothers and 22.5 percent of the babies died in 1861. In Stockholm in 1860, 40 percent of all women patients caught the fever and 16 percent died. In the General Hospital in Vienna, in the same ward where Semmelweis had shown twelve years earlier how the disease could be eradicated, 35 out of 101 patients died in the autumn of 1860.

Why did physicians and medical researchers ignore Semmelweis' theory? Even if they disagreed with the theory, why did they ignore his copious and undisputed statistics? Perhaps they found it hard to cope with the consequences of an idea which meant that each, with his own unwashed hands, had unwittingly sent many patients to their deaths. Then too, Semmelweis was not always as tactful as he could have been in trying to win acceptance for his ideas. His rhetoric was too strident. His propaganda was not sufficiently smooth and persuasive. Few facts could speak with greater emphasis and clarity than his did, but the facts were in no way sufficient to persuade physicians and medical researchers throughout Europe that their hands were spreaders of disease.

In the knowledge that many women were dying unnecessarily, and that no one would listen to his simple principles for preventing death, Semmelweis started cranking out somewhat hysterical letters. In an open letter of 1862 to professors of obstetrics, Semmelweis wrote: "If the Professors of Obstetrics do not soon comply by instructing their students in my doctrine . . . then will I myself say to the helpless public, 'You, father of a family, do you know what it is to summon an obstetrician or a midwife to your wife? . . . It is as much as to expose your wife and your yet unborn child to the danger of death. And if you do not wish to become a widower and if you do not wish that your still unborn child be inoculated with the germ of death, and if your children are not to lose their mother, then buy a single kreutzer's worth of chloride of lime, infuse it in some water, and do not allow the obstetrician and the midwife to examine your wife until they have washed their hands in the chlorine solution in your presence, and also do not permit the obstetrician and the midwife to make an internal examination until you have convinced yourself by touching their hands that the obstetrician and midwife have washed so long that their hands have become slippery.' "[7]

Semmelweis' mind began to wander. Some days he scarcely spoke at all; on others he would embarrass his colleagues by bursting out in a violent harangue. In 1865 he was induced by friends to visit a mental sanatorium. While the friends slipped out, he was forcibly restrained, confined to a straitjacket, and put in a dark room. He died two weeks later, on August 13, 1865. It was just one day earlier that Lister, whom Semmelweis had anticipated by a full fifteen years, first began to test the use of carbolic acid as an antiseptic agent. Once Lister had won his battle, and Pasteur had persuaded the medical profession that germs did really exist, then, some thirty years later than necessary, the doctors understood the *theory* by which they could make sense of the *facts* that said for them to wash their hands before undertaking obstetric examinations.

"But on principle it is quite wrong to try founding a theory on observable magnitudes alone. In reality the very opposite happens. It is the theory which decides what we can observe." So wrote Einstein to Werner Heisenberg, a year before Heisenberg formulated his indeterminacy principle in 1927. "It is the theory which decides what we can observe"—that is the exact reverse of the test-theory-by-facts methodology by which the philosophers say science always proceeds. Einstein's observation emphasizes that for scientists, just as for others, it is ideas and theories that are important. Ideas explain facts, theories make sense of the world. A fact by itself is trivial; it is interesting only if it sheds light on some underlying principle or theory. On psychological grounds alone, it is not surprising that scientists should often continue to believe in a theory, even when it is contradicted by experimental fact.

Sometimes the belief in theory over fact proves erroneous; sometimes it is well founded, because the contradictions turn out to be apparent, not real. When the American Physical Society heard in 1925 from its president, D. C. Miller, that he had discovered evidence that contradicted the Special Theory of Relativity (a "positive effect" in the Michelson-Morley experiment), the audience should instantly have abandoned the theory or at least assigned it to provisional status. "But no," comments physicist Michael Polanyi, "by that time they had so well closed their minds to any suggestion which threatened the new rationality achieved by Einstein's world picture, that it was almost impossible for them to think again in different terms. Little attention was paid to the experiments, the evidence being set aside in the hope that it would one day turn out to be wrong."[8] True, Miller's work is now thought to have been flawed by subtle experimental effects, but for scientists simply to presume that awkward results will turn out to be incorrect is a mere act of faith.

Verification of a theory, Polanyi points out, in fact requires the same kind of intuition about nature as did the devising of the theory in the first place. Intuition, a nonrational factor, does not enter into the philosopher's accounts. When discussing the verification of scientific laws, the philosophers always choose as examples laws about which there is not any doubt. "They are describing the practical demonstration of scientific law, and not its critical verification. As a result we are given an account of the scientific method which, having left out the process of discovery on the grounds that it follows no definite method, overlooks the process of verification as well, by referring only to examples in which no real verification takes place."

The first historians of science tended to see their subject matter in much the same light as did the philosophers and scientists themselves—as a straight-line, objective progression toward the truth. More recently, historians have begun to doubt that scientists always behave in the strictly objective manner prescribed by the hypothetico-deductive system of the philosophers. Some historians of science, writes Stephen G. Brush, "have been moving toward another conception of their role, based on the notion that scientists often operate in a subjective way and that experimental verification is of secondary importance compared to philosophical arguments, at least in some of the major conceptual changes that have occurred in science."[9]

Brush's own conversion to this view stemmed from his analysis of three topics in nineteenth-century physics—the wave theory of heat, the kinetic theory of gases, and interatomic forces—where theoretical considerations were given primacy by scientists over direct experimental facts that contradicted them. "While these decisions were made in the first instance by individual scientists, their colleagues did not protest the irrationality of the decisions but simply followed the leader; hence these cases provide legitimate evidence for the behavior of the scientific community," notes Brush. On the basis of the examples he has studied, Brush concludes that "improper behavior is not peculiar to a handful of great scientists but is characteristic of a much larger group. Indeed, the burden of proof would seem to be on anyone who claims that a majority of scientists habitually use the hypothetico-deductive method in the strict sense (that is, rejecting a theory if it fails to agree with all experimental facts)."

The human mind has a well-known capacity for retaining political or religious beliefs well beyond the point at which reason suggests they should be modified or abandoned. The claim of science is that it differs fundamentally from other belief systems in that it rests demonstrably upon reason alone. But the claim must be modified in light of what historians have to say about scientists' resistance to scientific ideas and their penchant for seeing the world through the prism of their own theories.

The fact is that the way in which science actually works, the process by which the existing stock of scientific knowledge is extended or restructured, is not by any means an entirely rational process. A logical structure can be discerned, post facto, in the substance of received scientific knowledge. The existence of a logical structure in scientific knowledge has led to the assumption that the structure was logically built. But the process of doing science, as distinct from the body of scientific knowledge, is created and governed by a different set of principles. Logical inference and the intent of being objective are important among them. But rhetoric, propaganda, appeal to authority, and all the usual arts of human persuasion are also influential in winning acceptance for a scientific theory.

Even the apparently logical mechanisms to which the philosophers have devoted so much attention, such as verification and replication, are in practice subject to nonrational decisions. Verification, the critical feature of science, which in the Logical Empiricists' view raised it above all other forms of knowledge, is dominated by scientists' expectations, and the strength of their belief in the theory under test, as much as by the facts. Replication is not a normal scientific procedure; it is undertaken only in special circumstances, such as with results of unusual importance or when fraud is suspected on other grounds.

To say that the process of science includes nonrational elements is not to say that rationality is absent. Science is both logical and illogical, rational and irrational, open-minded and dogmatic. The exact proportions of each ingredient vary from one discipline to another, depending on time, cause, and place. The degree of nonrational elements in scientific thinking is doubtless less than in other belief systems, but perhaps not significantly less. The burden of proof must lie on those who make special claims for science and scientists.

Some of the nonrational elements that govern the scientific process, such as intuition, imagination, or attachment to particular theories, are ones that most working scientists readily acknowledge. But others, such as rhetoric and propaganda, are denied any official role in science by scientific ideology, despite the fact they can play major, sometimes decisive, roles in the acceptance or rejection of hypotheses. Precisely because scientists believe themselves immune to these forms of argument, they are the more susceptible.

It is only when the existence of nonrational elements in science is conceded that the phenomenon of scientific fraud can be understood. Conversely, the study of fraud sheds light on how the nonrational elements operate in the scientific process. Fraud gains entry into science along with the nonrational elements, and is often successful because the same elements work in its favor.

Acceptance of fraud is the other side of that familiar coin, resistance to new ideas. Fraudulent results are likely to be accepted in science if they are plausibly presented, if they conform with prevailing prejudices or expectations, and if they come from a suitably qualified scientist affiliated with an elite institution. It is for the lack of all these qualities that radical new ideas in science are likely to be resisted.

Only on the assumption that logic and objectivity are the sole gatekeepers of science is the prevalence and frequent success of fraud in any way surprising. Only on the assumption that replication is the inexorable test to which all results are submitted is the persistence of fraud difficult to understand. Like sin among the faithful, fraud should not exist, let alone thrive, within the community of science. That it does is because practice differs from ideology.

For the ideologists of science, fraud is taboo, a scandal whose significance must be ritually denied on every occasion. For those who see science as a human endeavor to make sense of the world, fraud is merely evidence that science flies on the wings of rhetoric as well as reason.

CHAPTER 8

MASTERS
AND
APPRENTICES

One of the most dramatic scientific events of the 1960's was the discovery by radio astronomers in Cambridge, England, of a wholly novel class of stars. Known as pulsating radio stars, or "pulsars," they beamed out bursts of radio waves with extraordinary rapidity and precision. After a flurry of intense excitement, theoretical astronomers soon determined that pulsars were neutron stars, the long-postulated embers of stellar evolution that were assumed to be too faint ever to be detectable from earth. And the public who followed these events learned with a frisson of wonder that the Cambridge astronomers had for a time considered that the signals might have originated from another civilization, in honor of which they had nicknamed the pulsars LGM stars, for "Little Green Men."

These stirring events naturally attracted the attention of the Nobel prize committees in faraway Stockholm. In 1974, the Nobel prize for physics was awarded to Antony Hewish, leader of the Cambridge University group, "for his decisive role in the discovery of pulsars." There was just one problem. Pulsars were first discovered, and their nature as stellar objects was first recognized, not by Hewish but by a young woman graduate student of his named Jocelyn Bell.

The story of how Hewish walked away with a Nobel prize illustrates the first step of a problematic trend in the organization of the scientific workplace: the breakdown during the past few decades of the relationship between master and apprentice. Though founded on intellectual concern and sharing, the bond today is often based on material needs such as the purchase of equipment and the getting of grants. The dehumanization of the relationship has led to a variety of abuses, such as that seen in the discovery of pulsars. The appropriation of credit can expand to the point that large teams of junior researchers work almost exclusively for the glorification of a lab chief, even though the master has little or no day-to-day involvement in the work. Despite such remoteness, it is not unusual for the name of a prominent biomedical researcher to appear on as many as 500 or 600 papers produced by his juniors. As illustrated by several of the case studies in this chapter, the dislocation between work and reward can turn laboratories into a breeding ground for cynicism and outright fraud. Not that every overworked apprentice turns away from the strict canons of science. In the case of the discovery of pulsars, graduate student Bell merely decided to tell her side of the story.[1]

With a bachelor's degree in physics, Bell joined the radio astronomy group at Cambridge as a candidate for a Ph.D. degree in 1965. Though slight in stature, she could swing a twenty-pound sledgehammer by the time she left Cambridge, the result of spending the first two years of her doctoral apprenticeship physically constructing the radio telescope she was to use. Hewish had designed the telescope for a specific purpose: to study how radio waves from the sun affected the "twinkling" of stars seen from earth.

In July 1967 the telescope was ready to be switched on. Bell's task was to operate it single-handedly and analyze its data until she had enough material for a Ph.D. thesis. The analysis was not much less arduous than the construction work. The telescope churned out ninety-six feet of three-track paper every day. It took four days to cover the sky, so Bell had about 400 feet of paper chart to analyze for each complete coverage of the sky. Her job was to scan the chart by eye, mapping the signals that were true twinkling radio sources and discarding those that came from man-made sources of interference, such as French television, aircraft altimeters, and pirate radio stations. The temptation to cut corners must have been considerable. By October, Bell was 1,000 feet of chart behind and by the end of November she was lagging by a third of a mile.

It was in October that she discovered the pulsar. Its signal, which she describes as "a bit of scruff," occupied about half an inch of the 400 feet of chart. To the unpracticed observer, it differed hardly at all from the numerous other signals on the chart. To Bell, one thing stuck out from her memory—she had seen it before: "The first thing I noticed was that sometimes within the record there were signals that I could not quite classify. They weren't either twinkling or man-made interference. I began to remember that I had seen this particular bit of scruff before, and from the same part of the sky. It seemed to be keeping pace with twenty-three hours fifty-six minutes—with the rotation of the stars." Though much remained to be done, the nub of the discovery lay in that single instant of recognition.

Something that kept "sidereal time," as astronomers call the twenty-three hour fifty-six minute interval, was most probably some sort of star. But compelling counterevidence would soon emerge. Looking back through the records, Bell found the first time the scruff had appeared was on August 6, 1967. She discussed the signals with Hewish, and they jointly decided to look at them on the observatory's fast recorder to get a clearer picture of the signal's structure.

The recorder became available in mid-November, and Bell went out to the telescope at the time of day the source was passing through the beam. But for several weeks nothing happened. The signal, at all times variable, was too faint to appear. "Hewish was thinking at that stage that it was a flare star and that we had missed it," Bell recalls. "Finally one day I managed to catch it, and I got a series of pulses coming out of the recorder. They were almost exactly one and a half seconds apart. That is a very sort of man-made period. Tony Hewish had left the recording to me. I phoned him up to tell him about the pulses and he said, 'Oh, that settles it, it must be man-made.'"

Hewish came out to the observatory the next day to watch Bell make another fast recording. The signal was quite strong that day and she was able to produce a nice train of pulses for her supervisor's satisfaction. Hewish then went through the records and confirmed that the source was keeping sidereal time. "We had terrible trouble trying to sort out that conundrum," says Bell. The problem was that the fastest variable star then known had a period of one-third of a day, and no one could conceive of a star with a period of 1.5 seconds. But the source couldn't be man-made either because it appeared with each revolution of the stars, not with each rotation of the earth. Could it be radar signals bouncing off the moon, or a satellite in a peculiar orbit? That did not fit. Bell and Hewish then realized that the only people on earth who keep the twenty-three hour fifty-six minute schedules of sidereal time were other astronomers. "Hewish wrote round to all other observatories asking them if they had any program going since October." All wrote back saying no they didn't.

Then came the Little Green Men thesis. "Although they don't take it very seriously," remarks Bell, "radio astronomers are aware that they would probably be the first people to come into contact with other civilizations. So Hewish timed the pulses to see if there was a Doppler shift." The rationale was that the aliens would presumably be resident on a planet, and the orbital movement around its sun would produce a bunching of the pulses as the planet moved toward the earth and a spacing out of pulses as it moved away.

This moment in the investigation, when the Cambridge radio astronomy group was seriously considering that the pulses might be signals from another civilization, is described with notable terseness and understatement in the logbook that Bell kept at the time. Her entry for December 19, 1967, refers to a radio "source" under the remarkably prescient heading of "Belisha beacon." A Belisha beacon is the regularly flashing orange globe that warns motorists in England of a pedestrian crossing. Bell gave the source this private nickname—while the rest of the group called it the LGM star—*before* she had even detected the pulsation on the fast recorder.

As it happened, Hewish found no Doppler shift. At the same time, or slightly before, Bell took the step which finally settled the nature of the "source." She discovered another one. The day before she left Cambridge for her Christmas holiday, "I was working in the evening analyzing a chart. I saw something which looked remarkably like the bits of scruff we had been working with. This was in a bit of sky that wasn't very easy for the telescope to look at, but there was enough to confirm that there had been scruff. That particular bit of sky was to go through the beam at one A.M. It was a very cold night, and the telescope doesn't perform very well in cold weather. I breathed hot air on it, I kicked and swore at it, and I got it to work for just five minutes. It was the right five minutes, and at the right setting. The source gave a train of pulses, but with a different period, of about one and a quarter seconds."

Did she phone Hewish to tell him of the second discovery? "Not at three o'clock in the morning, oh, no. I dumped the recording on his desk and left for my holiday. I don't think he really believed that one. But he kindly kept the telescope running and the inkwells full of ink while I was away."

Hewish himself did a recording in the middle of the night in mid-January and confirmed the second source of pulses. "That removed the worry about the little green men, since there wouldn't be two lots signaling us at different frequencies. So obviously we were dealing with some sort of very rapid star. I threw up another two sometime in January." Those were the last two pulsars she discovered, because by mid-January it was time to start writing her Ph.D. thesis, to which pulsars appeared as an appendix.

When the article announcing the discovery of pulsars was published in *Nature*, Bell's name was second on the list of five authors. At the top of the list was Hewish. In the code of scientific writing, the authorship line of the article delivered a clear message to the scientific world: the discoverer of pulsars was Hewish, along with four members of his group.

Even if the facts about the discovery of pulsars were generally known among English astronomers, no one protested the downgrading of Bell's role until after the Nobel prize had been awarded to Hewish alone. Then in March 1975, the eminent theoretical astronomer Fred Hoyle described the award bluntly as a "scandal." Hoyle complained that Bell's original finding had deliberately been kept secret for six months while her supervisors "were busily pinching the discovery from the girl, or that was what it amounted to," Hoyle was quoted in *The Times* of London. In an explanatory letter to the newspaper a few days later, Hoyle remarked: "There has been a tendency to misunderstand the magnitude of Miss Bell's achievement because it sounds so simple—just to search and search through a great mass of records. The achievement came from a willingness to contemplate as a serious possibility a phenomenon that all past experience suggested was impossible. I have to go back in my mind to the discovery of radioactivity by Henri Becquerel for a comparable example of a scientific bolt from the blue."

In response to Hoyle's letter, Nobel laureate Hewish wrote *The Times*, saying in effect that Bell had been using his telescope, under his instructions, to make a sky survey which he had initiated. The possibility that the accidentally discovered pulsars were of human or alien origin was resolved under his direction, he said. Although the source had been first discovered in August 1967, it was not until January 1968, the month before publication, that the necessary tests could be completed.

Hewish's defense tended if anything to corroborate the general truth, though perhaps not the details, of Hoyle's accusation. To be sure, it was his telescope, but he had not told Bell to look for pulsars with it. He had instructed her to look for a completely different phenomenon. "She was told to plot scintillating radio sources, but she noted and pursued in her own way a different kind of signal," notes Thomas Gold, the Cornell University theoretical astronomer who explained the physical nature of pulsars. The problem of determining the human or extraterrestrial origin of pulsars, for which Hewish took credit, was decisively resolved by Bell's discovery of a second pulsar.

By any fair reckoning, the discovery of pulsars was a joint enterprise, Bell deserving the credit for first spotting the signals and diligently pursuing them, Hewish for acting as adviser and provider of the support equipment. But Hewish could not see it that way.

"Jocelyn was a jolly good girl but she was just doing her job," says the Nobel laureate. "She noticed this source was doing this thing. If she hadn't noticed it, it would have been negligent."

It is possible, but far from certain, that the next graduate student down the line would have made the discovery. Yet with this "what if" argument, almost every scientist could be stripped of his credit, in that every discovery would have been made by somebody else sooner or later. Moreover, with whatever strength Hewish's argument might apply to Bell, it applies to himself as well. The historical fact is that it was Bell, and not another individual, who discovered the pulsar signals.

The distribution of credit for the discovery of pulsars underlines a ubiquitous and significant feature of the modern scientific enterprise: that the supposed meritocracy of science rests on a power structure, and those who hold the reins of power are also influential in controlling the allocation of rewards and credit.

Central to the operation of contemporary science is the intensive educational procedure whereby new recruits are trained to become full-fledged members of the scientific community. The training period begins in earnest when a novice researcher enters on the three- to ten-year course that will end with his Ph.D. degree. It continues even beyond that, when the young holder of a Ph.D. degree, known as a "postdoc," takes his first independent research assignment, usually in a department different from that in which he gained his doctorate.

The professors who train these graduate students and postdocs stand in a fiduciary relationship to them, teaching them the art and craft of research, guiding their interests toward problems of scientific importance, and imbuing them with the tradition of serious research. In favorable circumstances, the relationship makes for the strongest of intellectual bonds. Like apprentices sitting at their masters' bench, the graduates learn the tools of their trade and means of future livelihood. The professor's true reward for sharing his knowledge is equally substantial: his graduates and postdocs will carry on the lines of inquiry he has initiated, and his work will live after him in the work of his students. The intimate bond that often grows up between the professor and his students is grounded in intellectual curiosity and a common commitment to the truth.

In contemporary science, the solemn bond of the master-apprentice relationship is often abused. Instead of being content with founding a research tradition, some professors seek the shorter-term goals of instant fame and recognition. The intellectual bond tends to be diminished, sometimes almost entirely replaced, by the elements of a business exchange. The lab chief trades job slots and patronage for the right to take credit for his subordinates' achievements.

How did the degradation of the master-apprentice relationship in science come about? Earlier in the century, research was still for many a calling, and the necessary ingredients for doing science were a sharp mind and perhaps some apparatus from a hardware store. With the professionalization of science, and the increasing expense of equipping a research laboratory, young researchers setting out on their careers must now find not just an intellectual master but a patron with command of a large government grant. For his part, the patron, simply to keep the grants flowing and to meet his payroll, must busily cultivate the appearance of success. There is doubtless nothing wrong with this system as long as the lab chief is providing the intellectual direction for his group. But there is no easy egress from the treadmill. Should the lab chief's attentions wander elsewhere, or his creative energies falter, he will experience strong pressures to continue by taking a large share of the credit for his subordinates' work. "After all," he may say to himself, "if it weren't for me, there wouldn't be the money for them to do research, and I would be at the bench too if I didn't have to spend all my time fund raising."

Today it is not unusual for the name of a prominent scientist to appear on many hundreds of papers. Such a prolific output was not so common in the past, although Lord Kelvin, the nineteenth-century physicist, is reputed to have published some 660 scientific papers in his lifetime. Now, however, a frequent reason for those prodigious numbers is not a great surge in creative energy and tireless devotion to the truth, but rather the deft exploitation of the lab chief system. Such a quantity of publication is often the result of graduates and postdocs working long hours in the lab, producing reports and papers to which the lab chief will graciously sign his name. They too are listed on the paper, at times in a subservient position. Given the hierarchical limbo they inhabit, the credit often will be seen in the scientific community as resting in the hands of the lab chief. In such an environment, scientific truth can become almost an accidental by-product. The laboratory can more accurately be considered a research mill, a factory for the mass production of scientific articles.

As the young scientist is pushed to publish papers in which he will appear as a minor light in the constellation of a senior scientist, the temptation to cut corners, to improve on the results, or even to fake data entirely, is often difficult to resist. The temptation is probably strongest where the workers by definition have no stake in the intellectual rewards of research: the process of publication. They work, but their names do not appear on the published papers. According to sociologist Julius A. Roth, who carried out an extensive study on what he calls hired-hand research: "Even those who start out with the notion that this is an important piece of work which they must do right will succumb to the hired-hand mentality when they realize that their suggestions and criticisms are ignored, that their assignment does not allow for any imagination or creativity, that they will receive no credit for the final product, in short, that they have been hired to do somebody else's dirty work. When this realization has sunk in, they will no longer bother to be careful or accurate or precise. They will cut corners to save time and energy. They will fake parts of their reporting."[2]

Roth uncovered several cases in which researchers admitted to inventing data. "Such behavior," he notes, "is not abnormal or exceptional, but rather is exactly the kind of behavior we should expect from people with their position in a production unit."

The disillusion that develops in subordinates who are under pressure to produce is illustrated by the case of Robert J. Gullis, a young doctoral candidate who worked between 1971 and 1974 at Birmingham University in England. His research concerned the chemical messengers produced by the brain. In essence, he showed during the course of his doctoral research that these messengers change the physical nature of cell walls all over the brain. His work was considered important by his peers, and one, William Lands of the University of Michigan, called it among the most interesting research he had seen in two years.

Gullis' line of research required patience, considerable skill, and long hours in the lab. A typical day would start at about 7 A.M. After three days of working late into the night, one experiment would be completed, and the next would start. "It took me nine months to get the ball rolling," Gullis told a reporter.[3] "I think I got nothing in the first six months." When his Ph.D. research was finally published in 1975, after four years of effort, it ran to thirty-three densely written pages of a professional journal. At the top of the paper, along with Gullis' name, appeared that of his supervisor, Charles E. Rowe.

It was not Rowe but scientists at the Max Planck Institute for Biochemistry in Germany, where Gullis went to work as a post-doc, who noticed that there was something wrong. After Gullis left the institute, having produced four papers on which the names of seven of his German colleagues appear, the staff tried to repeat some of his experiments. Several abortive attempts later, they asked Gullis to return. After a tense two weeks of trying to reproduce the results, he admitted that some of the data had been invented. It became clear that Gullis had performed the experiments but had falsified the results. Gullis was led to confess to his professor, Rowe, that earlier results, including his Ph.D. thesis, were also fraudulent. "The curves and values published are mere figments of my imagination," Gullis wrote in a letter to the respected journal *Nature*,[4] "and during my short research career I published my hypothesis rather than experimentally determined results." The episode led to the retraction of eleven papers in all.[5]

In the aftermath, lab chief Rowe voiced the typical plaint of a senior scientist who has been wronged by a junior. "I think if you work with anyone in scientific work, you have to take a certain amount on trust," he said, and without missing a beat, went on to state the essence of the matter, "otherwise you may as well do all the work yourself." While Gullis was at the University of Birmingham, Rowe had added his name to seven papers the doctoral candidate produced.

As for Gullis, he saw himself as victim of a system gone bad. "It's a problem you face everywhere. No one wants to bother too much with other people because they want to get on with their own work. This is silly for a university department because a university is a teaching place and a Ph.D. is also a place to learn, a place to learn how to do research properly. And if proper guidance is not there, then there is something wrong with the whole system." Gullis was particularly bitter on the subject of credit and the production of papers. "Not once was I ever rewarded for my work," he said. "They were very happy with the results. They were just after results and were quite glad when someone was there working really hard to get them out and get a Ph.D. at the same time."

Gullis was caught inventing data, and there could well be a self-serving element in his criticism of the system. But the neglect he describes, combined with a pressure to produce results, is not so rare. In Gullis' case, these circumstances led him into outright fraud. In the celebrated case of William T. Summerlin, the immediate cause of his downfall was a petty instance of "improving" the data.

Summerlin in 1974 was a junior colleague of the respected immunologist Robert A. Good. Both worked at the Sloan-Kettering Institute for Cancer Research, a Manhattan-based lab complex with a worldwide reputation. Good, fifty-two, an exceptionally bright scientist with a flair for teaching, had tremendous energy, drive, ego, and a penchant for promoting himself. In 1973 his picture appeared on the cover of *Time* magazine. Good was also the epitome of a well-organized lab chief. In a five-year period he had coauthored almost 700 scientific reports, a feat aided by establishing a large empire of research workers under his personal banner. Far from puffery, the papers he signed were highly regarded. Over a fourteen-year period, work with Good's name on it was cited by other scientists more than 17,600 times—making Good the most frequently cited author in the history of research.[6]

Summerlin was tall, balding, thirty-five, and affable. Born in a small town in South Carolina, he was sure of himself and his work. But he had little grant money to pursue his ideas. He had gone to work for Good in 1971, when Good was at the University of Minnesota and director of one of the nation's largest immunology research groups. The arrangement was to the benefit of both. Good had money to support Summerlin, and the unknown Summerlin wanted to follow up a breakthrough he believed he had made in transplantation research. The grants soon started to roll in. An early paper by Summerlin acknowledged funding from the National Institutes of Health, the Veterans Administration, and the National Foundation (March of Dimes). This paper was the first to which Good added his name.

It was a well-known fact among Minnesota researchers, however, that Good had less than continuous contact with his co-workers. He traveled a lot. When he was at the university, dozens of people vied for his attention. "Bob and I were not really working together," Summerlin told a reporter after the Sloan-Kettering affair erupted.[7] "In fact, it was often hard to get to talk to him. I used to have to get up at four or five o'clock in the morning to see him for a few minutes. But it did not matter too much then. The whole group there in Minnesota was very good, very friendly."

Soon after Summerlin's arrival, Good decided to move, with a retinue of fifty researchers, from the University of Minnesota to the Sloan-Kettering Institute, of which he had been invited to become director. Summerlin was now an established researcher and to a certain extent had to financially fend for himself, even though Good still signed papers he produced. In March 1973, Summerlin flew off to a science writers' meeting run by the American Cancer Society, where he presented an outline of his work in progress. Summerlin hoped that favorable coverage in newspapers and on TV and radio might help get him a grant from the society. He had applied for an award that over a five-year period would run to $131,564.

At the meeting, Summerlin reported to eager journalists that "after human skin is maintained in organ culture for four to six weeks, it becomes universally transplantable without rejection." Not only that, but he reported that he had transplanted human corneas, after culture, into rabbit eyes without rejection. It seemed that one of the major hurdles to transplant surgery of all kinds was about to be surmounted. The next day's edition of *The New York Times* carried a three-column headline declaring "Lab Discovery May Aid Transplants." Overnight, Summerlin had become a scientific celebrity.

Despite the public success, and lectures given by Summerlin at scientific meetings, other researchers were increasingly skeptical as they tried and failed to repeat his work. Good, supposedly the intellectual inspiration behind the research, reassured some immunologists, putting the strength of his own reputation behind his words. Most distressing was that the English immunologist Peter Medawar and his colleagues were unable to reproduce Summerlin's results.

Medawar had received a Nobel prize for his studies of transplantation. He was also a member of the Sloan-Kettering Institute's board. In October 1973 Summerlin, in a presentation to the board of his work with corneal transplants, produced a rabbit which he said had received corneal grafts in both its eyes. As Medawar later described the scene, "Through a perfectly transparent eye this rabbit looked at the board with the candid and unwavering gaze of which only a rabbit with an absolutely clear conscience is capable. I could not believe that this rabbit had received a graft of any kind, not so much because of the perfect transparency of the cornea as because the pattern of blood vessels in the ring around the cornea was in no way disturbed. Nevertheless, I simply lacked the moral courage to say at the time that I thought we were the victims of a hoax or confidence trick."[8]

Even people in Summerlin's own lab were having trouble with the experiments. The situation by March 1974 had deteriorated to the point that Good felt it would be necessary to publish a report by a junior member of Summerlin's lab announcing failure to repeat certain of Summerlin's experiments. The report would probably throw Summerlin's career into a tailspin. On the morning of March 26, at 4 A.M., Summerlin got up off the cot he kept in his office to sleep on in times of crisis, and prepared for a critical meeting with Good. His goal was to persuade Good that the negative report was unnecessary because success was just around the corner. A new experiment in transplanting skin between mice was going well, and Summerlin planned to show two of the animals to his mentor.

By 7 A.M. Summerlin was headed to Good's office. On his way, he whipped out a felt-tip pen and inked in some black patches on the white mice. The reason, Summerlin later explained, was simply to make the black patches of transplanted skin—so he claimed—stand out more clearly. Good did not notice Summerlin's handiwork. It was the lab assistant to whom the mice were returned who noticed the embellishment and informed his superiors. Summerlin was immediately suspended from duty.

Why did Summerlin stoop to deceit? The explanation seized on by administrators at Sloan-Kettering was that the man had gone out of his mind. Lewis Thomas, president of the center, announced in a formal statement of May 24: "I have concluded that the most rational explanation for Dr. Summerlin's recent performance is that he has been suffering from an emotional disturbance of such a nature that he had not been fully responsible for the actions he has taken nor the representations he has made. Accordingly, it has been agreed that the Center will provide Dr. Summerlin with a period of medical leave on full salary [$40,000], beginning now, for up to 1 year, to enable him to obtain the rest and professional care which his condition may require." It is a recurring theme. Episodes of deceit are often said to be caused by insanity, at least according to administrators where the deed was performed.

A more thoughtful explanation was provided by Medawar, who suggested that early in his career, Summerlin had perhaps successfully transplanted skin between genetically unrelated mice, but had been unable to repeat the experiment: "Being absolutely convinced in his own mind that he was telling a true story, he thereupon resorted, disastrously, to deception." Recent experiments suggest that Summerlin's approach may hold a certain promise, even if not in his hands.[9]

A committee set up by Thomas to look into the affair suggested that Good himself should share part of the blame for the Summerlin affair, in particular for allowing Summerlin's results to be trumpeted to the press before they had been adequately confirmed. The committee also opined that "Good was slow to respond to a suggestion of dishonesty against Dr. Summerlin at a time when several investigators were experiencing great difficulty in repeating Dr. Summerlin's experiments."

Despite the mild rebuke, however, the committee concluded by excusing Good on the grounds that a high-powered administrator like him was too busy to supervise a subordinate, and that "the usual presumptions of veracity and trustworthiness on the part of co-workers" would have made it difficult for him to entertain the notion of fraud. Medawar too came to Good's defense. The answers to the questions about Good's supervision of Summerlin, Medawar wrote in an article in *The New York Review of Books,* "do not wholly exculpate Good (and he himself does not think they do), but they show him in a very much better light than his enemies would like. In the first place it is a very much more endearing trait in the head of an institute to champion and promote the interests of his young than to let them get on with it while he busies himself with his own affairs." Medawar, himself a lab chief, found it easy to perceive the obligation owed by Summerlin to Good—"It was, indeed, Good's patronage in Minneapolis that made it possible for Summerlin to have a career at all"—but he said nothing about the other side of the relationship, the credit Good gained by being the coauthor of Summerlin's papers.

Summerlin himself, one of the most outspoken members of the scientific hall of shame, did not think that these arguments exonerated Good. "My error," he said in a formal statement, "was not in knowingly promulgating false data, but rather in succumbing to extreme pressure placed on me by the Institute director to publicize information. . . ." He expanded on this theme for a reporter from the *Journal of the American Medical Association:* "Time after time, I was called upon to publicize experimental data and to prepare applications for grants from public and private sources. There came a time in the fall of 1973 when I had no new startling discovery, and was brutally told by Dr. Good that I was a failure in producing significant work. [Dr. Good denies this.] Thus, I was placed under extreme pressure to produce."[10] Summerlin told another reporter that the painting of the mice was perhaps a kind of challenge to Good, to test his attention and acumen.[11]

When apprentices are discovered playing scandalously loose with data, the institution affected by the transgression often feels obliged to appoint a blue-ribbon committee to look into the affair. Such committees seldom deviate from a preordained script. Their basic role is to reassure outsiders that everything is well with the institutional mechanisms of science. A pro forma knuckle rap will be administered to the lab chief, but the weight of the blame is always placed on the errant apprentice. Since he has already been caught red-handed (always by his fellow apprentices, not the busy master), he has little choice but to play his allotted role of scapegoat, a custom in which, it might be noted, the cursed beast is sent off into the wilderness bearing not just his own sins but those of the whole community.

Thus when John R. Darsee was caught up in his crimes (as recounted in Chapter 1), his mentor was found totally free of guilt by an eight-person committee called together by the dean of the Harvard Medical School. The quick exoneration came despite the fact that the Darsee episode raised serious questions about issues of supervision and pressure to produce.[12] Eugene Braunwald was a busy administrator who was in charge of two complete labs, was physician-in-chief to two of Harvard's most prestigious hospitals, and was constantly heading symposia and meetings across the country. The lab where Darsee worked was run for Braunwald by a researcher who was in fact a year younger than Darsee. "For Darsee's earlier work," Braunwald told a reporter, "the reason we have complete confidence is that the raw data were inspected at the most fundamental level at the time they were gathered. But then his role changed. After eighteen months or so it is not the custom to hold on to a fellow's hand at every turn."

The blue-ribbon committee found that the problem centered totally on Darsee, who under Braunwald's direction at Harvard had published nearly one hundred abstracts and papers, many coauthored with his mentor.[13] "The present problem," wrote the committee, "does not appear to be at all referable to the existing Cardiac Research Laboratory standards, policies, or procedures nor to overpressure provided by its Director or Dr. Braunwald."

Robert Gullis, William Summerlin, and John Darsee were individual apprentices who betrayed the principles of their guild. Implausible as were the guild's assertions that all blame lay with the apprentice, this defense was even less applicable in the remarkable case that came to light at Boston University in 1978. Not one but a whole group of young researchers in a forty-member cancer research team claimed they had been pressured into falsifying data and records by the team leader, Marc J. Straus.

Straus, thirty-four, was a driving, intense research physician who specialized in lung cancer. He was highly successful in attracting private and federal funding for his work, being awarded nearly $1 million over a three-year period. He had published more than forty articles and a book, had organized a half-dozen cancer clinics in affiliated hospitals outside Boston, and had achieved a national reputation. One day in the spring of 1978, Straus sat with some of his staff in a fourteenth-floor classroom at Boston University Medical Center and daydreamed out loud about winning a Nobel prize.

Less than three months after the Nobel musings, however, the structure on which Straus had built his empire suddenly collapsed. Five members of his staff—two young physicians on fellowships and three nurses—went to officials at Boston University and said the team's reports contained numerous lies. The falsifications ranged from simply changing a patient's birth date here and there to reporting treatments and laboratory studies that were never done and inventing the existence of a tumor in one patient.

The five charged that the falsifications were made under Straus's orders. But others on Straus's staff said the fictions were perpetrated amid a general anxiety that a shortage of patients might threaten future funding for their research. Straus resigned under pressure, insisting that he did not know of the falsifications and that he had been the victim of a conspiracy.

Whether or not Straus had an overt role in the falsifications is a question still in vigorous contention. Straus still strongly maintains that he had no knowledge of the fakery. What is not debated, however, is that at least eight members of the staff did falsify data, and that they were caught up in a huge research combine whose output went to enhance the name and reputation of Marc J. Straus.

By most measures, Straus had built an impressive career with extraordinary rapidity. He arrived at University Hospital in the summer of 1974, having come from the National Cancer Institute (NCI) outside of Washington, D.C. He quickly built up a group of aides, nurses, and physicians for a special unit that he founded for the treatment of and research on lung cancer. He published a variety of reports in the best journals. In 1977 he was selected by the Boston Junior Chamber of Commerce as one of the "Ten Outstanding Young Leaders of Greater Boston."

One of the main medical programs in which Straus worked was a clinical trial sponsored by the Eastern Cooperative Oncology Group (ECOG), a prestigious forty-hospital international research team. At the time the falsifications were revealed, ECOG was performing several studies, one of them experimental treatment based on ideas promoted by Straus. The two-drug regimen was administered on a precise timetable that Straus believed would drastically improve the survival rate of cancer patients.

Data for the study were gathered, organized, and entered into the vast ECOG computer banks by nurses and physicians on Straus's staff. Little by little, according to team members,[14] data were falsified. Most falsifications, including the reporting of false laboratory or test results, were done either to conceal errors made by the team in following the specific requirements of ECOG studies or to permit physicians to diverge from the ECOG treatment without "losing credit" for the cases. Later, when Boston University conducted an investigation, officials found that nearly

15 percent of the data had been falsified. The cheaters came forward because some feared that falsified data, often kept in the patients' medical records, might result in wrong treatments. Around the time the staff performed some of the falsifications, Straus was in relative seclusion, working on an application for a three-year grant renewal.

In 1981, Straus, who after leaving Boston University went on to teach and perform research at New York Medical College in Valhalla, commented on the case for the first time in public.[15] "We had forty full-time people, including eight nurses and data managers, and we had a series of very good checks and balances, so I thought. And we had repetitive meetings, and we went up the ladder so that we could review whether patient consents were obtained, whether documents were proper, whether recording data was as accurate as possible.

"There are certain types of studies that are almost beyond the ability for absolute surveillance. ECOG would really be such an example. Here you have a national cancer cooperative trial which at that time had some forty-seven different studies ongoing. . . . When one generates an ECOG record, there are an average of several thousand pieces of data. And you must rely on the integrity of people who are going to fill in those multiplicity of little boxes correctly. . . . There is a certain level of surveillance in any operation, medicine or otherwise, that requires the belief that the persons under you are acting properly."

The modern research team has come a long way from the relative innocence of its past.

CHAPTER 9

IMMUNITY
FROM
SCRUTINY

On a March morning in 1979, an unusual letter arrived in the austere offices of Robert Berliner, dean of Yale University School of Medicine. It charged two members of his faculty with the high scientific crime of plagiary. Berliner, sixty-four, an urbane pipe-smoking administrator, had held top positions for two decades at the National Institutes of Health (NIH) before coming to Yale. He read through the letter, glanced at the enclosed manuscripts, and immediately concluded that things had been overstated.

So began an incident that provides a unique insight into the everyday practice of research in the United States. Since it concerned a case of fraud, the incident itself cannot be said to be wholly typical. Yet the general behavior of the many actors in the drama is strongly if not wholly representative of how many scientists behave in the day-to-day conduct of their research. In following the deeds and attitudes of those caught up in the affair, it is helpful to hold in mind the ideals that scientists say guide their behavior: a dispassionate commitment to truth; judging people and arguments on their merits alone; critical scrutiny of all research claims, regardless of the eminence or otherwise of their proponents; sharing in common all ideas and knowledge for the benefit of the community; and rigorous self-policing.

The letter that landed on Berliner's desk came from a young woman researcher at the NIH. She accused the Yale researchers of lifting more than a dozen passages from an unpublished manuscript of hers and putting them into a paper of their own. It went on to question the "authenticity" of their data, implying that the Yale study had materialized out of thin air. The letter closed with a request for an investigation.

Berliner had lived too long in the stormy world of research to be much moved by the request. A glance at the manuscripts showed that the so-called plagiarism consisted of a few unimportant phrases containing, in total, some sixty words. Such cribbing was clearly improper, but it was hardly criminal and was in fact almost understandable. The lead author, after all, was Vijay R. Soman, thirty-seven, a well-respected if not particularly creative assistant professor who had come to the United States in 1971 from Poona, India. He was still uncomfortable with the English language. Moreover, it was highly unlikely that the study had not been performed. The senior scientist who watched over Soman and who coauthored the study in question was Philip Felig, forty-three, a distinguished researcher. He had published more than 200 papers, received fifteen academic honors and awards, and pulled down an honorary degree from the Nobel-prize-giving Karolinska Institute in Sweden. At the Yale School of Medicine, Felig held an endowed chair, was vice chairman of the department of medicine, and chief of endocrinology research.

Just to be sure, Berliner requested from the researchers copies of the data sheets, the scientific foundation of the study. The sheets told of experiments on six women with anorexia nervosa (a morbid aversion to food). Thus equipped, Berliner wrote to the young NIH researcher, saying there was no question that the study had been done. Soman, moreover, had been reprimanded. "I hope," he wrote, "that you will now consider the matter closed."

She did not. For the next year and a half Helena Wachslicht-Rodbard wrote letters, made phone calls, threatened to denounce Soman and Felig at national meetings, and threatened to quit her job. She knew the plagiarism was self-evident. Now she wanted an investigation into the validity of the whole study because it was riddled with data that looked too good. She eventually got it. In the end, the investigation showed that the study in question was the least of the problems at Yale.[1]

Rodbard, a shy, soft-spoken Brazilian who avoids reporters and whose understated manner can lull an observer into overlooking her ardor and sense of adventure, came to NIH in 1975 on a fellowship. Two years and a promotion later, she went to work in the laboratory of Jesse Roth, forty-two, a diabetes specialist who had pioneered in a field of interest to her, the study of how insulin molecules bind to human blood cells in health and disease. A logical extension of Roth's work was to look at the way insulin binds in patients with anorexia nervosa, a mental disorder accompanied by an acute loss of weight. This was the task to which Rodbard, twenty-nine, set herself. The insulin-binding study was to be the acme of her career at NIH, and her first as the chief researcher of a team. She threw herself wholeheartedly into the project.

As senior author, Rodbard on November 9, 1978, had submitted a paper to the *New England Journal of Medicine*, the leading journal for medical researchers, entitled "Insulin Receptor Abnormalities in Anorexia Nervosa: Mirror Image of Obesity." The manuscript was coauthored by her lab chief, Roth, and a psychologist who had monitored the condition of the patients. As is standard practice, the article was reviewed for the journal by two referees, one recommending acceptance, the other rejection.

On January 31, 1979, Arnold Relman, the influential editor of the journal, wrote to Rodbard apologizing for the two-and-a-half-month delay, saying her study had "engendered considerable differences of opinion." A third referee had been called in, and the editorial board of the *New England Journal of Medicine* had decided the manuscript would not be acceptable unless it was revised. The delay was a sizable setback for the young researcher. What Rodbard did not know was that the negative review touching off the delay had come from quiet and unannounced rivals of hers at Yale, Soman and Felig.

Soman had arrived at the Albany Medical College in 1971 after teaching at a medical college in Poona, India. A photograph on file at the New York State Board of Education shows a boyish, trusting Soman with smooth round face, large features, wide-set eyes, and hair neatly combed off to one side. A co-researcher at Albany says Soman was "a highly capable, honorable, honest researcher." During this period he published three papers. In 1975, Soman took a giant step in his career by landing a fellowship at

Yale. Better yet, next year he was appointed to the Yale faculty. In 1977, now an assistant professor of medicine, he won support from NIH for two grant proposals, one of them, entitled "Glucagon and Insulin Receptors in Glucose Homeostasis," picking up a much-coveted Clinical Investigator Award. Soman worked under the guidance of Felig, who had a reputation in his department as something of a taskmaster, expecting and getting a good deal of publishable material from his subordinates. Soman did not disappoint him. By 1980, Soman's rate of production had multiplied many times over. He had coauthored fourteen papers since arriving at Yale and was receiving nearly $100,000 in NIH support.

Early in his career at Yale, in 1976, Soman received permission from the Institutional Review Board to perform an insulin-binding study on patients with anorexia nervosa. For more than two years he seemed in no haste to write a paper, but the glint of competition soon spurred him on.

In November 1978, Felig received a request from the *New England Journal of Medicine* asking him to review Rodbard's manuscript. Though it went against the practice of the journal, Felig passed the manuscript to his subordinate Soman. With this new information that the Rodbard manuscript provided, the pace of Soman's project picked up considerably. It was clear that Rodbard's study was identical to the one Soman had first conceived back in 1976 and on which he had allegedly been working ever since, along with his myriad other tasks. After reading Rodbard's manuscript, Soman started busily assembling the data of his own study.

Felig returned Rodbard's paper to the *New England Journal of Medicine,* and, under his own signature, recommended that they reject it. He did not mention that his junior associate Soman had seen the paper and was privately working on an identical study. Meanwhile, unbeknownst to Felig, Soman had made a copy of Rodbard's manuscript and was using it in preparation of his own.

In late December 1978, just one month after reviewing the Rodbard manuscript, Soman mailed off a paper entitled "Insulin Binding to Monocytes and Insulin Sensitivity in Anorexia Nervosa." Soman was listed as lead author, Felig as coauthor. The paper was sent to the *American Journal of Medicine,* where Felig was an associate editor.

The arrival of the Rodbard manuscript told Felig that his associate Soman was in a losing position in the race to publish first. Did he try to help Soman reverse the position? Felig, a man precise in speech and cool in manner, claims he recommended rejection of Rodbard's paper purely on its merits, not so as to buy more time for Soman. He says he had no reason to vie for priority or even care about acquiring another publication, because he already had 200 papers to his name. The relationship with Soman, Felig contends, was one in which Soman was the chief beneficiary. "In essence," he told the Congressmen at the Gore hearings, "I was providing Soman a cloak of scientific credibility." In contrast, Soman clearly had a motive to vie for priority, according to Felig. Soman was pushing himself hard, working his way into the higher reaches of the U.S. academic hierarchy.

Felig's description, while doubtless accurate as far as it goes, neglects to cite the assistance his subordinates may have given him in accruing publications and influence. Despite his claim to 200 papers, Felig is sole author of only 35. On the other papers his name is surrounded by coauthors. In the early days of his career, these fellow authors were undoubtedly senior researchers who at best made minimal contributions to the published work. In the later days, the situation was reversed, and the Somans of the world were undoubtedly giving Felig's career something of a lift. When Felig rejected Rodbard's paper, might he at the same time have strongly advised Soman to hurry up with his anorexia project? Felig denies this possibility. Soman, however, may have referred to it after admitting to an investigator that he had fudged much of his data. "[My] actions," he said, "were done in the midst of significant pressure so as to obtain priority. . . ." He never spelled out the nature of that pressure.

In any event, the manuscript that Soman mailed to the *American Journal of Medicine* was sent off for review, and, as fate would have it, the manuscript was sent to Roth at NIH. He in turn passed it on to his junior associate Rodbard.

She was aghast. Here was her paper, complete with verbatim passages and even a formula she had devised for working out the number of receptor sites per cell. Yet other than her colleagues and the editors of the *New England Journal of Medicine*, no one had seen her paper—no one, that is, except for the three anonymous referees. Upon closely reading over their comments, and comparing the printed typefaces with that of the manuscript she had just been handed, she guessed, correctly, that it was Felig who had written the negative review of her paper. In a controlled fury, she fired off a three-page letter to Relman at the *New England Journal of Medicine,* enclosing a copy of the Soman-Felig manuscript.

She accused Felig and Soman of plagiarism, of a conflict of interest in reviewing her paper, and of trying to slow down the acceptance of her work. "We recognize the problems encountered by Editors," she noted, "and by the entire peer review system, when two or three laboratories are working in a competitive field. For our own part, we shall promptly inform the *American Journal of Medicine* that we will decline the role of impartial and fair referee, in view of the obvious conflict of interest."

Relman in part agreed with Rodbard's criticisms. "The plagiarism was really trivial," he later said. "I thought it was bad judgment for an Indian associate of Felig's to copy some of the standard phrases, but it was not a lethal accusation." For Soman and Felig to have reviewed her paper, however, was "a conflict of interest that was direct and immediate. It wasn't just a question of working on the same subject, but a question of timing and priority, putting them head to head."

"Surprised and disappointed," Relman called Felig one day in late February 1979 to talk over the conflict-of-interest charges. Felig replied that the review had been based on the merits of the Rodbard paper, and that the work by Soman had been initiated two years previously. He also told Relman that their work had been completed before the Rodbard paper had arrived. Felig later found out this statement was false. Relman was upset by the whole situation, and soon published the Rodbard paper,[2] although he now denies that the conflict-of-interest revelations prompted his quick change of mind about the paper.

On the same day that Relman telephoned, Felig also received a call from Rodbard's boss and coauthor at NIH, Roth. Roth was a pillar of the NIH community, a distinguished researcher and chief of the diabetes branch of the National Institute of Arthritis, Metabolism, and Digestive Diseases. In addition, Roth was no stranger to Felig. They were competitors but also close friends who had grown up together in Brooklyn and had gone to the same grade school. Roth told Felig that he had no doubts Soman had worked independently of Rodbard, but that they ought to discuss the problem further.

Less than a week later, Felig flew down to NIH for a meeting, and on Saturday, March 3, he and Roth compared the papers during a private meeting at the Holiday Inn in Bethesda. The plagiary, though not extensive, was unmistakable. Felig agreed to go back and confront Soman. In a bid to settle the matter quickly and quietly, the two lab chiefs also worked out a plan to correct the wrong they now agreed Soman had done. It was a plan, as Felig later commented in a memo for his files, meant "to avoid even the perception of impropriety on our part." He told Roth he would (i) include a reference in the Soman-Felig paper to the work of Rodbard, (ii) delay publication until 1980 so that Rodbard's paper would have clear priority, and (iii) mention Rodbard's work in his presentation at the American Federation for Clinical Research meetings that were scheduled to be held in May. As a final concession, Felig promised to withhold publication of the manuscript "so long as any legitimate questions" remained about the independence of the work. This final point would later come back to haunt him.

On Sunday, Felig phoned Rodbard, saying he was chagrined by what had happened and offering his plan to put things right. He also suggested, Rodbard later recalled, that the plan would go into effect "in exchange for a letter of exoneration."[3] Rodbard had little enthusiasm for the plan.

Back in New Haven on Monday, Felig met with his Indian associate, and Soman confessed to having kept a copy of the Rodbard paper and to using it as a crutch to prepare his own.

How had Soman been able to perform his misdeeds without Felig knowing? Felig was later to explain that one factor was campus geography. Soman worked at a laboratory in the Farnum building of the Yale medical school complex, some two city blocks away from Felig's office in the Hunter building. Another factor was spelled out by Felig at the subsequent congressional hearings.[4] "Our relationship had been based on one of trust, in which in the earlier stage of his career he had been doing work under my guidance in specific techniques where I was intimately familiar. There was no evidence in those earlier interactions of any aspect that would suggest dishonesty." Auditors would later find evidence to the contrary. Felig continued to describe his relationship with Soman: "He then went on to develop new techniques and in the development of those techniques he had established his own laboratory, obtained his own funds, and as is often the case, with a collaboration one accepts a certain element of what one's colleagues are doing as being honest. . . ."

When Soman confessed to Felig in March 1979 that he had kept a copy of Rodbard's manuscript as a "crutch," his lab chief demanded to see copies of the laboratory notes so that the dates when Soman studied the patients could be established. That same day, Felig got a second call from Roth saying Rodbard now believed the Soman-Felig study had been entirely fabricated on the basis of her paper. Roth added that he was dissociating himself from those charges. He wrote to Felig later that same day saying he had no doubt that the Soman-Felig studies had been initiated independently and "were largely or entirely completed" before Rodbard's manuscript had been reviewed. Roth had asked Rodbard to cosign the letter, he noted, but she had refused. This March 5, 1979, letter from Roth to Felig was written without benefit of the actual evidence. On March 13, Felig sent Roth copies of the data sheets, with a cover sheet that showed the dates of the studies.

Rodbard was frustrated with things on the home front. She felt a serious wrong had been done by both Felig and Soman, and that something more should be done about it. Early publication of her paper in the *New England Journal of Medicine* was not enough. Frustrations were further heightened because she felt her own superior was trying to shut her up. She and Roth had argued heatedly over the matter and had exchanged chilly memos, with Roth eventually ordering her to stop using NIH stationery and time to pursue her grievance. At this point, Rodbard momentarily gave up pursuing the matter from within NIH and turned to the dean of the Yale School of Medicine, Berliner. It was then that the young researcher wrote the letter that was to eventually throw the Yale medical school into turmoil. She asked Berliner's help "in resolving a serious ethical matter." She had been shocked, explained her letter of March 27, 1979, to discover "that the paper by Drs. Soman and Felig contained more than a dozen passages which were verbatim with the paper which I had previously submitted to the *New England Journal of Medicine.*" She went on to discuss why an investigation was needed to establish "the authenticity of the data." Among her reasons:

- "The names of the physicians and/or psychiatrists responsible for conducting behavior modification therapy were not specified, nor was the hospital where the studies were performed."
- "There were a number of unusual aspects of the data. Remarkably, all patients resumed menses following therapy contrary to general experience."

Rodbard's first point was more significant than it might have seemed. The scientific discovery reported by both studies was that patients with anorexia nervosa tend to bind more insulin molecules to blood cells than normal, but when cured of the illness, the blood cells behave in a more usual fashion. Recovery from the disease, however, often calls for close attention by a physician or psychiatrist. One would certainly expect the Yale researchers at the least to have named their psychiatric colleague or, like Rodbard, to have included him as a coauthor.

What also fueled Rodbard's suspicions was that most of the data in the Soman-Felig study were uncannily precise. The data displayed on graphs normally lie close to, but seldom dead on, ideal curves and lines. In the Soman-Felig study, however, the graphs were nearly perfect. Rodbard did not mention this suspicion in her letter to Berliner, because it was a matter of judgment that could be argued away. Instead, she stressed a fact that could not be pooh-poohed, the plagiary. A quick glance at the two manuscripts and the conclusion of plagiary was inescapable, though Berliner and Yale in general played it down as being a matter of only sixty-odd words. Yet Soman's appropriation of Rodbard's few phrases was almost certainly the key factor that eventually forced Rodbard's complaints to be given a serious hearing. Had this clear offense not been beyond contention, Rodbard's criticisms might have been ignored, and the skeletons in the laboratory at Yale might have remained buried forever in the vast unscrutinized underworld of research.

On April 9 Felig supplied, at Berliner's request, the names of the patients and the dates on which they had been studied, together with the data sheets compiled by Soman. Though he would later dearly regret it, Felig had not looked to see if the data compared accurately to the notebooks or the patients' hospital charts. In a cover memo to Berliner attesting to the authenticity of the work, Felig noted that "my main concern at this point is what further harassment we will be subjected to and what if anything can be done about it."[5] In explaining the situation to a reporter, Yale officials at times referred to Rodbard as a "hysterical female." Berliner wrote on April 17 to Rodbard, saying "the data were collected over a period going back to November 1976. . . . All but one of the studies were complete before your paper was submitted to the *New England Journal.*" Referring to the Roth-Felig agreement that called for mention of Rodbard's work at the clinical meetings, Berliner said he thought this "a very generous resolution of the matter."

Not Rodbard. She complained to Roth and told him that if there was not an investigation she would stand up at the May clinical meetings and denounce the Soman-Felig study. Roth eventually conceded, telling her before the meeting that he would arrange an investigation.

In June 1979, Roth proposed that an audit at Yale be conducted by his superior, Joseph E. Rall, fifty-nine, who was the director of intramural research at his institute. Both Felig and Rodbard accepted this arrangement. Most everyone, however, seemed to think that Rodbard was overreacting and that the problem if left alone would simply evaporate. Roth had been satisfied with the data sheets supplied by Felig. Rall too thought an audit would be effort wasted. "I just found it hard to believe that Felig had engaged in any hanky-panky," he would later remark. "I saw the validity of the complaints in the Rodbard letter, but my feeling by and large was that people don't falsify data and don't plagiarize things."

A busy administrator at NIH, Rall gave the visit a low priority, saying he would get around to it in the fall. Meanwhile, Rodbard quit NIH and her ambitions in research in July and started working as an ordinary physician in a Washington, D.C., hospital.

September came and went, as did October and November. By the time December rolled around, and the investigation still had not materialized, Rodbard picked up the pace of her phone calls to her former boss, Roth, complaining about the lack of action. Roth eventually confronted Rall, and Rall said he did not think he was going to be able to get to New Haven. Maybe it would be better, he said, to get someone "more familiar with the subject matter."

Felig at this point had every reason to hope that the whole episode might fade from view and be forgotten, for the greatest opportunity of his career had just appeared. A search committee from Columbia University's prestigious College of Physicians and Surgeons had recommended that he be appointed Samuel Bard Professor and chairman of the department of medicine. Felig accepted, with the intention of starting in June 1980, apparently feeling the storm had blown over. In January 1980, he took Soman to Columbia, introduced him to officials, and recommended that he be appointed an assistant professor.

But the calm that Felig evidently perceived was merely the lull before a far angrier storm. At Rodbard's continued urging, Roth in January 1980 lined up a new inspector for the long-postponed investigation. Unlike the former candidate, he was young and energetic. Jeffrey S. Flier, though only thirty-one, was chief of the diabetes metabolism unit at Beth Israel Hospital in Boston, and an assistant professor at the Harvard Medical School. Flier said he would perform the audit in February, and would send the results directly to Roth, with a copy to Felig.

Felig still had no idea of the gathering storm about to break. One indication of this is that in January 1980 the *American Journal of Medicine*[6] published the Soman-Felig paper that had been under fire for nearly a year, despite the fact that Felig had promised to withhold publication as long as "legitimate questions" remained about the independence of the work. Nor was Felig alone in expecting that the impending investigation would clear the Yale group of Rodbard's charges. "Nobody," says Dean Berliner, "was taking the audit seriously, so there was no reason to stop publication." But a certain defiance lurks within the printed pages of the Soman-Felig study; it includes all but two of the passages lifted from the Rodbard manuscript.

On February 5, nearly one year after Rodbard originally called for an investigation, Flier boarded a train in Boston bound for

New Haven, ready to carry out an audit, a highly unusual procedure in research. Having met Soman some years earlier and having watched his prodigious and very elegant output in the scientific literature, Flier was sure he would find no evidence of overt fraud at Yale. Waiting on the station platform at New Haven was Soman. He drove Flier to his office, where he had laid out on his desk a number of hospital records, data sheets, and notebooks. Flier later told a reporter[7] that Soman seemed somewhat nervous, and kept saying, with a giggle, things like, "Isn't it silly that you have to be bothered with this?" In an attempt to ease the tension, Flier made small talk about the research each was pursuing. "After half an hour," Flier recalls, "I thought we were ready, so I said, 'Well, Vijay, I guess we have to get on with this.' I asked to look first at the data on the individual patients, and we began to go through their hospital charts. There were only five of them, rather than six, and Soman didn't say why one was missing. But I could see that the five patients had all, as reported, been diagnosed as having anorexia nervosa and had all gained significant amounts of weight in the course of treatment.

"Next, I asked Soman for evidence that insulin-binding had been done on these patients before and after treatment. He handed me a data sheet for the first patient. I was surprised. I had expected graphs for each patient, showing the data plotted out and curves drawn through the points, but what he gave me was just a sheet of raw numbers. 'Don't you have graphs?' I asked him. He seemed flustered, and said, 'Well, we threw away the individual graphs after a year because we had no storage space.' I started to feel uneasy. You don't throw away graphs with data that have just been published. It made no sense.

"So I studied that first sheet and visualized what the graph would look like, and it was clear, as their paper had reported, that there was more binding of the insulin when the patient was anorexic than after she gained weight. But it was also clear that the numbers on the data sheet did not at all conform to the kind of curve we always get in insulin receptor studies—nor to the curve published in the Soman-Felig paper, which was said to represent all the pooled findings on all six patients.

"I said, 'Vijay, it's funny that instead of having a sharp falloff, as in the published curve, this all looks very flat. It doesn't look like what you reported or what we'd normally expect.' He looked at the sheet and said, 'Gee, you're right. That must have been a bad one. Let's look at another case.' We did, but it was no better. One by one we went through the print-outs, and all of them proved to be deficient in one way or another. Something was seriously wrong. There was no way that the beautiful composite curve they had in the paper could have been derived from the data I had been looking at."

Flier recalls that he then, with some trepidation, asked, "Vijay, what am I to think about this? It looks as if the published data don't conform to the data you're showing me." Soman, looking increasingly distressed, blamed the inaccuracies on a technician, but Flier asked, "Even if this was the fault of the technician, wouldn't you have decided not to publish if the data weren't good?

"Somewhere about then," Flier says, "I used the word 'fudged' for the first time: I said something like, 'Were the published data fudged? Were they made to look good?' Soman fumbled around and then said, basically, yes, they had been fudged. Felig hadn't known about it. Nobody had. I also asked about some discordant data that seemed to have been suppressed, and he admitted to doing that, too."

Flier says he felt "pretty devastated" by Soman's confession, but with some effort continued to play his role: "I said, 'You know how serious this is?' and he said, 'Yes,' and started to defend himself. He said he'd been under great pressure to publish as soon as possible so as to obtain priority for the finding. He said that the laboratory he worked in was oriented toward productivity and success."

With the fudged data sheets spread out before them both, Soman started saying maybe he didn't need to continue in the field of research. Maybe practicing clinical medicine would be enough. "Earlier in his career," Flier recalls, "Soman felt he had been totally reputable, but something that led him to fabrication came over him in this busy group."

In hindsight, Flier realizes that he and his colleagues had marveled at the beauty of Soman's published data. Yet even though Flier and friends had not been able to achieve such clean results, they never suspected that the elegant data were the result of deliberate fraud. "You'd shake your head and say, 'How did they ever get such beautiful data?'"

It was one week after the audit, on February 12, that Felig returned to New Haven (his mother had died) and heard the results. The falsified article was already published, and now, in three hours, Flier had made a simple discovery that Felig had overlooked for more than a year. Felig called the chairman of his department, Samuel Thier, an athletic man in his mid-forties, and told him the news. The two men conferred with Dean Berliner, who said Soman had to go.

Soman was called into Felig's office. It was Thier who took the lead. As he recalls: "I said, 'Vijay, this and this is what's been presented to me. What's going on?' He looked very shaken and went through several denials that didn't hold up. Then he repeated what he'd told Phil [Felig] about Flier's being prejudiced in some way. I said: 'Vijay, this doesn't make sense. There's no reason for this man to come here and make false statements about your work. Now what, in fact, happened?' Finally, he said, 'I smoothed out the data. I took the curves and smoothed them out,' and he began to cry. It was dreadful."[8]

Both men tried to extract from Soman the reason for his deceit, but he only mumbled something about this being his fate. After a while Soman asked, "What do I do now?" and Thier told him that the best choice was to resign and to give up research. Soman agreed to do so and to leave Yale.

During the next few days Felig repeatedly asked Soman why he had doctored the data. Unlike Flier, Felig remembers Soman saying nothing about pressure or the cutthroat pace of research. Every time the subject came up, says Felig, Soman's reply was always the same as the one mumbled in the office. Fate. One day, however, Soman told Felig a story about how his father in India had been trained as an engineer but made his living as a farmer. Soman's father did this, Felig recalls, because he felt that a person who engaged in a profession other than farming would sooner or later be corrupted.

Amid the upheaval at Yale and the concomitant stir down at NIH over the results of the audit, a rather remarkable observation made by Flier seemed to escape notice. "It would appear that the insulin receptor studies that were performed were carried out during out-patient visits to the Diabetes Unit at Yale-New Haven," he wrote in a four-page report of his findings, "as there were no specific notations in their medical records regarding blood drawn for insulin receptor studies." In other words, the audit showed that five patients in the Yale Hospital had clearly been followed by Felig and Soman, but there was no evidence, other than that submitted by Soman in his notebooks, that they had been the object of insulin-binding studies. "It was a rather remarkable thing," Flier later said, "but nobody made a big deal about it." The observation implied that Soman might have dreamed the whole thing up out of thin air. At the very least, it was clear Soman had lacked a sufficient number of anoretic subjects at the time he saw the Rodbard paper. In November 1978, he took one patient, whom he had been following for another condition, and for the purposes of the falsified study called her anoretic. "Her weight has always been just right," says her mother. The patient herself says she was studying at Central Connecticut State College in New Britain during the period Soman allegedly performed the binding studies on her at Yale in New Haven.

Soman left Yale within a few weeks of his confession and by summer was back in Poona, India. For Felig, however, a period of considerable inconvenience had just begun. The Soman-Felig paper would have to be retracted, a minor scandal, and another investigator would have to be called in to examine the rest of Soman's data. Not to do so would leave Yale open to charges of a coverup. Felig, Thier, and Berliner decided to impound all of Soman's notes, records, and charts. Berliner wrote to Jerrold M. Olefsky, thirty-seven, an endocrinologist at the University of Colorado, who agreed to come to Yale in March.

Felig, meanwhile, was faced with the delicate task of telling his would-be superiors at the Columbia College of Physicians and Surgeons about the problems at Yale. The situation called for candor, for a conversation with the dean. Late in February 1980, he went to the school to conduct a seminar, and afterward broke the news.

Dark and serious portraits of Samuel Bard professors peered down from the walls as Felig, sitting in the office of Columbia Dean Donald F. Tapley, recounted the events. Felig mentioned the junior researcher he had planned on bringing to Columbia, Vijay Soman. Now, he said, that would be impossible. An audit at Yale revealed that Soman had fudged data, and he had been fired. A Soman-Felig paper with doctored data was being retracted, he said. Another audit was in the offing, and there might be further retractions.

What Felig did not mention to Tapley or any other official at Columbia was the battle for priority, the year-old charges by a rival researcher, the months-long delay in the audit, and the admission of plagiarism by Soman. These omissions later proved to be quite significant.

On a blustery day in late March, after Felig's talk with Tapley, Olefsky flew into New Haven with the notion that he would examine a total of fourteen papers in which Soman had taken part. He was mistaken. When Felig had impounded Soman's notes, he was dismayed to find that most of what was needed was missing. He asked Soman what had happened to the data sheets and books, and Soman replied that many of them had been discarded. So Olefsky sat down to work with what was presented—data for five papers. In a report to Dean Berliner, he told of his two-day odyssey: he had found from a quarter to half the data missing; as for what remained, he concluded that "one is left with the impression that there has been a general tendency to smooth the data up a bit." In three of the papers for which data were available, some of the conclusions were simply false, because they did not follow from the data. Of the fourteen papers, Olefsky was able to give his approval to only two. The remaining dozen either were suspect because the data were missing or were cases of outright fraud. Ten of these papers were coauthored by Felig.

Getting wind of the Olefsky audit, Rodbard called him at the University of Colorado on April 17, 1980, and heard for the first time about the missing data books. She then wrote to Berliner on April 30, saying that this lack of data meant that the Olefsky audit had been restricted to looking at only the "tip of the iceberg." Her understanding of the agreement for an investigation, she wrote, was that "the data as published in the literature must be a faithful representation of the real data, or else the papers must be retracted." She also noted with some chagrin in the letter to

Berliner that both Felig and Thier had called her a few days earlier to say the latest audit indicated everything was OK. "As you can understand," she wrote, "this is quite different information from that which we have received directly from Dr. Olefsky. It is difficult for us to understand the basis for this discrepancy."

One week after Rodbard mailed this letter, the powers that be responded in their own way. A letter was sent from Yale to the *American Journal of Medicine*, retracting the paper that had started the uproar in the first place. The retraction came more than one and a half years after Soman's plagiary. By the end of May, letters retracting a total of twelve papers had gone out from Yale. A little more than two months later, in early August, a faculty committee at the Columbia College of Physicians and Surgeons forced Felig to resign from his new post in part because of his failure to tell the whole story right from the start. Administrators there had heard about the bevy of retractions through the rumor mill rather than from Felig. Though perhaps not the most significant omission, it was Felig's not telling Dean Tapley of the admission of plagiary that most upset the committee. The plagiarism was mentioned in every "conclusion" of the seven-page faculty report. Members of the committee repeatedly said that "plagiarism is plagiarism," even though they in fact had not laid eyes on the manuscripts.

In the aftermath of one of the most serious shake-ups in the history of biomedical research, the principals carry on, though sometimes in ways unknown. Nothing in scientific circles is known of Soman's life in India. Philip Felig, after having his case reviewed by the Yale medical school for more than three months, was rehired. He was not, however, returned to his endowed chair. In addition, he is no longer an associate editor at the *American Journal of Medicine*. Since he was not found personally responsible for any acts of fraud by a team of investigators from NIH, his major grant has been renewed. Other funding agencies such as the American Diabetes Association have followed suit. He has not given up on team research, but is still, after more than a dozen years, corresponding with researchers at the Karolinska Institute in Stockholm on a project that may result in three or four papers. In addition, he continues working on five team projects at Yale, though he says he is much more careful about signing a paper in which a subordinate has developed the methods. "When a senior scientist is not too familiar," Felig told the Gore congressional hearing "he or she should exercise even greater care in reviewing the original data of the junior scientist, or his or her name should not be included on the paper. I further deem it advisable that consultation from outside experts be sought before permitting the material to be published with the senior scientist's name."

Helena Wachslicht-Rodbard completed her residency in internal medicine and entered private practice. Research, she tells friends, does not hold the attraction it once did.

The Yale imbroglio shows science at work in a far more real sense than do the heroic case studies of the scientific textbooks. To be sure, few experiments are based on fabricated data; but Soman's fraud was a mechanism that brought to light the actual behavior patterns and attitudes of a segment of the scientific community. Moreover this was not just any segment; Yale and the NIH are part of the scientific elite.

Researchers are formally committed to the search for truth, but in the day-to-day conduct of their activities, it is not so much this abstract ideal but competition with rivals and colleagues that is the spur to action. When Felig was asked to review Rodbard's manuscript for the *New England Journal of Medicine*, he gained sight of the cards in Rodbard's hands without her seeing those in his. The advantage was unfair, because from that moment on, Felig and Soman knew they were in a race, while Rodbard had no idea that she was pitted against the Yale team. In recommending rejection of the paper, even if solely on its merits, Felig can hardly have failed to perceive that his action would delay Rodbard and buy more time for Soman.

The elitism that permeates the world of research ensures that the feats of scientific celebrities and their proxies will be more widely noticed than the equivalent deeds of lesser-known researchers. Philosophers and sociologists of science contend that skepticism keeps science pure by weeding out research that is either bad or fraudulent. Yet the power of the elite to shelter itself from skeptical inquiry is a sign that this mechanism is not universally applied in science. Despite Rodbard's well-documented complaint, it took a year and a half before an investigation was launched and the fraud found out.

Being part of the elite perhaps shaped the actions of the players in ways that otherwise are hard to explain. Why, for instance, did Felig go ahead and publish the challenged study even after he knew that Soman had plagiarized parts of it? Why did he not conduct a complete review of Soman's data and methods, instead of just glancing at the data sheets, as soon as Rodbard leveled the charges? Since Rodbard was pressing for an audit, prudence might have suggested a routine check that everything was in order. But perhaps Felig and his senior colleagues at Yale shared the natural assumptions of their counterparts at NIH. Roth was convinced, before even seeing the evidence, that Soman had conducted his study independently. Roth's chief, Rall, appointed as first auditor, never got around to going to Yale, because, as he put it, "I just found it hard to believe that Felig had engaged in any hanky-panky." The Yale authorities simply took for granted that they were above reproach.

The same immunity from scrutiny that protected Felig also extended to his protégé Soman. When Flier and his colleagues saw the various data being published by Soman, they didn't suspect deceit; instead, they just marveled at the beauty and speed of his work. And even when Soman went beyond smoothing up data and produced results that were totally incorrect, it was not by the replication of experiments, that supposed guarantor of scientific truth, that the fraud was discovered. Replication did not and could not detect the crime. It took the almost unprecedented method of an examination by Flier and a two-day audit by Olefsky to uncover the misdeeds in the Yale laboratory.

Without the audit, the fraud would have passed unnoticed into the ocean of unchecked and uncheckable scientific results. So the extreme difficulty with which that audit was triggered bears some pondering. Science is supposed to be a meritocracy in which people and ideas are taken on their merits. It is not. Just as in other walks of life, scientists pay a great deal of attention to rank and pecking order. Rodbard was a young, unknown scientist. Even Roth, her own lab chief, dissociated himself from her charges beyond a certain point. The Yale authorities were even more inclined to pooh-pooh her accusations. In everything she said, she proved to be exactly right, and they wrong. Yet the merit of her case did not suffice to gain her a prompt hearing, because in science, rank counts. Had it not been for the obvious plagiary, rank would have outweighed the facts of her case.

Like any other profession, science is ridden with clannishness and clubbiness. This would be in no way surprising, except that scientists deny it to be the case. The pursuit of scientific truth is held to be a universal quest that recognizes neither national boundaries nor the barriers of race, creed, or class. In fact, researchers tend to organize themselves into clusters of overlapping clubs. Felig was both the beneficiary and the victim of the club. Columbia University withdrew his appointment not when he first told them of the Soman problem, but when the whiff of scandal reached the campus. The members of the faculty committee then pounced on the plagiary, without even troubling to read the two manuscripts to gauge its extent, and cited that as one of the main reasons for demanding his resignation. In fact the plagiary was minor, and in any case was none of Felig's doing.

Fraud apart, the episode at Yale is representative of the attitudes and customs that prevail in many scientific laboratories. The picture of research it reveals bears little resemblance to the idealized portrait so beloved by writers of textbooks and defenders of the scientific status quo. An understanding of the way science really works is important because the process does not take place in a vacuum. Scientists are a part of society. What they do and how they behave affect the general public in a way perhaps more profound than any other profession. The attitudes and customs of the scientific establishment created an environment that could nurture a Soman, and the results of Soman's research had implications for the care of young women with anorexia nervosa. It is here, in the interaction with society at large, that scientific fraud shows its most pernicious side.

CHAPTER 10

RETREAT UNDER PRESSURE

Basic research, the kind designed to increase knowledge for knowledge's sake, is mostly undertaken at universities, in an atmosphere as free as possible of political and social pressures. The independence of science from society is important for several reasons, not least of which is that corrupt motives in one institution can often infect and distort arrangements in the other. As is described in this chapter, the pathology of Lysenkoism starkly illustrates the falsifications that result when a political ideology is imposed on science. The reverse process, discussed in Chapter 11, is the corruption of society by false science, a disease with less conspicuous symptoms but even graver consequences.

In the search for legitimacy, political ideologies often turn to science, especially to biology and the difficult issues of genetics and evolution. In the nineteenth century the Social Darwinists in England and the United States cited the theory of evolution and natural selection as support for conservative, laissez-faire policies; just as natural selection lets the fit survive and the weak perish, they argued, so should governments let the wealthy prosper and the poor sink or swim. Radicals and liberals, on the other hand, have found the theory of Darwin's rival, Lamarck, more useful for their purposes. If acquired characteristics can be inherited, as Lamarck suggested, then the prospects of reforming society through education are much brighter and the claims by all individuals for equal opportunity are that much the stronger.

Not content with merely drawing upon biology, some ideologists have tried to shape biology more positively to their liking. In the celebrated but still ambiguous case of Paul Kammerer and the midwife toads, it may have been his political views that led him to forge evidence in support of Lamarckism. An Austrian biologist with legendary skill in breeding amphibians and other animals, Kammerer led an active political and social life in Vienna in addition to pursuing his scientific career. He was an ardent pacifist and socialist. He fell in love with Alma Mahler, widow of the composer, and threatened to shoot himself on Gustav Mahler's grave unless she married him. Alma married several distinguished men, such as the architect Walter Gropius, and had affairs with a great many others, including the painter Oskar Kokoschka; but her relationship with Kammerer was restricted to the historically more significant role of being his laboratory asistant for a time.

In science, Kammerer became a well-known advocate of the Lamarckian view that newly acquired characteristics can be inherited, as opposed to the Darwinian view that they cannot. By the 1920's, the debate between the Lamarckians and the Darwinians had been bubbling along for more than half a century. Soon to be abandoned by the rest of the world, Lamarckism was to reach its climax in the rise of Lysenkoism in the Soviet Union, a development with which Kammerer's life was strangely connected.

Though on the retreat, Lamarckian ideas were still espoused by serious scientists. In 1923, for example, the eminent Russian physiologist I. P. Pavlov announced a spectacular series of experiments in which he claimed that learned behavior was inherited by mice. The new experiments, said Pavlov, "show that conditioned reflexes, i.e., the highest nervous activity, are inherited." Mice were trained to run to their feeding place at the sound of a bell. The first generation of mice required 300 lessons. Their offspring learned the same task after only 100 trials, the third generation needed 30 lessons and the fourth only 10. "The last generation which I saw before leaving Petrograd," Pavlov said at a lecture given on July 7, 1923, at Battle Creek, Michigan, "learned the lesson after five repetitions. The sixth generation will be tested after my return. I think it very probable that after some time a new generation of mice will run to the feeding place on hearing the bell with no previous lesson."[1]

For doctrinaires intent on improving the human race, the discovery that learning could be inherited was of the utmost importance. Unfortunately the experiment with the six generations of mice was in error. Announcing that he had been misled by a laboratory assistant, Pavlov retracted the result a few years later. Pavlov "would not have been so gullible if he had not shared the Lamarckian predisposition, common to Russian bioscientists— and to the intelligentsia in general—even before the Revolution . . ." commented one observer.[2] But Pavlov retained enough interest in Lamarckian ideas to invite Paul Kammerer to come to Russia and build a laboratory affiliated with his institute.

The invitation came at a difficult time for Kammerer. His work was under heavy attack from the Darwinians, notably the geneticist William Bateson in England and Kingsley Noble of the American Museum of Natural History in New York. The focus of their attention was an experiment performed by Kammerer with the midwife toad, a species that usually breeds on land. The male midwife toads lack "nuptial pads," rough patches on the hands with which the males of other species grasp the slippery back of the female while mating in water.

Kammerer had found that if he forced midwife toads to mate in water for several generations, the descendants eventually came to be born with the nuptial pads characteristic of other toads. It was Kammerer's opponents, not he, who claimed that this was the crucial experiment favoring the inheritance of acquired characteristics. Kammerer regarded another experiment, one with sea squirts, as his best evidence for Lamarckism. As for the midwife toads, they might be acquiring and inheriting the capacity for nuptial pads, but equally well this might be just an inherent capacity coming to light again, Kammerer believed.

By 1923 Kammerer had only one specimen left of a male midwife toad with nuptial pad. He showed it to Bateson on a visit to England. Later Bateson asked to re-examine it but was told it couldn't be sent from Vienna. Meanwhile, Noble in New York decided that in microscope sections published by Kammerer certain glands in the nuptial pad did not look right. On a visit to the Biological Experimental Institute in Vienna in 1926 Noble examined the pad in the one remaining specimen. He announced his findings in the August 7 issue of *Nature:* the black coloring that marked the pad was nothing but India ink.[3]

Kammerer was on the point of leaving Vienna to become professor of biology at Moscow University. On September 22, 1926, he wrote to the Academy of Sciences in Moscow: "After having read the attack [in *Nature*], I went to the Biological Experimental Institute for the purpose of looking over the object in question. I found the statements of Dr. Noble completely verified. Indeed, there were still other objects (blackened salamanders) upon which my results had plainly been 'improved' post mortem with India ink. Who besides myself had any interest in perpetrating such falsifications can only be very dimly suspected. But it is certain that practically my whole life's work is placed in doubt by it.

"On the basis of this state of affairs I dare not, although I myself have no part in these falsifications of my proof specimens, any longer consider myself the proper man to accept your call. I see that I am also not in a position to endure this wrecking of my life's work, and I hope that I shall gather together enough courage and strength to put an end of my wrecked life to-morrow."[4] The following day Kammerer took a walk in the mountains and shot himself through the head.

Kammerer's suicide provided the last dramatic detail needed to make the episode into an object lesson about the folly of scientific fraud: foe of Darwin's fakes data, is inevitably found out, and takes his own life in remorse. But the truth is more ambiguous than the clear-cut moral that has been drawn for the benefit of generations of science students. Kammerer did not regard the experiment as proof of Lamarckism, and the profession of innocence in his suicide note deserves serious consideration. The writer Arthur Koestler has devoted a whole book to arguing Kammerer's innocence.[5] In Koestler's view, the pads really existed at one time, and were perhaps touched up by an overzealous lab assistant in preparation for Noble's visit; another possibility, in Koestler's view, is that the clumsy forgery was done deliberately by someone who wished to discredit Kammerer.

On the other hand, Lester Aronson, a former assistant to Noble, believes Koestler has whitewashed the considerable evidence of Kammerer's suspect scientific behavior.[6] Alma Mahler noted of her experiences as Kammerer's lab assistant that "I kept very exact records. That too annoyed Kammerer. Slightly less exact records with positive results would have pleased him more."[7] Kammerer's guilt or innocence cannot now be established, but there is a perceptive account which suggests that the truth lay somewhere in between. "I do not believe that Kammerer was an intentional forger," wrote Richard B. Goldschmidt of the University of California in 1949: "He was a very highstrung, decadent but brilliant man who spent his nights, after a day in the laboratory, composing symphonies. He was originally not a scientist, but what the Germans call an 'Aquarianer,' an amateur breeder of lower vertebrates. In this field he had immense skill, and I believe that the data he presented upon the direct action of the environment are largely correct. . . . He then conceived the idea that he could prove the inheritance of acquired characters and became so obsessed with this idea that he 'improved' upon his records. . . . In later years he probably became so absorbed with the necessity for proving his claims that he started inventing results or 'doctoring' them. Though the actual results of all this amounted to falsification, I am not certain that he realized it and intended it. He probably was a nervous wreck in the end."[8]

Goldschmidt's interest in Kammerer had been aroused some twenty years earlier when walking down a street in Leningrad, in 1929, he saw a poster for a film called *Salamandra*. An ardent piece of propaganda for the doctrine of Lamarckism, the film's central character was the tragic figure of Kammerer. He is set up by his laboratory assistant, who injects a critical specimen of a salamander with ink and reveals the forgery after Kammerer has given a brilliant lecture on the inheritance of acquired characteristics. Expelled from the university, Kammerer is about to take his own life when he receives a message from Anatoly V. Lunacharsky, the people's commissar for education, inviting him to the Soviet Union.

The plot might be fantasy, but the film portended the sober reality of a cataclysm about to descend on Russian science. Lamarckism had the highest blessing of the Soviet state. *Sala-*

mandra was commissioned by Education Commissar Lunacharsky, who played himself in the film. And while Lunacharsky did not try to impose Lamarckism on Soviet scientists, he created the climate for those who did.

The Lysenko affair is usually recounted, in simplified form, for the purpose of warning politicians never to jeopardize the autonomy of science. The moral is correctly drawn, but the full version of the complex history contains another, less obvious lesson: that scientists and their institutions do not always possess the inner strength to protect their deepest principles from political encroachment.

Trofim Denisovich Lysenko was born in 1898, the son of a Ukrainian peasant. He graduated from the Kiev Agricultural Institute with a doctoral degree in agricultural science. He first came to the attention of the Soviet public in 1929 with his announcement of "vernalization": by soaking and chilling winter wheat, it could be planted as late as spring and would give greater yields than spring wheat, Lysenko claimed. The experts dismissed him but Lysenko proved them wrong: at his request, his peasant father soaked forty-eight kilos of winter wheat, grew it beside spring wheat, and reaped a better harvest.

Vernalization was seized on and massively promoted by the politicians as a way of improving the notoriously unproductive system of Russian agriculture. The campaign was started before further tests of the technique had even begun. One season's success on half a hectare had launched Lysenko on his career.

Vernalization was not, as Lysenko claimed, a discovery of his own, but an ancient peasant technique. It may raise yields in some circumstances, but there is now known to be no scientific basis for the far-reaching claims that Lysenko made. Lenin had decreed that in matters of science the party bosses must defer to the authority of autonomous specialists. But the politicians were in a hurry to do something about agriculture. The scientists were offering results in five years' time; Lysenko had a scheme that could be put into effect immediately. The politicians wanted the scientists to take Lysenko seriously, and for a debate to begin as to which side was right. But the vast majority of Soviet biologists either stayed on the sidelines or made conciliatory remarks praising Lysenko. According to the Russian physiologist Zhores Medvedev, "It must be noted that the rational elements in the first publications of Lysenko were supported by many scientists. . . . The then President of the Academy of Sciences, Komarov, Professor Rikhter, Academician Keller, and many other physiologists and botanists appraised this work favorably."[9]

The scientific community's initial tendency to compliance and conciliation was the first wrong step in a road that led to disaster. Was there any choice? True, from 1929 to 1932 the Party decreed the extinction of all "bourgeois" specialists, meaning those with an outlook independent of the Party. But this constraint fell upon the whole scientific community; it was not linked in any way to Lysenkoism.

The only scientists who took public issue with the Lysenkoites in the early 1930's were those who had been trying to develop a Communist position in science before 1929, such as Nikolai I. Vavilov. A brilliant plant collector and ambitious scientific administrator, Vavilov came under criticism for not doing more to help Soviet agriculture. At first he praised Lysenko, hailing his method in *Izvestia* (November 6, 1933) as a "revolutionary discovery of Soviet science." "It was a useless tactic," comments David Joravsky, author of a studiously careful and subtle history of Lysenkoism.[10] Lysenko and his disciples accepted the praise but declined to accept the scientific explanations that came with it. Says Joravsky, "They preferred the freedom of their own makeshift explanations, though they achieved that freedom by flouting science. Only a small number of militant scientists dared to say so vigorously, without debilitating concessions and restraint. . . . The bulk of the scientific community simply watched in silence."

Up until 1935 the Soviet government had given more support to mainstream scientists than to the eccentrics like Lysenko. But in 1935 it suddenly subordinated the mainstream scientists to the eccentrics. It was an act of willful desperation. The bureaucrats realized they were not making much progress with the agricultural situation; the "discussion" they had ordered between the Lysenkoites and the scientists produced no clear answers since the two sides talked right past each other. So the bureaucrats chose a bureaucratic solution, which was to put someone in charge and let him cope with the problem. Unfortunately the person they chose was Lysenko.

The conception of Lysenko prevalent among Western scientists is that he instituted a reign of terror, forcing biologists to abandon genetics or risk imprisonment and death. The truth is more complex. It was not until 1948 that he acquired the administrative power to remove geneticists from their posts. To be sure, there were reigns of terror directed by Stalin against various sectors of society, but it was in large measure a random process. Seldom mentioned is the fact that the Stalinist terror struck down Lysenkoites as well as orthodox geneticists. "Any way one searches it, the public record simply will not support the common belief that the apparatus of terror consciously and consistently worked with the Lysenkoites to promote their cause," says Joravsky.*

From 1935 onward Lysenko and his followers steadily consolidated their power, aided by the pliant attitudes of the plant pathologists. He tried to subordinate all plant pathology to the principle of vernalization. "Plant physiologists defended their discipline against the crippling vagueness and confusion that Lysenko pressed upon it, but almost always they weakened their defense by conceding practical utility to Lysenko and confessing a comparative lack of it in their own. Only a few brave souls dared to suggest, in rather delicate language, that Lysenko's practical successes might be as meretricious as his contributions to science," notes Joravsky. Textbooks and articles would commonly adopt the "chimera" defense—matters of science would be sandwiched between thick layers of Lysenkoist claptrap.

Lysenko did not really begin to attack the theoretical bases of

* The case of Vavilov illustrates the ambiguities. "Vavilov has come to be regarded as one of the outstanding geneticists of the twentieth century, a symbol of the best aspects of Soviet science, and a martyr for scientific truth," notes the *Dictionary of Scientific Biography*. But Vavilov was also a politician, a man who showed complete loyalty to the Party although without becoming a Party member. He was arrested in 1940 while on a plant-collecting expedition in the Ukraine, found guilty of "spying for England," and died in prison in 1943, probably from malnutrition. But did he die for his political activities, as did many other leaders in Soviet society, or for his scientific beliefs? True, he was publicly denounced by two Lysenkoites before his arrest—but they both followed him to jail.

biology, and the subject of genetics in particular, until after the Second World War. It was then that he declared himself a Lamarckist as a way of countering the Darwinian arguments made by his scientific critics. At the same time the politicians' faith in his quick-fix practical remedies was beginning to waver. Once again they called for a period of "discussion," only to decide in July 1948 that Lysenko should be given supreme power in all matters affecting agricultural science.

A meeting held in the Academy of Sciences in 1948 showed the desperate state to which Soviet biology had then been reduced. Those who spoke included Lysenkoites celebrating their total victory, honest hypocrites humiliating themselves to save their institutes, and careerists intent on preserving their own positions regardless of their colleagues or their principles. To the question of whether a scientist's professional commitment would enable him to resist political pressure, the answer in this instance was no. Reading the transcript of this meeting revolted historian Joravsky: "The Lysenkoites had forced political salts into the bowels of Soviet scientists, and some began to void themselves in public, the honorable ones fouling themselves alone, the dishonorable trying to rub it off on others."

The plant scientists, by and large, accommodated to Lysenko. As long as they paid lip service to his nonsensical theories, they were allowed to ply their trade in peace. But the price of their appeasement left their colleagues in genetics to face the Lysenkoites alone. Working in a methodologically more rigorous science, the geneticists had less room for accommodation. Very few betrayed their profession, and when they were forced to resign after 1948, their profession ceased to exist in the Soviet Union. Of the thirty-five members of the Academy of Sciences' Institute of Genetics in 1935, only four turned Lysenkoite in 1940 when Vavilov was replaced by Lysenko as director, and these four were almost the only Soviet geneticists to do so.

If 1948 marked the triumph of Lysenkoism, it also contained the seeds of his downfall. From the moment that he was clearly in charge, he was also responsible for what happened in improving agricultural productivity. However hard it may be to believe from their actions, the Party bosses prided themselves on being practical men above all else. That was why they kept choosing Lysenko over the ivory-tower theorists, because his stock in trade was the emphasis of practice over theory.

But Lysenko was running out of tricks. The cleverness of his schemes was that generally they cost little and didn't do any harm. What the practical Party bosses at last began to realize, after some twenty years, was that Lysenko's schemes weren't doing any good either. Even so, it took another eleven years after Stalin's death for his successors to change their minds. One reason why it took so long was presumably the abject passivity to which the community of Soviet biologists had been reduced. With the geneticists destroyed, no one in a position to know dared say the simple truth, that all of Soviet biology was dominated by a charlatan and his sycophants.

The Academy of Sciences is one of the few semiautonomous bodies in the Soviet Union: under its grant of authority from Peter the Great, it retains a precious privilege, the right to a secret ballot for electing its members. In June 1964, N. I. Nuzhdin, a particularly unpopular Lysenkoite and one of the four geneticist turncoats, was proposed for membership and approved by the biology section of the Academy. But at the general meeting, Nuzhdin's candidacy was too much to stomach. It was a young physicist, then unknown in the West, Andrei Sakharov, who delivered a vehement protest against Nuzhdin's election. His speech concluded as follows:

SAKHAROV: As for myself, I call on all those present to vote so that the only "ayes" will be those who, together with Nuzhdin, together with Lysenko, bear the responsibility for the infamous, painful pages in the development of Soviet science, which fortunately are now coming to an end. (*Applause*)

KELDYSH (President of the Academy): . . . I do not think that we can approach . . . the election from this point of view. It would seem to me inappropriate to open up here a discussion on the problems of development of biology. And from this standpoint, I consider Sakharov's speech tactless . . .

LYSENKO: Not tactless, but slanderous! The presidium . . .

KELDYSH: Trofim Denisovich, why should the presidium defend itself? It was Sakharov's speech, not the presidium's. It is not supported, at least not by me. . . .

It was the pliancy of scientific leaders such as Keldysh that helped perpetuate the long lunacy of the Lysenkoite era. A crank and publicist whose ideas deserved five minutes' currency managed to mesmerize the highest political leaders of the Soviet Union for close to thirty-five years. The basic fault should of course be sought in the pathology of the society in which Lysenko flourished. But the point is that the scientific community within that society was unable to preserve either its principles or a central part of its beliefs under pressure from outside. That pressure was at times reinforced by the Stalinist reign of terror but was in no way identical with it. Even in 1964, with the protection of a secret ballot, some 22 members of the Academy of Sciences voted for the hack Nuzhdin, 126 against.

Lysenko was dismissed from his post as director of the Academy's Institute of Genetics in February 1965. An expert committee sent to investigate Lysenko's experimental farm in the Lenin Hills above Moscow returned with a devastating report that accused Lysenko of misreporting and the deliberate falsification of scientific data. His current scheme at the time was a method for raising the butterfat yield in milk. But the committee found that though the percentage of butterfat in milk was raised by Lysenko's method, the total yield of milk, and of butterfat, went down. "Even according to his own data, the methods recommended by Lysenko for application throughout the country were economically unsound and by 1965 were causing serious losses," comments Medvedev. Lysenko's power was finally broken. For years afterward his gaunt figure could be seen around the Academy of Sciences in Moscow, a haunting reminder of its years of humiliation. He died in 1976.

It is easy to dismiss the bizarre episode as a unique disease of Soviet society, and maybe only in the Soviet Union could the disease have lasted for so long. But many of the ingredients that kept Lysenko in power are present in most countries. The leaders of the Soviet Union did not set out with the intention of destroying the study of Mendelian genetics in their country, although that was a consequence: their aim was to modernize Soviet agriculture in a hurry. As for the Soviet scientists faced with the problem of Lysenkoism, the episode showed that there exist clear limits to the ability of the scientific method to resist encroachment by nonscientific ideologies.

The terrifying feature of Lysenkoism, remarks the English physicist and science watcher John Ziman, "was the apparent normality of the scientific organization within which this false doctrine existed. The tragedy lies not with those few who were forced, by irresistible threats of violence, to keep silent or to say the opposite of their thoughts: it is with the many who seem to have accepted the doctrine as it was taught to them and failed to subject it to their own tests of rationality. We cannot blame a half-educated crank for believing his own theories and trying to get them accepted: we must ask what was wrong with a whole scientific community that it allowed itself to be captured by such crazy notions."[11]

The Lysenko episode shows how far a supposedly autonomous scientific community will accommodate toward conscious pressure from the society of which it is part. In Western countries, such pressure is generally viewed as inappropriate, which is not to say that the politicians don't try it from time to time.* For Western societies, with their openness and greater receptivity to new ideas, the greater threat is the other way around: when the body politic is infected by false science, or by social dogma disguised as science, which scientists have failed to unmask. The melancholy history of ability testing is an egregious example.

---

* In 1953 the United States Secretary of Commerce, Sinclair Weeks, fired the director of the National Bureau of Standards, Allen V. Astin, because his scientists persisted in declaring that a certain battery additive, AD-X2, was useless, which it was.

CHAPTER 11

THE FAILURE
OF
OBJECTIVITY

The essence of the scientific attitude is objectivity. The scientist is supposed to assess facts and test hypotheses while rigorously excluding his own expectations or desires as to the outcome. In the public's eye, objectivity is the distinguishing feature of the scientist, for it keeps his vision pure from the distorting effects of dogma and allows him to see the real world as it is. Objectivity does not come easily, and researchers undergo a lengthy training to acquire it.

With some scientists, nevertheless, objectivity is only skin deep, not a sincerely felt attitude toward the world. Under its guise, a scientist can foist his own dogmatic beliefs on the world far more easily than could a plain demagogue. But there is a more important issue at stake than that of individual scientists who become the prisoners of their own dogmas.

Science is meant to be a community of intellectuals, dedicated to a common goal. If one scientist falls prey to dogma, and tries to promote doctrinaire beliefs in the name of science, won't his colleagues immediately perceive the error and take action to correct it? History shows that, to the contrary, a community of scientists is often ready to swallow whole the dogma served up to them, as long as it is palatable and has the right measure of scientific seasoning. Just as replication is no sure defense against error, objectivity often fails to resist infiltration by dogma.

The episodes discussed in this chapter include cases both of deliberate fraud and of self-deception. As far as the community of scientists is concerned, of course, it makes no difference by which origin an error is introduced: the challenge of expunging it is the same. The episodes concern a theme that poses a severe test of scientific objectivity—the question of how and in what respective measure heredity and environment shape the properties of organisms, and of humans in particular. The issue is seldom treated with detachment because it affects people's political and social preconceptions. In crude terms, the hereditarian view, that intelligence or other abilities tend to be innate, appeals to conservatives since it seems to justify the status quo and their position in society. The environmentalist view, on the other hand, suggests that human abilities are limited only by society and that privilege receives no justification from nature. Time and again, over the last century and a half, the scientific community has permitted dogmatists posing as scientists to wave the flag of science in their various discreditable causes.

Samuel G. Morton was a prominent Philadelphia physician and a well-known scientist in his day. Between 1830 and his death in 1851, he amassed a collection of more than 1,000 human skulls of people of different races. Morton believed that the volume of the skull is a measure of intelligence. His ranking of races by skull volume put whites on the top, blacks on the bottom, and American Indians in between. Among the whites, Western Europeans were above Jews. The results conformed exactly with the prejudices of his time. But they were of course presented as the inevitable conclusions compelled by objective, scientific facts.

What is striking about the Morton case is how thoroughly he allowed his prejudices to permeate his scientific work. His dogma shaped not just his theory but the very data from which it was supposedly derived. He juggled the numbers to get the results he wanted. The juggling was done right out in public, on the open page of his scientific reports, so he was evidently doing it unconsciously. The final paradox in the extraordinary story is that no contemporary scientist spotted the errors, glaring though they were. They did not come to light until 1978 when Stephen Gould, a paleontologist at Harvard, recomputed Morton's data and showed that, on Morton's own evidence, all races in fact have approximately equal skull volumes.[1] Had Morton looked at his data with a trace of objectivity, he could have seen that the major determinant of skull size is body size.

Morton was not some eccentric plowing a lone furrow. He represented the cream of American science. "Probably no scientific man in America enjoyed a higher reputation among scholars throughout the world than Dr. Morton," declared an obituary in the *New York Tribune*. He was widely praised in his day for having replaced speculation with a body of objective fact. According to Gould, Morton's tables of skull volumes "were reprinted repeatedly during the nineteenth century as irrefutable 'hard' data on the mental worth of human races." They were used to justify the institution of slavery. The *Charleston Medical Journal*, the leading magazine of its kind in the South, proclaimed on Morton's death that "we of the South should consider him as our benefactor, for aiding most materially in giving to the negro his true position as an inferior race."

The way Morton fudged his figures is in retrospect childishly obvious. Essentially he would include subgroups with small skulls when he wanted to bring down a group average and exclude them when he wanted to raise a group average. Thus a large set of Incas, with generally small skulls, was included in assessing American Indians, but Morton explicitly left out the small-headed Hindus so as not to drag down the Caucasian mean. Failing to notice that men, being generally larger than women, have larger skulls, Morton neglected to correct for the effect of sex. His tables show that Englishmen have a skull volume of 96 cubic inches, compared with 75 cubic inches for Hottentots, yet the Englishmen are based on an all-male sample and the Hottentots on an all-female sample. In addition, Morton made a number of straight arithmetical errors, all in favor of his preconceptions about racial hierarchy.

Gould has recalculated Morton's data, with the results shown in the table on page 196. "My correction of Morton's conventional ranking reveals *no* significant differences among races for Morton's own data," Gould concludes.

The finagling in Morton's data was never discovered by the sci-

Table
Internal skull volume by race, in cubic inches.

RACE	ACCORDING TO MORTON	RECALCULATED BY GOULD
Caucasian (whites)	87	87 (Modern)
		84 (Ancient)
Mongolian	83	87
Malay	81	85
American (Indians)	82	86
Ethiopian (blacks)	78	83

entists who relied on his results. His tables remained unchallenged in the scientific literature and sank from sight only when the entire subject of ranking races by skull volume fell into disrepute.

Yet throughout the nineteenth century the search continued to find "scientific" measures of man that would rank some groups above others. The searchers invariably proclaimed the strict objectivity of their undertaking and the impossibility of bias in their results. Time and again, the rankings they came up with just so happened to justify certain controversial social arrangements of the time, whether slavery, the subjection of women, or European dominion over other peoples. And invariably the parameters on which the rankings were based—whether brain weight, the size of certain parts of the brain, or the time at which brain sutures close—were measures that are now known to be quite meaningless for the purpose to which they were put.

In his book *The Mismeasure of Man*, Gould has chronicled the sorry story of these exercises in scientific dogmatism.[2] The common thread is the reclothing of prejudice in scientific garb. A scientist, believing in some current social dogma of his time, will try to prove it "scientifically"—in other words, by appeal to the objective test of the scientific method. But in looking at the data in the real world, he will unconsciously select mostly those data that support the initial supposition. He will then proclaim the supposition to be proved. The argument is always presented as a straight line from data to conclusion whereas in fact it is invariably a circular journey, from conclusion to selected data and back to conclusion.

It was not just the cranks but the best scientists as well who were caught up in these misdirected efforts. Paul Broca, the eminent French anatomist after whom the speech area in the brain is named, was a leading exponent of ranking by brain size. "In general, the brain is larger in mature adults than in the elderly, in men than in women, in eminent men than in men of mediocre talent, in superior races than in inferior races," he wrote in 1861. When an egalitarian opponent observed that Germans have larger brains than Frenchmen despite their obviously being less intelligent, Broca invoked the factors such as body size that actually do influence brain size, but only for the purpose of correcting the German brains down to a smaller size than the French cerebral organs. On another occasion, five eminent professors at the University of Göttingen, having previously given their consent, had their brains weighed after death. When the weights turned out to be embarrassingly close to average, Broca preferred to suggest that the professors weren't so eminent after all than to abandon his theory. Broca might have allowed the facts a fairer hearing had he known that his own brain would weigh in at only a few grams above mediocre.

Theories, says Gould, "are built upon the interpretation of numbers, and interpreters are often trapped by their own rhetoric. They believe in their own objectivity, and fail to discern the prejudice that leads them to one interpretation among many consistent with their numbers. Paul Broca is now distant enough. We can stand back and show that he used numbers not to generate new theories but to illustrate a priori conclusions. . . . Broca was an exemplary scientist; no one has ever surpassed him in meticulous care and accuracy of measurement. By what right, other than our own biases, can we identify his prejudice and hold that science now operates independently of culture and class?"

It is easy to laugh at the delusory antics of men such as Morton and Broca—easy, but a mistake. They were not just harmless nineteenth-century cranks: each was regarded as one of his country's best scientists. The circular journey that each traversed has been gone around by many others since then. Twentieth-century scientists have proved themselves every bit as capable of falling into the identical trap: it's just the trappings that are different. Today it is not skull volume or brain weight that is proclaimed as the measure to rank different peoples: the chimera is still pursued just as eagerly but under a different guise—that of the IQ score.

Intelligence tests were invented by a Frenchman, Alfred Binet. He laid down three cardinal principles for their use, which were systematically ignored and perverted by his American imitators. Binet's Rule 1 was: The scores do not define anything innate or permanent. Rule 2: The scale is a rough guide for identifying and helping learning-disabled children; it is not a way of measuring normal children. Rule 3: Low scores don't mean a child is innately incapable. Binet's tests were translated and introduced to America by H. H. Goddard, director of research at the Vineland Training School for Feeble-Minded Girls and Boys in New Jersey. Soon after, Goddard developed a scale of mental deficiency using Binet test scores, based on the assumption that he was identifying intelligence as a single real entity, and thus breaking Binet's Rule 1. In addition, he took it for granted that intelligence is inherited, violating Rules 2 and 3. From this Goddard argued that the existing class structure of society is justified and immutable, because those at the bottom of the heap, witless by birthright, require the leadership of their hereditarily superior masters.

Goddard did not flinch from describing the awesome truths to which his premises led. "We must learn that there are great groups of men, laborers, who are but little above the child, who must be told what to do and shown how to do it. . . . There are only a few leaders, most must be followers," he said in 1919. He perceived another consequence of his ideas: that the "feeble-minded"—as identified by Goddard—should not be allowed to breed lest they reduce still further the average intelligence level of the population.

In proof of this argument he traced the ancestry of a New Jersey family whose ancestor had married twice, first a feeble-minded barmaid and then a worthy Quakeress. From the first union had come paupers and morons; from the second, only upstanding citizens. The Kallikak family, as Goddard referred to it, became famous in the eugenics movement for several decades as a classic study of pedigree. "There are Kallikak families all about us," warned Goddard. "They are multiplying at twice the rate of the general population, and not until we recognize this fact, and work on this basis, will we begin to solve these social problems."[3]

Photographs of the feeble-minded descendants were published by Goddard in a book about the Kallikaks. The reader can see at a glance that their eyes have a depraved, satanic look, and their mouths are twisted in evil leers. Unfortunately, the ink has faded in Goddard's books, revealing that the photographs are fakes. The eyes and mouths have been touched up to give the Kallikaks their manic demeanor.[4]

Goddard introduced Binet's tests to the United States, but it was Lewis M. Terman, a psychologist at Stanford University, who produced the revised version known as the Stanford-Binet, the model for almost all IQ tests that followed. Terman believed in the godlike power of his tests to identify bad genes and to eventually rid society of their owners. "It is safe to predict that in the near future intelligence tests will bring tens of thousands of these high-grade defectives under the surveillance and protection of society. This will ultimately result in curtailing the reproduction of feeble-mindedness and in the elimination of an enormous amount of crime, pauperism, and industrial inefficiency," he wrote in 1916. Terman advocated that everyone should be tested, as a means not only of weeding out defectives but of channeling acceptable members of society into professions suited to their mental capacities.

There is one thing that IQ scores measure for certain: performance on IQ tests. Claims that they give a measure of anything beyond that, such as "intelligence," are inferential. In the many capacities of the human mind that probably contribute to what is called intelligence, there are undoubtedly components that are inherited. But whatever is inherited is shaped and reworked and reformulated by the environment in which an individual grows up. The IQ testers of the early twentieth century had a hereditarian bias so strong that it blinded them to the evidence of environmental influence that cried out from their data. All they could see was the reflection of their own dogmatic beliefs which, just like those of Samuel Morton, echoed the prejudices of their time and social class.

Lysenko became a byword for errant science because he was able to impose his crankish dogma on science. It was not for lack of trying that the hereditarians failed to install themselves as the gatekeepers of a society strictly regimented by their tests. On the day the United States entered the First World War, Robert M. Yerkes, the president of the American Psychological Association, urged his fellow council members to press their services on the military. What emerged was a massive program for applying psychological tests to military recruits. Fortunately the Army paid almost no attention to the results, but the psychologists used the massive test results to bolster their own claims for the technique. In 1924 Terman, a former president of the American Psychological Association, proclaimed: "Now that psychology has tested and classified nearly two million soldiers; has been appealed to in the grading of several million school children; is used everywhere in our institutions for the feeble-minded, delinquent, criminal, and insane; has become the beacon light of the eugenics movement; is appealed to by congressmen in the reshaping of national policy on immigration . . . no psychologist of to-day can complain that his science is not taken seriously enough."

The results of the army mental tests were published in 1921 in a massive 800-page monograph, *Psychological Examining in the United States Army*, by Robert Yerkes. According to Stephen Gould, the "facts" derived from the tests influenced American social policy for long after their original source had been forgotten. The three main conclusions were, first, that the average white American adult had a mental age of thirteen, just above moronity; second, European immigrants could be graded by their country of origin, with the fair-skinned Nordic races being more intelligent than the Slavs and the dark-skinned peoples of southern Europe; and third, that blacks come at the bottom of the scale with a mental age of 10.41, lower even than Italians at 11.01 and Poles at 10.74. Instead of doubting their ludicrous findings that the average man of most nations is a moron, the psychologists were led to discuss whether democracy is a viable system when half the electorate is incompetent to vote.

By any scientific standards, despite the psychologists' usual claims for objectivity, the army tests were hopelessly invalid. The questions in the tests were highly culture bound, the rushed pace and inadequate conditions under which they were conducted made a mockery of the procedure, and there is clear evidence that in many cases the recruits failed to understand what they were supposed to do, which should have rendered the test results null and void. Nevertheless, through the mass of flawed data looms the unmistakable effect of environment on intelligence. It was not that Yerkes missed the effect; more curiously, he would always contrive to explain it away in favor of a hereditarian account. He found a strong correlation between average score and infestation with hookworm. Mightn't that suggest that the state of health, and in particular diseases related to poverty, affects a person's score? Yerkes preferred another explanation, that stupid people were more likely to get sick: "Low native ability may induce such conditions of living as to result in hookworm infection," he said.

Yerkes' figures showed that blacks from northern states had an average score almost double that of blacks from the South, and that the average black score for the four highest northern states in fact exceeded the white score for nine southern states. Might that just possibly reflect the better schooling available to blacks in the North compared with the discrimination and mandatory segregation they then faced in the South? Of course not; Yerkes had found that blacks scored lower than whites who had spent an equal number of years in school. True, the schools for whites might be a little better in quality, but this variability, said Yerkes, "certainly cannot account for the clear intelligence differences between groups."

Perhaps the clearest evidence of an environmental effect was that the average test scores of foreign recruits rose steadily the longer they had resided in the United States. Didn't that mean simply that the greater their familiarity with American ways, the better they did on the tests? Yerkes admitted the possibility, but paid it no further attention. "The army mental tests," concludes Gould, "could have provided an impetus for social reform, since they documented that environmental disadvantages were robbing from millions of people an opportunity to develop their intellectual skills. Again and again, the data pointed to strong correlations between test scores and environment. Again and again, those who wrote and administered the tests invented tortuous, ad hoc explanations to preserve their hereditarian prejudices."

Yerkes was not a fringe scientist. As professor of psychology at Harvard and then at Yale, he was a pillar of the psychological establishment. Nor was his bending of science to support his prejudices a harmless intellectual exercise. American psychologists after the First World War were trying to get maximum publicity for their newly founded discipline. One practical issue on which they strenuously brought their expertise to bear was the congressional debates leading to the rewriting of the immigration laws. The army mental tests, it was pointed out, provided a scientific basis for defining which nations produced desirable immigrants and which produced a class of people whom it would be better to keep away from America's shores.

There is some difference of opinion as to how influential the psychologists were. Congressional debates "continually invoke the army data," says Gould. On the other hand Franz Samelson of Kansas State University considers that the psychologists "had a limited influence on the legislation despite their claim to possess conclusive scientific data."[5] Even if the psychologists had no effect, it was not from want of trying. The Immigration Restriction Act of 1924 reduced immigration from southern and eastern Europe to a trickle. While the psychologists cannot be held responsible for an event in which they played at most a minor role, they did endorse a misguided course of action that contributed to tragedy. "Throughout the 1930s," comments Gould, "Jewish refugees, anticipating the holocaust, sought to emigrate, but were not admitted. The legal quotas, and continuing eugenical propaganda, barred them even in years when the inflated quotas for western and northern European nations were not filled. . . . We know what happened to many who wished to leave but had nowhere to go. The paths to destruction are often indirect, but ideas can be agents as sure as guns and bombs."

It might be said that in their mistaken notions about the mental inferiority of immigrant races, blacks, and lower-class whites, the intelligence testers were only expressing the prejudices shared by Congressmen and public opinion of the time. That might excuse the testers, but not the discipline they represented. The claim of science to represent a reliable body of knowledge rests foursquare on the assumption of objectivity, on the assertion that scientists are *not* influenced by their prejudices or are at least protected from them by the methodology of their discipline.

The failure of the scientific method to afford a protection against prejudice is particularly disconcerting when the failure extends beyond an individual to the colleagues in his own discipline. What is science if it is not a method for seeing the world objectively? Is it merely a label pasted on the package after the contents have been determined?

In general, a group should never be condemned for the errors of one of its members. But a scientific community has a special problem when it persistently fails to detect gross and manifest error in a finding central to the discipline. The initial findings of the intelligence testers, writes Samelson, "had fitted well enough with the common-sense observations and cherished prejudices of the United States to be absorbed into the folklore. The price for the initial errors was paid not by those who committed them, but by their subjects who had been saddled with the 'scientific' marks of inferiority. There is little doubt that intelligence testing has served as an equalizer of opportunity and vehicle for upward mobility for some. . . . Yet even after the removal of explicit group stigmatization by a more liberal, environmentalist approach to intelligence, the effect of ability testing in the United States may well have been—as its critics claim—largely one of maintaining (and justifying) the existing social stratification."

The failure of psychologists to spot dogma masquerading as objective truth is even more pronounced in the extraordinary case of Sir Cyril Burt. Burt's chief work, a study of intelligence which emphasized its high degree of heritability, was not merely wrong; it was riddled with glaring statistical errors, later shown to be a sign of wide-scale fraud. Since it purported to be the largest collection of IQ data of its kind, it was repeatedly cited by both proponents and critics of the hereditarian view. Yet throughout the heat of the debate, the scientists who rested their case on Burt's data failed to spot its flagrant inconsistencies. Perhaps even more remarkably, the critics of Burt's position also missed the red flags that leaped out from his disputed writings.

Cyril Burt, one of the pioneers of applied psychology in England, was a man of brilliance and great culture. He became professor of psychology at University College, London, and was the first psychologist to receive a knighthood for his services. The American Psychological Association gave him its Thorndike prize in 1971, the first time that the high honor had been awarded to a foreigner. When he died, the same year, the obituaries proclaimed him "Britain's most eminent educational psychologist" and even "dean of the world's psychologists." "Everything about the man," wrote Arthur Jensen of Stanford University, "—his fine, sturdy appearance; his aura of vitality; his urbane manner; his unflagging enthusiasm for research, analysis and criticism; . . . and, of course, especially his notably sharp intellect and vast erudition— all together leave a total impression of immense quality, of a born nobleman."[6]

But the man who impressed Jensen with his nobility of intellect possessed a grievous intellectual flaw: he was a cheat. He invented data out of whole cloth to support his own theories and confound his critics. He used his mastery of statistics and gift of lucid exposition to bamboozle alike his bitterest detractors and those who acclaimed his greatness as a psychologist.

What was more remarkable still, Burt attained a great part of his eminence in the field of IQ testing not because of any thoroughgoing program of research, of which he did little worth the name, but through his skills of *rhetoric*. If a real scientist is one who wants to discover the truth, Burt was no scientist, because he already knew the truth. He used the scientific method with great effect, but not as an approach to understanding the world. In Burt's hands the scientific method can be seen most clearly for its utility as a purely rhetorical device, a method of argument with which to assume a position of moral superiority, to pretend to greater learning or diligence. According to his biographer L. S. Hearnshaw, "He was fond of accusing his opponents of basing their criticisms 'not on any fresh evidence or new researches of their own, but chiefly on armchair articles from general principles.' 'My co-workers and I,' on the other hand, were engaged in on-going research. It was a powerful argument with which to belabor the environmentalists; but to sustain it there had to be co-workers, and these co-workers had to be currently engaged in data collection."[7] But there were no new data, and no co-workers. The lonely and embattled Burt sat in his armchair, summoned both data and co-workers from the vasty deep of his tormented imagination, and clothed them so well in the semblance of scientific argument that the illusion fooled all his fellow scientists for as much as thirty years.

Burt's work was influential, in different ways, on both sides of the Atlantic. In England, he served as a consultant to a series of blue-ribbon committees that restructured the English educational system after the Second World War. The crux of the new system was a test applied to children at the age of eleven, the results of which determined their assignment to a higher- or lower-quality education. The 11+ exam, as it was called, was based on the assumption that a child's educability and future potential can fairly be assessed at that age. Burt cannot be held responsible for the 11+ exam, which was the decision of many people, but his persuasive insistence that intelligence is more than 75 percent a fixed, inherited ability was certainly influential in shaping the climate of opinion among English educators from which the 11+ was born.

The 11+ exam and the selective system of education that was based on it began to come under heavy attack in the 1950's, after Burt had retired from his professorship at University College, London. To defend his theory against the critics, Burt started to publish a series of articles in which striking new evidence for the hereditarian view was produced. The new evidence, Burt explained, had mostly been gathered during the 1920's and 1930's when he was the psychologist for the London school system. It had been updated with the help of his co-workers, Miss Margaret Howard and Miss J. Conway. The pearl of Burt's impressive IQ data was that derived from separated identical twins, the largest single such collection in the world. With the same heredity but different environments, separated identical twins afford uniquely ideal subjects for testing the interplay of the two effects on intelligence. Burt's data on twins and other kinship relations "were widely quoted, widely accepted as valid, and were among the strongest piece of evidence for the preponderantly genetic determination of intelligence," says Hearnshaw.

In 1969, after the 11+ had been abolished and England's selective education replaced with a comprehensive system, Burt published an article purporting to document a decline in educational standards. The intention of the article was clearly to influence educational policy.[8]

Meanwhile, the authority and crispness of Burt's new twin data was attracting the eager attention of hereditarian psychologists in the United States. Arthur Jensen made considerable use of Burt's findings in his 1969 article in the *Harvard Educational Review,* a furiously debated tract in which he argued that since the genetic factor determines 80 percent of intelligence, programs of compensatory education addressed to lower-class black and white children were useless and should be scrapped.[9] Burt's twin data were relied on even more heavily by Richard Herrnstein of Harvard in his September 1971 article in *The Atlantic* arguing that social class is based in part on inherited differences in intelligence. "The measurement of intelligence," the Harvard psychologist proclaimed in his widely influential article, "is psychology's most telling acomplishment to date."[10] Pride of place was given to Burt's twin studies.

When Burt died in October 1971, at the age of eighty-eight, his theories were at the peak of their influence in the United States, even if educational policy in Britain had turned away from them. His oeuvre crumbled only after his death, and the collapse was quite sudden, because the edifice was a mere façade of scholarship. The man who had eyes to see the emperor's outrageous state of undress was Leon Kamin, a Princeton University psychologist who had never ventured into the IQ field until a student urged him to read one of Burt's papers in 1972. "The immediate conclusion I came to after 10 minutes of reading was that Burt was a fraud," says Kamin.[11]

Kamin noticed first that Burt's papers are largely innocent of the elementary trappings of scholarship, such as precise details of who had administered what tests to which children and when. This peculiar vagueness is evident in Burt's first major summary of his IQ and kinship studies, an article published in 1943, and continues thereafter. But in Burt's twin studies, Kamin spotted something much more serious.

Burt published the first full report on the IQ of his separated identical twins in 1955, when he claimed to have located twenty-one pairs.[12] A second report in 1958 mentioned "over 30" pairs,[13] and the final accounting in 1966 cited fifty-three pairs, by far the largest collection in the world.[14] The correlation between the IQ scores of the separated twins, Kamin noticed, was given as 0.771 —*in all three studies.* For a correlation coefficient to remain unchanged, to three decimal places, while new members are added to the sample on two occasions, is highly improbable. But it was not the only case. The correlation in IQ of identical twins reared together stuck at 0.944 through three sample sizes. All together there were twenty such coincidences in a table of sixty correlations. Kamin summarized his study of Burt's work in a book published in 1974. His review was biting, ironic, and devastating. He concluded, in words that will always be part of the history of psychometrics, "The absence of procedural description in Burt's reports vitiates their scientific utility. . . . The marvelous consistency of his data supporting the hereditarian position often taxes credibility; and on analysis, the data are found to contain implausible effects consistent with an effort to prove the hereditarian case. The conclusion cannot be avoided: The numbers left behind by Professor Burt are simply not worthy of our current scientific attention."[15]

Kamin was excluding Burt from the scientific literature. Jensen, to his great credit, did the same, though in politer language. Hearing of Kamin's conclusions from a lecture he gave in 1972, Jensen quickly realized that the invariant correlations "unduly strain the laws of chance and can only mean error, at least in some of the cases"; therefore Burt's data "are useless for hypothesis testing," Jensen wrote in an article of 1974.[16] That still left the problem of what had gone wrong. Were the errors in Burt's papers due to mere carelessness, or something worse?

Although Kamin suspected fraud from the beginning, he did not explicitly accuse Burt of fraud in his book. The first printed accusation of fraud came in an article in the London *Sunday Times* of October 24, 1976, by its medical correspondent Oliver Gillie.[17] Gillie based the charges in part on Kamin's findings and on his own failure to discover any record of the existence of Burt's two co-workers in collecting the twin data, Miss Howard and Miss Conway.

Despite the unchallenged statements published by Kamin and Jensen two years earlier, the actual charge of fraud evoked spasms of indignation from psychologists on both sides of the Atlantic. The very suggestion, said Herrnstein, "is so outrageous that I find it hard to stay in my chair. Burt was a towering figure of 20th century psychology. I think it is a crime to cast such doubt over a man's career."[18] Hans Eysenck, a leading IQ expert at the Institute of Psychiatry in London, wrote to Burt's sister that the whole affair "is just a determined effort on the part of some very left-wing environmentalists determined to play a political game with scientific facts. I am sure the future will uphold the honour and integrity of Sir Cyril without any question."[19]

In effect, the task of deciding exactly what had gone wrong was left to Leslie Hearnshaw, professor of psychology at the University of Liverpool. Hearnshaw, an admirer of Burt's, had given the eulogy at his funeral, as a result of which he had been commissioned by Burt's sister to write a biography. To his growing amazement as he continued his research, Hearnshaw found that Burt had indeed invented data in several of his crucial papers. "As I read Burt's correspondence I was surprised, and shocked, by his contradictions and demonstrable lies—lies which were not benign, but clearly cover-ups," Hearnshaw says.[20] The evidence from Burt's detailed personal diaries showed that he had not carried out the research he claimed to have done. "The verdict must be, therefore, that at any rate in three instances, beyond reasonable doubt, Burt was guilty of deception," his official biographer concluded.

Published in 1979, Hearnshaw's study of Burt is a sympathetic and subtly drawn portrait.[21] It shows a man of great gifts, but with a pathological streak in his character that found expression in his jealous treatment of critics, rivals, and even former students. Introverted, private, ambitious, there was a duality in Burt's nature that allowed his talents to be bent to demeaning ends. His twin data are at least partly spurious, Hearnshaw believes, because he could not have added twins to his collection after his retirement in 1950, yet the papers of 1958 and 1966 state this to be the case. Burt may once have worked with the elusive Misses Conway and Howard, but not in this period: he had no co-workers and did no research. For the same reason, his paper of 1969 purporting to document a decline in educational standards over the period 1914 to 1965 must also be fictitious, at least in part. The third case of proven falsification, in Hearnshaw's view, lies in Burt's claim to have invented the technique of factor analysis. Although Kamin suspects that possibly everything Burt did was fraudulent, right from his first research paper in 1909, Hearnshaw believes that the earliest work there is any reason to doubt dates from 1943. "From 1943 onwards Burt's research reports must be regarded with suspicion," he concludes.

"The gifts which made Burt an effective applied psychologist," observes Hearnshaw, ". . . militated against his scientific work. Neither by temperament nor by training was he a scientist. He was overconfident, too much in a hurry, too eager for final results, too ready to adjust and paper over, to be a good scientist. His work often had the appearance of science, but not always the substance." How could a man who had only the appearance of being a scientist rise to the height of his academic profession, to the senior chair of psychology in Britain? If science is a self-policing, self-correcting community of scholars, always checking one another's work with rigorous and impartial skepticism, how could Burt get so far and stay undetected for so long?

If Burt's fraud is taken as starting in 1943, he remained undetected for thirty-one years, until Kamin's book of 1974. For psychology as a discipline, the point is not so much that the fraud itself passed unnoticed, but that the glaring procedural and statistical errors—there for whatever reason—were not picked up earlier. During the sixteen years that Burt was editor of the *British Journal of Statistical Psychology*, numerous articles signed by pseudonyms (such as Conway) appeared and in unmistakably Burtian style heaped praise on Burt and criticism on his opponents. At least from 1969 onward, his data occupied a central position in controversy, in a subject that is presumably no less rigorous than other disciplines. Why did journal editors and referees not require that he report his results in scientific form? Why did scholars reading his papers not spot the flaws?

Burt's figures were unlikely enough to have prompted several requests from American psychologists for further information. At least one, Sandra Scarr-Salapatek of the University of Minnesota, did so because she thought the data "looked funny."[22] In his final twin paper of 1966, Burt reported, as a clinching blow to the environmentalists, that his separated pairs of twins had been brought up in homes whose social backgrounds were entirely uncorrelated, a surprising fact since adopted children are usually placed in homes of similar backgrounds to their own. One psychologist who doubted the data at the time was Philip Vernon of the University of Calgary, Alberta: "I could not stomach that, I could not believe that. I didn't know what he had done," says Vernon, a former collaborator of Burt's. Asked why no one had publicly disputed the result, Vernon says that "there were certainly grave doubts although nobody dared to put them into print, because Burt was enormously powerful."[23] Burt's power stemmed not from patronage but apparently from the formidable prose style in which he would take out after those who dared criticize him.

Even if those close to Burt or his work had their doubts, no one until Kamin raised in print the central problem. "The sober fact is that scholarly penetration of the literature, and endless delving into primary sources, occurs only very rarely," comments Liam Hudson, a psychologist at the University of Edinburgh. "It reflects on all of us that these figures should have been in the literature of a highly contentious and important area for more than a decade before anyone went back to examine them as Kamin did. It strikes me as very damaging to us as a profession that articles were coming from someone called Conway whom no one had ever heard of. That is not the way that a community of scholars should be working."[24]

Kamin's interpretation is that Burt's data remained unchallenged because they confirmed what everyone wanted to believe: "Every professor knew that his child was brighter than the ditch-digger's child, so what was there to challenge?" There may be something to the argument, but it cannot be the whole story because Burt's critics also failed to catch the flaws.

The most plausible answer, not just to the Burt affair but also to many of the other episodes cited in this chapter, is that many scientific communities do not behave in the way they are supposed to. Science is not self-policing. Scholars do not always read the scientific literature carefully. Science is not a perfectly objective process. Dogma and prejudice, when suitably garbed, creep into science just as easily as into any other human enterprise, and maybe more easily since their entry is unexpected. Burt, with the mere appearance of being a scientist, worked his way to the top of the academic ladder, to a position of power and influence in both science and the world beyond. He used the scientific method as a purely rhetorical tool to force the acceptance of his own dogmatic ideas. Against such weapons, the scientific community that harbored him was defenseless. Against rhetoric and appearance, the scientific method and the scientific ethos proved helpless. Against dogma disguised as science, objectivity failed.

CHAPTER 12

FRAUD AND THE STRUCTURE OF SCIENCE

The conventional ideology of science cannot satisfactorily explain the phenomenon of fraud. It deals with fraud only by denying it to be a problem of any prevalence or significance. In point of fact, fraud is a significant phenomenon that has occurred throughout the history of science and is no less in evidence today. It is not fraud that must be dismissed, but the conventional ideology.

The analysis of fraud sheds considerable light on how science works in actual practice. It illuminates both the motivation of the individual researcher and the mechanisms by which the scientific community validates and accepts new knowledge.

From its earliest days, science has been an arena in which men have striven for two goals: to understand the world and to achieve recognition for their personal efforts in doing so. This duality of purpose lies at the foundation of the scientific enterprise. Only through recognition of the double goal can the motives of scientists, the behavior of the scientific community, and the process of science itself be properly understood.

The scientist's two purposes for the most part work hand in hand, but in certain situations conflicts arise. When an experiment does not come out exactly as expected, when a theory fails to win general acceptance, a scientist will face a spectrum of temptations that range from improving the appearance of his data in various ways to outright fraud. Some who commit fraud do so to persuade their refractory colleagues of a theory they know is right. Newton manipulated the fudge factor to confound the critics of his theory of gravitation. Mendel's statistics of his pea ratios, for whatever reason, are too good to be true. Millikan was outrageously selective in his use of data to describe the charge on the electron.

If history has been kind to scientists such as these, it is because the theories turned out to be correct. But for the moralist, no distinction can be made between an Isaac Newton who lied for truth and was right, and a Cyril Burt who lied for truth and was wrong. Newton and Burt each lied for what he thought he knew to be truth. Probably each turned to fraud also in part for reasons of personal vindication, for the vanity of having his professional colleagues acknowledge the validity of his theory.

Most scientists, no doubt, do not allow the thirst for personal glory to distort their pursuit of the truth. Yet the temptation to which even Ptolemy, Gallileo, Newton, Dalton, and Millikan succumbed grew even stronger as science became professionalized in the nineteenth and twentieth centuries. The remarkable career of Elias Alsabti illustrates how completely the desire for credit can vanquish the honest search for truth. Alsabti's behavior is by no means typical. But it demonstrates in extreme form the ambition and careerism that are regular ingredients of modern scientific life. More importantly, Alsabti's success shows how ineffectually the social mechanisms of science operate to check the excesses of ambition and careerism.

Much of science does not work in this way, and most scientists do research because they like it, not because they are trying to climb some career ladder to scientific stardom. There is no single social organization of science but rather a spectrum of structures that range from the ideal community of equal colleagues to the hierarchically organized research mill. Perhaps the prevalence of fraud is an indication of how well these various structures work. No sure generalization can yet be made, but an apparent pattern is that fraud seems to be committed most often either by loners, such as Alsabti and Burt, or by members of research mills.

If anything, the social mechanisms of science are designed to promote careerism. The hierarchically structured research mills, in which the lab chief often takes an automatic share of the credit for the work done by his junior colleagues regardless of how insignificant his own contribution may have been, allow one scientist to amass glory at the expense of others. Those whose efforts are exploited go along with the practice because they see it as an unchangeable part of the system, from which they too hope to profit in their turn.

The lab-chief system encourages not only careerism but also cynicism because, by its structure and organization, it tends to force a disjunction between the scientist's two goals, the pursuit of truth and the desire for credit. The system, with its heavy emphasis on results, on producing papers, on winning the next research grant, sets up pressures that favor glory-getting and credit-grabbing over the dispassionate pursuit of truth.

Science to a large extent is hard and discouraging work. For every second of cognitive exaltation at a pretty idea or an experiment that finally works, the researcher must put in hours of frustrating labor at the laboratory bench, trying to master a new technique, to iron out the bugs, to wrest a clear answer from the confusing substance of nature. To persevere in research requires a high degree of motivation, for which glory is often the incentive, denial of grant money the goad. But that motivation can easily turn to cynicism if younger researchers see that their elders are more preoccupied with chasing of scientific honors than in dispassionate examination of nature.

Sociologists have emphasized the community of science, portraying it as a band of colleagues dedicated to a common goal, the pursuit of truth. But this is only part of the picture. Science is also a race, an often furious competition in which individuals strive to be first—for without priority, discovery is a bitter fruit. Under the pressure of competition, some researchers yield to the temptation of cutting corners, of improving on their data, of finagling their results, and even of outright fraud.

Science may in one sense be a community, but in another, equally important, it is a celebrity system. The social organization of science is designed to foster the production of an elite in which prestige comes not just on the merits of work but also because of position in the scientific hierarchy. Members of the scientific elite control the reward system of science and, through the peer review system, have a major voice in the allocation of scientific resources.

Like the paper factories of the lab chiefs, the celebrity system favors the search for personal glory over the search for truth. It also interferes with the normal mechanisms for communal evaluation of results, because it gives undue prominence and immunity from scrutiny to the work of the elite. Members of the scientific elite cannot be held directly responsible for the cases of fraud that occur quite regularly in the elite institutions of science, but they are the product and beneficiaries of a social organization that fosters careerism and creates the temptations and opportunities for fraud. William Summerlin, Vijay Soman, and John Darsee were members of laboratories where a large number of articles were produced, in part for the greater glory of the lab chief. John Long traded on the prestige of his institution and scientific affiliations to spin a research career out of nothing.

Fraud is revealing not only of the sociological structure of science but also of scientific methodology. Fraud and self-deception generate incorrect data that pose a challenge to the self-corrective mechanisms of science, in particular to the verification of scientific results. As is shown by many of the frauds discussed here, the replication of an experiment is often undertaken only as a last resort, and usually to confirm suspicions arrived at for other reasons. Exact replication is not a regular part of the scientific process. The reason is simple: there is no credit to be gained from replicating someone else's experiment.

Replication is not the engine of scientific progress. A closer description of the central validation method of science would be to say that recipes that work are adopted into the general cuisine. Science is in some respects a profoundly pragmatic enterprise. Theory may get the attention but the working scientist depends on his ability to make experiments work. If a new experiment or technique is successful, it will be adapted by other scientists to their own ends. It is by a continuous succession of small improvements on existing recipes that the scientific juggernaut inches forward. Only rarely are bad recipes demonstrated to be the product not of chefs but of charlatans. More often they just fall by the wayside, to be ignored along with a great mass of other forgettable, insignificant, or somehow erroneous research.

Science is pragmatic, but scientists are also as susceptible as others to all the arts of persuasion, including flattery, rhetoric, and propaganda. The careerist will make full use of these weapons to aid in the acceptance of his ideas. No one showed better how the scientific method could be wielded as a purely rhetorical weapon than did Cyril Burt. By merely claiming to be more scientific than his adversaries, by his mastery of statistics and brilliantly lucid exposition, Burt hoodwinked the community of educational psychologists in both England and the United States for some thirty years.

To the extent that rhetoric is persuasive in science, it can be so only at the expense of objectivity. The study of fraud indicates that the ideal of objectivity is often departed from. Objectivity is perhaps best thought of as a retrospective virtue of science. That accumulation of dispassionate fact in the scientific textbooks seems to stand quite independently of its human originators. Yet the attitude of detachment, however highly applauded by the philosophers and sociologists, is one that is hard to maintain in the competitive, results-oriented atmosphere of modern science. Nor is it evident that objectivity is a necessary qualification for the practicing scientist. Most researchers believe passionately in their work, in the techniques they rely on and the theories they are trying to prove. Without such an emotional commitment, it would be hard to sustain the effort. When the technique proves to be ambiguous or the theory untenable, the researcher learns to pick up the pieces and start over anew. Many scientists want passionately to know the truth. It is only the literary conventions of scientific reporting that compel scientists to feign detachment and pretend that when they put on a white coat they turn into logical automatons. Objectivity is an abstraction of the philosophers, a distraction for the researcher.

How is scientific knowledge validated, if not by replication and objective analysis? The economist Adam Smith explained in his classic work how private greed leads to public good. Even though everyone in the marketplace strives only to maximize his personal gain, the public good is served because an efficient market brings supply and demand into equilibrium at the lowest prices. A similar mechanism operates in science. Each scientist in the research forum tries to win acceptance for his own ideas or recipes: on balance, over time, the better recipe for dealing with nature generally prevails, so that the stock of useful knowledge grows steadily greater. The more vigorously that scientists pursue their own personal goals, the more efficiently does truth emerge from the competing claims.

In the realm of economics, Adam Smith invoked the "Invisible Hand" as the miraculous mechanism that produced public good out of private gain. The analogous mechanism that operates in science might be called the "Invisible Boot." The Invisible Boot kicks out all the incorrect, useless, or redundant data in science. It tramples over almost every scientist's work without discrimination, treading down into oblivion the true and the false, the honest and the dishonest, the keepers of the faith and the betrayers of the truth. Over time it stamps out the nonrational elements of the scientific process, all the human passions and prejudices that shaped the original findings, and leaves only a desiccated residue of knowledge, so distant from its human originators that it at last acquires the substance of objectivity.

The philosophers have described logical deduction, objective verification of results, and the construction of theories as the pillars of the scientific method. The analysis of fraud suggests a different picture. It shows science as pragmatic and empirical, something of a trial-and-error procedure in which the competitors in a given field try many different approaches but are always quick to switch to the recipe that works best. Science being a social process, each researcher is trying at the same time to advance and gain acceptance for his own recipes, his own interpretation of the field. He will use all rhetorical techniques that are likely to be effective, including appeal to scientific authority, emphasis on the thoroughness of his own methods, explanation of how his recipes agree with or support current theory, and other approved modes of discourse.

It would be extreme to state that science is nothing but recipes and rhetoric, with the Invisible Boot kicking out the useless and incorrect research over the course of time. But it is equally extreme to portray science as an exclusively logical process, guided by objective tests of verification and motivated solely by the search for truth. Science is a complex process in which the observer can see almost anything he wants provided he narrows his vision sufficiently. But to give a complete description of science, to understand the process as it really works, the temptation to seek out ideals and abstractions must probably be avoided.

The chief abstraction, of course, is the philosopher's search for the scientific method. It may be that there is no one scientific method. Scientists are individuals and they have different styles and different approaches to the truth. The identical style of all scientific writing, which seems to spring from a universal scientific method, is a false unanimity imposed by the current conventions of scientific reporting. If scientists were allowed to express themselves naturally in describing their experiments and theories, the myth of a single, universal scientific method would probably vanish instantly.

For a rounded understanding of how science works, the disciplinary abstractions of the philosophers, sociologists, and historians of science must be recognized as single aspects of a multifaceted object, not taken for the whole picture, as the conventional ideology assumes. Science is first and foremost a social process: the researcher who discovers the secret of the universe and keeps it to himself has not contributed to science. Secondly, it is a historical process: it moves forward with time, it is an integral part of civilization and history, and cannot properly be understood when wrested out of its context. Thirdly, science is the cultural form that allows fullest opportunity for the expression of the human propensity for rational thought.

It is the third aspect of science that has perhaps been subject to the greatest amount of misinterpretation. The presence of a strong rational element in science has been taken to mean that that is the only significant element of scientific thought. But creativity, imagination, intuition, persistence, and many other nonrational elements are also essential parts of the scientific process, and other less vital qualities such as ambition, envy, and the propensity to deception also play a role. The existence of fraud in science is proof of nonrational elements at work, both on the part of the individual who fakes data and the community that accepts them.

The rationality evident in science has also been misinterpreted to mean that science is the only rational exercise of intellect in society, or at least the highest and most authoritative. Some scientists, in their public appearances, can be noticed playing up to this role, which seems to invest them as cardinals of reason propounding salvation to an irrational public. It is probably a misperception to think of science as different in kind from other exercises of the human intellect. At the least, the burden of proof should be on those who make special claims for science, and any claim founded solely on what the philosophers say about science must be rejected as partial.

In addition, scientists are put in a false position by those who would make them the sole guardians of rationality in society. Historians who have attempted to arrogate to science all credit for social or material progress, or for the triumph of reason over the forces of darkness and ignorance, also render science vulnerable to blame for all the deficiencies of modern societies. To a probably insalubrious degree, science has replaced religion as the fundamental source of truth and value in the modern world.

The rigidity imposed by consciousness of such a role is perhaps evident in the typical response of the scientific establishment to fraud. Establishment spokesmen generally find it difficult to suggest that a certain background level of fraud should be expected in science as much as in any other profession. They are also disinclined to concede that the practices or institutions of science should shoulder any part of the blame for fraudulent behavior. Only by abandoning the conventional ideology of science would it be possible for them to accept fraud for what it most probably is, a small, but not insignificant, endemic feature of the scientific enterprise.

The rejection of fraud as a serious issue leaves the profession of science in an awkward position, most especially when the implications of scientific fraud move beyond the world of pure research to the realm of public policy. Here fraud can become a matter of immediate practical significance. The testing of drugs and food ingredients is a case in point. Government agencies, not the institutions of science, have taken the initiative in trying to control the wide-scale fraud that has occurred in biological testing.

Another significant impact of fraud has been in the unhappy field of measuring human abilities. Fraud and self-deception have played major parts in studies that have influenced public attitudes on matters of class and race, and in shaping public action on issues such as immigration and education. Scientists' deception of themselves and others in this context illustrates the more general principle: that objectivity is often the first victim when scientists enter battle on social issues.

Besides the practical damage done by some scientific frauds, there is the harm done by each new revelation of laboratory legerdemain to the public credibility of science. Without a serious effort on the part of scientists to address the issue, pressure will build for Congress to take action of some sort, perhaps by instituting a laboratory police force modeled on the inspection system of the Food and Drug Administration.

Congress would probably take such a step only with great reluctance, because of its deep belief that scientific research and universities should be autonomous from government. But at a period when initiatives against waste and fraud are being pursued in all other areas of government, Congress is unlikely to indulge science as a haven where fraud can continue just as usual.

Political considerations aside, it would in any case be in the interests of science to remedy the causes of fraud. In general, there is no absolute defense against fraud that would not bring the whole machinery of science grinding to a halt. But the detection of fraud is of far less importance than its prevention. What is required first and foremost are steps to diminish the inducement to fraud.

By and large, those features in the social organization of science that encourage and reward careerism also create the incentive for fraud. The excesses of the careerist system spread cynicism among young researchers, who sometimes respond to pressure by imitating the worse aspects of their elders' behavior. This is the atmosphere in which the finagling of data or the wholesale invention of results is perhaps most likely to occur. Scientists should be more skeptical of elitism, and particularly of young superstars in elite institutions who seem to do too much too fast. A branch of knowledge that claims to be universal should ensure that its own internal tests are evenly applied.

A simple but valuable reform would be for the scientific community to set itself more formal guidelines for the assignation of credit, in particular for that critically important part of a scientific paper—the authorship line. Two principles might be established. First, all people named as authors should have made a definably major contribution to the work reported. Any minor contribution should be explicitly acknowledged in the text of the article. Second, all authors of a paper should be prepared to take responsibility for its contents in precisely the same measure as they stand to take credit.

Such steps, if generally accepted, would curtail the inherently dishonest practice of lab chiefs signing their name to work in which they have been only peripherally involved, if at all. It would also spare the public the ludicrous spectacle of lab chiefs who hog credit for everything that goes well but disclaim responsibility when fraud is discovered. If a lab chief is not close enough to a research project to know whether data is being falsified, he should not put his name on the paper. For the papers he does sign, he should take full responsibility. To most nonscientists, such principles probably seem too obvious to be worth stating.

A specific area in urgent need of reform is that of medical research. The pressures put on students trying to enter medical school encourage and reward a kind of competition that often includes deception. "Stories of cheating among premedical students are common, and the race for high grades so as to insure admission to medical school is hardly designed to encourage ethical and humanitarian behavior," says the former dean of the Harvard Medical School, Robert H. Ebert. When those accustomed to cheating experience the fierce competitive pressures of the medical world and the prestige that attaches to doing research, they do not find it too unnatural to clean up data or even invent experiments. The "bad apples" who commit fraud in medical research are a special fruit of the system. One solution would be a wider degree of separation between medical research and medical education.

A problem that affects research in general is the excessive proliferation of scientific papers. Too many scientific articles are published. Many are simply worthless. Moreover the worthless papers clutter up the communications system of science, preventing good research from receiving the attention it deserves and protecting bad research from scrutiny. Alsabti and his fellow plagiarists were able to achieve success only because of the shelter given them by the ocean of unread and unreadable articles of which the scientific literature is so largely composed.

As the system now stands, researchers are rewarded for extracting the maximum number of separate articles out of a single piece of research, so as to amplify the list of their published work. This pernicious habit makes reviewing the literature almost impossible. Scientists who fragment their results should be criticized rather than rewarded.

The root of the publication problem lies in a system that is carefully protected from market constraints. The research journals that publish the articles that no one needs to read are twice subsidized, both times by the taxpayer. Their publishers levy page charges on authors to defray the printing costs. The scientific libraries that buy the journals are also subsidized. Both the page charges and the library funds come from researchers' government grants. The subsidies underlie the ease with which almost any scientific article, however poor, can get into print.

Attempts to tighten up the refereeing process are seldom successful, because a paper turned down by one journal will eventually be published in another. What is needed is greater competition brought about by a sharp reduction in the number of journals, especially in medicine and biology. Many of these journals serve as little more than what publishers call a vanity press, with the taxpayer supporting the vanity through the grants given to researchers. The practice of page charges should be sharply curtailed. Market forces of supply and demand should be introduced wherever possible into the game of academic publishing.

Just as the emphasis in publication should be shifted from quantity to quality, so promotions and grant renewals should not be handed out on the basis of a long list of seemingly important publications. Administrators should develop sophisticated means of reading and evaluating a research record, such as citation analysis, where the influence of a scientist can be measured by the number of times his work is cited by other researchers. Such techniques tell much more about the real worth of a scientist than a long list of publications on a curriculum vitae.

A reduction in the number of scientific articles of course suggests a more radical kind of surgery, that of a reduction in the number of scientists. The available evidence indicates that the great majority of research responsible for the advance of science is produced by a small number of scientists. This small elite depends overwhelmingly on the research of other members of the elite, not on that of the wider majority. The pace of scientific advance would not obviously be slowed if this majority did not exist. It might even be enhanced if pursued by a leaner and fitter community of researchers. Perhaps there are too many scientists. Perhaps basic scientific research would be more appropriately supported by private patrons, as economist Milton Friedman has suggested, instead of by the government.

In his book *The Decline of the West*, the philosopher Oswald Spengler cited fraud by scholars as one of the signs of a decadent civilization. It is not necessary to believe Spengler's thesis to be alarmed by the persistent, even if minor, presence of fraud in science. The idea of progress is a sustaining value of Western societies, and scientific research is an important means to that end. Scientists are professionally committed to ascertain the truth on society's behalf; when they betray the truth for personal gain, the signs of a possibly serious corrosion of principle should not be ignored.

For the public, a better understanding of the nature of science would lead to their regarding scientists with less awe and a dash more skepticism. A more realistic attitude would be healthy for both. But a proper understanding of science must begin with scientists themselves, and should embrace the concept that there is no discontinuity between scientific and other modes of intellectual creation. The phenomenon of fraud underlines the importance of the human side of science. It suggests that the logical structure of scientific knowledge is not a proper basis for placing science in a different category from other intellectual activities. Science is not removed from the wellsprings of art or poetry, nor is it the only cultural expression of rationality.

Science is not an abstract body of knowledge, but man's understanding of nature. It is not an idealized interrogation of nature by dedicated servants of truth, but a human process governed by the ordinary human passions of ambition, pride, and greed, as well as by all the well-hymned virtues attributed to men of science. But the step from greed to fraud is as small in science as in other walks of life. Usually the misrepresentation amounts to no more than a sweetening or prettification of the data; less often, to outright fraud.

"Truth is the daughter," Bacon remarked, "not of authority, but time." Time and again, the truth has been betrayed by scientists, whether unintentionally, or for their own ends, or because they presumed to lie on truth's behalf. Scientific authorities deny that fraud is anything more than a passing blemish on the face of science. But only by acknowledging that fraud is endemic can the real nature of science and its servants be fully understood.

KNOWN OR SUSPECTED CASES OF SCIENTIFIC FRAUD

"Strangely enough, deliberate, conscious fraud is extremely rare in the world of academic science. . . . The only well-known case is 'Piltdown Man.'"—J. M. Ziman, NATURE, *227, 996, 1970.*

"Indeed, a number of old stories are being exhumed and revived, as though to reveal a pattern of habitual falsehood in the process of science. . . . These can, if you like, be made to seem all of a piece, part of a constantly spreading blot on the record of science. Or, if you prefer (and I do prefer), they can be viewed as anomalies, the work of researchers with unhinged minds, or, as in the cases of Newton and Mendel, the gross exaggerations of the fallibility of even superb scientists."—Lewis Thomas, DISCOVER, *June 1981.*

Following is a list of cases of known or strongly suspected fraud in science, from ancient Greece to the present day. The list represents merely those cases that have come to our attention, and is not the result of an exhaustive search. Each case is described in summary form, with a single reference for the reader to obtain further information.

We would be glad if those knowing of cases not cited here would bring them to our attention, c/o Simon & Schuster, 1230 Avenue of the Americas, New York, N.Y. 10020.

CASE: Hipparchus (Greek astronomer)
DATE: Second century B.C.
- Published star catalog taken from Babylonian sources as if it were the result of his own observations.

REFERENCE: G. J. Toomer, "Ptolemy," *Dictionary of Scientific Biography* (Charles Scribner's Sons, New York, 1975), p. 191.

CASE: Claudius Ptolemy (Egyptian astronomer whose theory of the solar system held sway for 1,500 years)
DATE: Second century A.D.
- Claimed to have performed astronomical measurements which he did not.

REFERENCE: Robert R. Newton, *The Crime of Claudius Ptolemy* (Johns Hopkins University Press, Baltimore, 1977).

CASE: Galileo Galilei (physicist and founder of scientific method)
DATE: Early seventeenth century
- Exaggerated the outcome of experimental results.

REFERENCE: Alexandre Koyré, *Metaphysics and Measurement: Essays in Scientific Revolution* (Harvard University Press, Cambridge, 1968).

CASE: Isaac Newton (first modern physicist)
DATE: 1687–1713
- Introduced fudge factors into his magnum opus so as to increase its apparent power of prediction.

REFERENCE: Richard S. Westfall, "Newton and the Fudge Factor," *Science,* 179, 751–758, 1973.

CASE: Johann Beringer (German dilettante and collector of fossils)
DATE: 1726
- Hoaxed by rivals in publishing book of fake fossils.

REFERENCE: Melvin E. Jahn and Daniel J. Woolf, *The Lying Stones of Dr. Johann Bartholomew Adam Beringer* (University of California Press, Berkeley, 1963).

CASE: Johann Bernoulli (mathematician who refined calculus)
DATE: 1738
- Plagiarized his son's discovery of the "Bernoulli equation,"

backdating his own book so it appeared to have been issued before his son's.

REFERENCE: C. Truesdell, in introduction to Euler's *Opera Omnia,* Ser. II, Vol. II, p. xxxv.

CASE: John Dalton (father of modern atomic theory)
DATE: 1804–1805
• Reported experiments that cannot now be repeated, and which probably could not have happened as described.
REFERENCE: Leonard K. Nash, "The Origin of Dalton's Chemical Atomic Theory," *Isis,* 47, 101–116, 1956.

CASE: Orgueil (a meteorite shower that fell on France)
DATE: 1864
• Unknown hoaxster tampered with piece of meteorite so it seemed to bear organic remains, implying the existence of extraterrestrial life.
REFERENCE: Edward Anders *et al.,* "Contaminated Meteorite," *Science,* 146, 1157–1161, 1964.

CASE: Gregor Mendel (father of genetics)
DATE: 1865
• Published statistical results too good to be true.
REFERENCE: Several papers in Curt Stern and Eva R. Sherwood, *The Origin of Genetics: A Mendel Source Book* (W. H. Freeman and Co., San Francisco, 1966).

CASE: Admiral Peary (American explorer)
DATE: 1909
• Alleged he had reached the geographic North Pole when in fact he knew he was hundreds of miles away.
REFERENCE: Dennis Rawlins, *Peary at the North Pole: Fact or Fiction?* (Robert B. Luce, Washington-New York, 1973).

CASE: Robert Millikan (American physicist and winner of Nobel prize)
DATE: 1910–1913
• Kept unfavorable results out of published papers while publicly maintaining that he had reported everything.

REFERENCE: Gerald Holton, "Subelectrons, Presuppositions, and the Millikan-Ehrenhaft Dispute," *Historical Studies in the Physical Sciences,* 9, 166–224, 1978.

CASE: Piltdown
DATE: 1912
   • Hoaxster planted fake fossils in gravel pit, presumably to cast Britain as birthplace of the human race.
REFERENCE: J. S. Weiner, *The Piltdown Forgery* (Oxford University Press, London, 1955).

CASE: Adriaan van Maanen (American astronomer at Mount Wilson Observatory)
DATE: 1916
   • Misreported the reliability of key astronomical observations.
REFERENCE: Norriss S. Hetherington, *Beyond the Edge of Objectivity,* unpublished book MS.

CASE: Paul Kammerer (Viennese biologist)
DATE: 1926
   •Kammerer or assistant faked breeding results with toads.
REFERENCE: Arthur Koestler, *The Case of the Midwife Toad* (Hutchinson, London, 1971).

CASE: Cyril Burt (English psychologist)
DATE: 1943(?)–1966
   • Fabricated data to support theory that human intelligence is 75 percent inherited.
REFERENCE: L. S. Hearnshaw, *Cyril Burt, Psychologist,* Hodder and Stoughton, London, 1979, 370 pp.

CASE: James H. McCrocklin (president of Southwest Texas State College from 1964 to 1969)
DATE: 1954
   • Pirated parts of old report in Ph.D. thesis.
REFERENCE: *Texas Observer,* March 7, 1969, pp. 6–8.

CASE: "Traction" (pseudonym)
DATE: 1960–1961

• A young researcher falsified work at Yale, then was hired by Fritz Lipmann at the Rockefeller Institute, where he published falsified work with Lipmann and was eventually found out.

REFERENCE: William J. Broad, "Fraud and the Structure of Science," *Science,* 212, 137–141, 1981.

CASE: P. G. Pande, R. R. Shukla, and P. C. Sekariah (at Indian Veterinary Research Institute)
DATE: 1961
• Claimed to have discovered parasite in hens' eggs, but photomicrographs had been lifted from another publication.

REFERENCE: The editorial board of *Science,* "An Unfortunate Event," *Science,* 134, 945–946, 1961.

CASE: "Fraley" (pseudonym)

DATE: 1964
• A visiting professor in David E. Green's University of Wisconsin lab faked several important experiments, leading Green to announce retractions at a national meeting.

REFERENCE: Joseph Hixson, *The Patchwork Mouse* (Doubleday, New York, 1976), pp. 146–148. Hixon refers to the perpetrator of the frauds as Fraley.

CASE: Robert Gullis (biochemist from Birmingham University)
DATE: 1971–1976
• Faked series of experiments on messenger chemicals used by the brain.

REFERENCE: Mike Muller, "Why Scientists Don't Cheat," *New Scientist,* June 2, 1977, pp. 522–523.

CASE: Walter J. Levy (parapsychologist and protégé of father of parapsychology, J. B. Rhine)
DATE: 1974
• Faked results of experiment in which rats were to influence equipment by brain power, a phenomenon known as psychokinesis.

REFERENCE: J. B. Rhine, "A New Case of Experimenter Unreliability," *Journal of Parapsychology,* 38, 215–255, 1974.

CASE: William Summerlin (immunologist)
DATE: 1974
- In an attempt to bolster research that was under fire, Summerlin faked results of skin transplants with mice.
REFERENCE: Joseph Hixson, *The Patchwork Mouse* (Doubleday, New York: 1976).

CASE: Stephen S. Rosenfeld (undergraduate researcher at Harvard)
DATE: 1974
- Forged letters of recommendation and allegedly faked series of experiments in biochemistry.
REFERENCE: Robert Reinhold, "When Methods Are Not So Scientific," *The New York Times*, December 29, 1974, p. E7.

CASE: Zoltan Lucas (surgeon at Stanford University)
DATE: 1975
- Admitted to faking citations to research papers of his that did not exist. Some of the fakery was aimed at winning NIH grants.
REFERENCE: Series of news releases put out by Stanford University News Service, August 1981.

CASE: Wilson Crook III (graduate student in geology at University of Michigan)
DATE: 1977
- Regents at the university in 1980 rescinded Crook's master's degree, saying he had fraudulently claimed to have discovered a natural mineral called "texasite," which in reality was a synthetic compound. Crook denied the charges.
REFERENCE: Max Gates, "Regents Rescind Student's Degree, Charging Fraud," *The Ann Arbor News*, October 18, 1980, p. A9.

CASE: Marc J. Straus (cancer researcher at Boston University)
DATE: 1977–1978
- Group of Straus's researchers and nurses admitted falsifying data in clinical tests and charged that some of the fakery was done on Straus's orders. Straus denied any wrongdoing.
REFERENCE: Nils J. Bruzelius and Stephen A. Kurkjian, "Cancer Research Data Falsified; Boston Project Collapses," *Boston Globe*, five-part series starting June 29, 1980, p. 1.

CASE: Elias A. K. Alsabti (Iraqi medical student who worked at several research centers in the United States)
DATE: 1977–1980
- Plagiarized scientific papers, perhaps sixty in all.
REFERENCE: William J. Broad, "Would-be Academician Pirates Papers," *Science*, 208, 1438–1440, 1980.

CASE: Stephen Krogh Derr (radiation chemist at Hope College in Holland, Michigan)
DATE: 1978
- Published allegedly invented results of remarkable treatment said to remove plutonium from the bodies of poisoned workers.
REFERENCE: Lawrence McGinty, "Researcher Retracts Claims on Plutonium Treatment," *New Scientist*, October 4, 1979, pp. 3–4.

CASE: John Long (research pathologist at the Massachusetts General Hospital)
DATE: 1978–1980
- Forged data in the course of a research career spent studying cell lines that turned out to come not from humans but from a brown-footed Columbian owl monkey.
REFERENCE: Nicholas Wade, "A Diversion of the Quest for Truth," *Science*, 211, 1022–1025, 1981.

CASE: Vijay R. Soman (biomedical researcher at Yale)
DATE: 1978–1980
- Falsified results in three papers, threw away raw data in others, forcing retraction of twelve papers in all.
REFERENCE: Morton Hunt, "A Fraud That Shook the World of Science," *The New York Times Magazine*, November 1, 1981, pp. 42–75.

CASE: Mark Spector (rising young biochemist at Cornell University)
DATE: 1980–1981
- A series of elegant experiments by Spector that pointed to a unified theory of cancer causation turned out to be fakes. Spector denied any wrongdoing, saying somebody else spiked the test tubes.
REFERENCE: Nicholas Wade, "The Rise and Fall of a Scientific Superstar," *New Scientist*, September 24, 1981, pp. 781–782.

CASE: M. J. Purves (physiologist at University of Bristol)
DATE: 1981
- Falsified work presented in paper to International Congress of Physiological Science. Retracted paper, resigned his post after university investigation.

REFERENCE: "Scientific Fraud: In Bristol Now," *Nature*, 294, 509, 1981.

CASE: John R. Darsee (cardiologist at Harvard Medical School)
DATE: 1981
- Admitted faking one experiment and blue-ribbon committee found two others highly suspect.

REFERENCE: William J. Broad, "Report Absolves Harvard in Case of Fakery," *Science*, 215, 874–876, 1982.

CASE: Arthur Hale (immunologist at Bowman Gray School of Medicine at Wake Forest University)
DATE: 1981
- Investigation by Wake Forest officials found Hale faked one experiment and did not have adequate raw data for twenty others. Hale resigned, denying any wrongdoing.

REFERENCE: Several articles by Winston Cavin, *Greensboro News & Record*, January 31, 1982.

NOTES

CHAPTER 1
THE FLAWED IDEAL

1. *Fraud in Biomedical Research.* Hearings before the Subcommittee on Investigations and Oversight of the Committee on Science and Technology, U.S. House of Representatives, Ninety-Seventh Congress, March 31–April 1, 1981 (U.S. Government Printing Office, No. 77-661, Washington, 1981), pp. 1–380.
2. Nicholas Wade, "A Diversion of the Quest for Truth," *Science,* 211, 1022–1025, 1981.
3. William J. Broad, "Harvard Delays in Reporting Fraud," *Science,* 215, 478–482, 1982.
4. William J. Broad, "Report Absolves Harvard in Case of Fakery," *Science,* 215, 874–876, 1982. Also see "A Case of Fraud at Harvard," *Newsweek,* February 8, 1982, p. 89.

CHAPTER 2
DECEIT IN HISTORY

1. C. Kittel, W. D. Knight, M. A. Ruderman, *The Berkeley Physics Course,* Vol. 1, *Mechanics* (McGraw-Hill, New York, 1965). This passage, together with an interesting analysis of the scientific textbook writers' use of history, is quoted in an article by Stephen G. Brush, "Should the History of Science Be Rated X?" *Science,* 183, 1164–1172, 1974.

2. Dennis Rawlins, "The Unexpurgated Almajest: The Secret Life of the Greatest Astronomer of Antiquity," *Journal for the History of Astronomy*, in press.

3. Robert R. Newton, *The Crime of Claudius Ptolemy* (Johns Hopkins University Press, Baltimore, 1977). For a summary of the argument see Nicholas Wade, "Scandal in the Heavens: Renowned Astronomer Accused of Fraud," *Science*, 198, 707–709, 1977.

4. Owen Gingerich, "On Ptolemy As the Greatest Astronomer of Antiquity," *Science*, 193, 476–477, 1976, and "Was Ptolemy a Fraud?" preprint No. 751, Center for Astrophysics, Harvard College Observatory, Cambridge, 1977. See also a news article summarizing an attempt to absolve Ptolemy, *Scientific American*, 3, 90–93, 1979.

5. Cecil J. Schneer, *The Evolution of Physical Science* (Grove Press, New York, 1960), p. 65.

6. I. Bernard Cohen, *Lives in Science* (Simon & Schuster, New York, 1957), p. 14.

7. Some research has suggested that Galileo could have easily carried out certain experiments, and that historians who claim they were all imaginary are overstating the case. See Thomas B. Settle, "An Experiment in the History of Science," *Science*, 133, 19–23, 1961. See also Stillman Drake, "Galileo's Experimental Confirmation of Horizontal Inertia: Unpublished Manuscripts," *Isis*, 64, 291–305, 1973. See also James MacLachlan, "A Test of an Imaginary Experiment of Galileo's," *Isis*, 64, 374–379, 1973.

8. Alexandre Koyré, "Traduttore–Traditore. A Propos de Copernic et de Galilée," *Isis*, 34, 209–210, 1943.

9. Alexandre Koyré, *Études Galiléennes* (Hermann, Paris, 1966). This is a reprint of three articles published between 1935 and 1939.

10. Richard S. Westfall, "Newton and the Fudge Factor," *Science*, 179, 751–758, 1973. See also various letters in response in *Science*, 180, 1118, 1973.

11. William J. Broad, "Priority War: Discord in Pursuit of Glory," *Science*, 211, 465–467, 1981.

12. J. R. Partington, *A Short History of Chemistry* (Harper & Brothers, New York, 1960), p. 170. Also see Leonard K. Nash, "The Origin of Dalton's Chemical Atomic Theory," *Isis*, 47, 101–116, 1956.

13. J. R. Partington, "The Origins of the Atomic Theory," *Annals of Science*, 4, 278, 1939.

14. Charles Babbage, *Reflections on the Decline of Science in England* (Augustus M. Kelley, New York, 1970), pp. 174–183.

15. Loren Eiseley, *Darwin and the Mysterious Mr. X* (E. P. Dutton, New York, 1979).
16. Stephen J. Gould, "Darwin Vindicated," *The New York Review of Books,* August 16, 1979, p. 36.
17. Francis Darwin, *The Life and Letters of Charles Darwin* (John Murray, London, 1887), p. 220.
18. L. Huxley, *Life and Letters of Thomas Henry Huxley* (Macmillan, London, 1900), p. 97.
19. For this and other Darwin quotes on ambition see Robert K. Merton, *The Sociology of Science: Theoretical and Empirical Investigations* (University of Chicago Press, 1973), pp. 305–307.
20. R. A. Fisher, "Has Mendel's Work Been Rediscovered?" *Annals of Science,* 1, 115–137, 1936. For reprints of this and several other papers on Mendel see Curt Stern and Eva R. Sherwood, *The Origin of Genetics: A Mendel Source Book* (W. H. Freeman and Co., San Francisco, 1966), pp. 1–175.
21. L. C. Dunn, *A Short History of Genetics* (McGraw-Hill, New York, 1965), p. 13.
22. For Wright's analysis see Curt Stern and Eva R. Sherwood, *The Origin of Genetics: A Mendel Source Book* (W. H. Freeman and Co., San Francisco, 1966), pp. 173–175.
23. B. L. van der Waerden, "Mendel's Experiments," *Centaurus,* 12, 275–288, 1968.
24. Anonymous, "Peas on Earth," *Hort Science,* 7, 5, 1972.
25. Peter B. Medawar, *The Art of the Soluble* (Barnes & Noble, New York, 1968), p. 7.
26. Gerald Holton, "Subelectrons, Presuppositions, and the Millikan-Ehrenhaft Dispute," *Historical Studies in the Physical Sciences,* 9, 166–224, 1978.
27. Allan D. Franklin, "Millikan's Published and Unpublished Data on Oil Drops," *Historical Studies in the Physical Sciences,* 11, 185–201, 1981.
28. For an account of the Stanford discoveries see "Fractional Charge," *Science 81,* April 1981, p. 6.

CHAPTER 3
RISE OF THE CAREERISTS

1. For an overview of the Alsabti episode, see William J. Broad, "Would-Be Academician Pirates Papers," *Science,* 208, 1438–

1440, 1980; and Susan V. Lawrence, "Let No One Else's Work Evade Your Eyes . . . ," *Forum on Medicine,* September 1980, pp. 582–587.

2. E. A. K. Alsabti, "Tumor Dormancy (A Review)," *Neoplasma,* 26, 351–361, 1979. This is actually just one of three identical Alsabti articles based on Wheelock's grant application and manuscript. See also "Tumor Dormancy: A Review," *Tumor Research* (Sapporo), 13, 1–13, 1978, and "Tumor Dormancy," *Journal of Cancer Research and Clinical Oncology,* 95, 209–220, 1979.

3. Daniel Wierda and Thomas L. Pazdernik, "Suppression of Spleen Lymphocyte Mitogenesis in Mice Injected with Platinum Compounds," *European Journal of Cancer,* 15, 1013–1023, 1979. For Alsabti's copy of this article see: Elias A. K. Alsabti *et al.,* "Effect of Platinum Compounds on Murine Lymphocyte Mitogenesis," *Japanese Journal of Medical Science and Biology,* 32, 53–65, 1979.

4. Elias A. K. Alsabti, "Tumor Dormancy: A Review," *Tumor Research,* 13, 1–13, 1978; "Carcinoembryonic Antigen (CEA) in Plasma of Patients with Malignant and Non-Malignant Diseases," *Tumor Research,* 13, 57–63, 1978; "Serum Immunoglobulins in Acute Myelogenous Leukemia," *Tumor Research,* 13, 64–69, 1978.

5. Takanobu Yoshida *et al.,* "Diagnostic Evaluation of Serum Lipids in Patients with Hepatocellular Carcinoma," *Japanese Journal of Clinical Oncology,* 7, 15–20, 1977. Alsabti's version of this paper: Elias A. K. Alsabti, "Serum Lipids in Hepatoma," *Oncology,* 36, 11–14, 1979.

6. William J. Broad, "Would-be Academician Pirates Papers," *Science,* 208, 1438–1440, 1980; "An Outbreak of Piracy in the Literature," *Nature,* 285, 429–430, 1980; William J. Broad, "Jordanian Denies He Pirated Papers," *Science,* 209, 249, 1980; William J. Broad, "Jordanian Accused of Plagiarism Quits Job," *Science,* 209, 886, 1980; William J. Broad, "Charges of Piracy Follow Alsabti," *Science,* 210, 291, 1980; "One Journal Disowns Plagiarism," *Nature,* 286, 437, 1980.

7. "Must Plagiarism Thrive?" *British Medical Journal,* July 5, 1980, pp. 41–42.

8. "Plagiarism Strikes Again," *Nature,* 286, 433, 1980.

9. Lawrence, *op. cit.*

10. Stephen M. Lawani, unpublished letter, *Science.*

11. Jonathan R. Cole and Stephen Cole, "The Ortega Hypothesis," *Science,* 178, 368–375, 1972.

12. William J. Broad, "The Publishing Game: Getting More for Less," *Science*, 211, 1137–1139, 1981.
13. Roy Reed, "Plagiarism Charge Is Stirring Political Fight at Texas College," *The New York Times*, March 10, 1969; "McCrocklin Attempts Defense," *Texas Observer*, March 7, 1969, pp. 6–8; "The McCrocklin Resignation," *Texas Observer*, May 9, 1969, p. 17.
14. Philip M. Boffey, "W. D. McElroy: An Old Incident Embarrasses New NSF Director," *Science*, 165, 379–380, 1969.
15. Morton Mintz, "Top U.S. Alcohol Expert Hit on Book Similarities," *Washington Post*, April 10, 1971, p. 1.
16. Daniel S. Greenberg, "Alcoholism Post Stirs Conflict," *Science & Government Report*, May 15, 1971, p. 3.
17. "Plagiarism strikes again," *Nature*, 286, 433, 1980.

CHAPTER 4
THE LIMITS OF REPLICATION

1. Lewis Thomas, "Falsity and Failure," *Discover*, June 1981, pp. 38–39.
2. *Fraud in Biomedical Research*. Hearings before the Subcommittee on Investigations and Oversight of the Committee on Science and Technology, U.S. House of Representatives, Ninety-Seventh Congress, March 31–April 1, 1981 (U.S. Government Printing Office, No. 77-661, Washington, 1981), p. 12.
3. Address by Charles P. Snow to the annual meeting of the American Association for the Advancement of Science. *Science*, 133, 256–259, 1961.
4. Robert K. Merton, "The Normative Structure of Science," in *The Sociology of Science*, Norman W. Storer, ed. (University of Chicago Press, 1973), pp. 267–278. Merton's view has evolved over the years from his earlier and more idealistic formulations; see Robert K. Merton, "Priorities in Scientific Discovery," in *The Sociology of Science*, Norman V. Storer, ed. (Chicago: University of Chicago Press, 1973) pp. 308–316. Also, for a comprehensive review of fraud from the Mertonian school, see Harriet Zuckerman, "Deviant Behavior and Social Control in Science," in *Deviance and Social Change*, Edward Sagarin, ed. (Beverly Hills: Sage Publications, 1977) pp. 87–138.
5. June Goodfield, *Cancer Under Siege* (Hutchinson, London, 1975), p. 218.

6. The first public description of the Spector case was by Jeffrey L. Fox, "Theory Explaining Cancer Partly Retracted," *Chemical and Engineering News,* September 7, 1981, pp. 35–36. Two later but more general accounts are: Nicholas Wade, "The Rise and Fall of a Scientific Superstar," *New Scientist,* September 24, 1981, pp. 781–782; and Kevin McKean, "A Scandal in the Laboratory," *Discover,* November 1981, pp. 18–23. Parts of this account first appeared in the *New Scientist* article, © 1981, *New Scientist.*

7. Efraim Racker and Mark Spector, "The Warburg Effect Revisited: Merger of Biochemistry and Molecular Biology," *Science,* 213, 303–307, 1981.

8. *Ibid.*

9. Judith Horstman, "Famed Cornell Scientist Retracts Major Cancer Discovery," *Ithaca Journal,* September 9, 1981.

10. Mark Spector, Robert B. Pepinsky, Volker M. Vogt, and Efraim Racker, "A Mouse Homolog to the Avian Sarcoma Virus *src* Protein Is a Member of a Protein Kinase Cascade," *Cell,* 25, 9–21, July 1981.

11. William J. Broad, "Fraud and the Structure of Science," *Science,* 212, 137–141, 1981.

12. Leroy Wolins, "Responsibility for Raw Data," *American Psychologist,* 17, 657–658, 1962.

13. James R. Craig and Sandra C. Reese, "Retention of Raw Data: A Problem Revisited," *American Psychologist,* 28, 723, 1973.

14. Jonathan R. Cole and Stephen Cole, "The Ortega Hypothesis," *Science,* 178, 368–375, 1972.

15. Franz Samelson, "J. B. Watson's Little Albert, Cyril Burt's Twins, and the Need for a Critical Science," *American Psychologist,* 35, 619–625, July 1980.

16. Nicholas Wade, "Physicians Who Falsify Drug Data," *Science,* 180, 1038, 1973.

17. *Pharmaceutical Manufacturers Association Newsletter,* June 1, 1981, p. 4.

18. Constance Holden, "FDA Tells Senators of Doctors Who Fake Data in Clinical Drug Trials," *Science,* 206, 432–433, 1979.

19. R. Jeffrey Smith, "Creative Penmanship in Animal Testing Prompts FDA Controls," *Science,* 198, 1227–1229, 1977.

20. Joann S. Lublin, "A Lab's Troubles Raise Doubts About the Quality of Drug Tests in U.S.," *The Wall Street Journal,* February 21, 1978.

21. Hank Klibanoff, "A Major Lab Faces Big Test of Its Own," *Boston Globe,* May 11, 1981; "U.S. Charging 4 Falsified Reports on

Drugs in Lab," *The New York Times*, June 23, 1981. The case had not come to trial at the time this book went to press.

22. Linda Garmon, "Since the Giant Fell," *Science News*, July 4, 1981, p. 11.

23. Smith, *op. cit.*

24. Howie Kurtz, "Agencies Re-examining Hundreds of Products," *Washington Star*, July 5, 1981.

25. Joann S. Lublin, "FDA Is Tightening Control over Drug Studies on Indications Some Doctors Have Faked Them," *The Wall Street Journal*, May 15, 1980.

26. John Ziman, "Some Pathologies of the Scientific Life," *Nature*, 227, 996, 1970.

27. Quoted in Joseph Hixson, *The Patchwork Mouse* (Doubleday, New York, 1976), p. 147.

28. Susan Lawrence, "Watching the Watchers," *Science News*, 119, 331–333, 1981.

29. William Broad, "Harvard Delays in Reporting Fraud," *Science*, 215, 478–482, 1982.

30. Theodore Xenophon Barber, *Pitfalls in Human Research* (Pergamon Press, New York, 1973), p. 45.

31. Stephen J. Gould, "Morton's Ranking of Races by Cranial Capacity," *Science*, 200, 503–509, 1978.

32. Ian St. James-Roberts, "Are Researchers Trustworthy?" *New Scientist*, 71, 481–483, 1976.

33. Ian St. James-Roberts, "Cheating in Science," *New Scientist*, 72, 466–469, 1976.

34. R. V. Hughson and P. M. Cohn, "Ethics," *Chemical Engineering*, September 22, 1980.

35. Deena Weinstein, "Fraud in Science," *Social Science Quarterly*, 59, 639–652, 1979.

CHAPTER 5
POWER OF THE ELITE

1. Robert Merton, "The Normative Structure of Science," in *The Sociology of Science*, Norman W. Storer, ed. (University of Chicago Press, 1973), pp. 267–280.

2. Parts of the episode concerning John Long originally appeared in Nicholas Wade, "A Diversion of the Quest for Truth," *Science*, 211, 1022–1025, 1981, © 1981, American Association for the Advancement of Science.

3. John C. Long, Ann M. Dvorak, Steven C. Quay, Cathryn Stamatos, and Shu-Yuan Chi, "Reaction of Immune Complexes with Hodgkin's Disease Tissue Cultures: Radioimmune Assay and Immunoferritin Electron Microscopy," *Journal of the National Cancer Institute*, 62, 787–795, 1979.

4. Nancy Harris, David L. Gang, Steven C. Quay, Sibrand Poppema, Paul C. Zamecnik, Walter A. Nelson-Rees, and Stephen J. O'Brien, "Contamination of Hodgkin's Disease Cell Cultures," *Nature*, 289, 228–230, 1981.

5. Paul C. Zamecnik and John C. Long, "Growth of Cultured Cells from Patients with Hodgkin's Disease and Transplantation into *Nude* Mice," *Proceedings of the National Academy of Sciences*, 74, 754–758, 1977.

6. Letter from Ronald W. Lamont-Havers, Director for Research Administration, Massachusetts General Hospital, to Ronald Lieberman, National Cancer Institute, May 5, 1980.

7. Zamecnik and Long, *op. cit.*

8. John C. Long, Paul C. Zamecnik, Alan C. Aisenberg, and Leonard Atkins, "Tissue Culture Studies in Hodgkin's Disease," *Journal of Experimental Medicine*, 145, 1484–1500, 1977.

9. *Fraud in Biomedical Research*. Hearings before the Subcommittee on Investigations and Oversight of the Committee on Science and Technology, U.S. House of Representatives, Ninety-Seventh Congress, March 31–April 1, 1981 (U.S. Government Printing Office, No. 77-661, Washington, 1981), pp. 65–66.

10. Robert H. Ebert, "A Fierce Race Called Medical Education," *The New York Times*, July 9, 1980.

11. Isabel R. Plesset, *Noguchi and His Patrons* (Fairleigh Dickinson University Press, Rutherford, N.J., 1980).

12. Hugh H. Smith, "A Microbiologist Once Famous," *Science* 212, 434–435, 1981.

13. Jonathan R. Cole and Stephen Cole, "The Ortega Hypothesis," *Science*, 178, 368–374, 1972.

14. Robert Merton, "The Matthew Effect in Science," in *The Sociology of Science*, Norman W. Storer, ed. (University of Chicago Press, 1973), pp. 439–459.

15. Stephen Cole, Leonard Rubin, and Jonathan R. Cole, "Peer Review and the Support of Science," *Scientific American*, 237, 34–41, 1977.

16. Stephen Cole, Jonathan R. Cole, and Gary A. Simon, "Chance and Consensus in Peer Review," *Science*, 214, 881–886, 1981.

17. Quoted in Bernard Barber, "Resistance by Scientists to Scientific Discovery," *Science*, 134, 596–602, 1961.
18. *Ibid.*
19. Robert K. Merton and Harriet Zuckerman, "Institutionalized Patterns of Evaluation in Science," in *The Sociology of Science,* Norman W. Storer, ed. (University of Chicago Press, 1973), pp. 460–496.
20. Douglas P. Peters and Stephen J. Ceci, "A Manuscript Masquerade," *The Sciences*, September 1980, 16–19, 35.
21. Michael J. Mahoney, "Publication Prejudices: An Experimental Study of Confirmatory Bias in the Peer Review System," *Cognitive Therapy and Research*, 1, 161–175, 1977.
22. P. G. Pande, R. R. Shukla, and P. C. Sekariah, "Toxoplasma from the Eggs of the Domestic Fowl (Gallus gallus)," *Science*, 133, 648, 1961.
23. Editorial board of *Science*, "An Unfortunate Event," *Science*, 134, 945–946, 1961.
24. Joseph Hanlon, "Top Food Scientist Published False Data," *New Scientist*, November 7, 1974, pp. 436–437.
25. Michael T. Kaufman, "India Stepping Up Money for Science," *The New York Times*, January 17, 1982.

CHAPTER 6
SELF-DECEPTION AND GULLIBILITY

1. It is interesting to note that historians espousing the conventional ideology of science have tried to save appearances by assuming that Hooke and Flamsteed were observing another phenomenon, known as stellar aberration, which they innocently mistook for the stellar parallax. This explanation will not wash. Stellar aberration is an apparent displacement similar to which a raindrop seen from a moving car seems to fall slantwise instead of straight down. It was discovered in 1725 by James Bradley in the very course of trying to repeat Hooke's observation of the stellar parallax. Bradley himself specifically stated that Hooke's data could not be measurements of stellar aberration. Hooke's observations were "really very far from being either exact or agreeable to the phenomena," Bradley reported. "It seems that Hooke found what he expected to find," notes Norriss Hetherington of the University of California, Berkeley, in an account of this episode ("Ques-

tions About the Purported Objectivity of Science," unpublished MS).

2. Robert Rosenthal, *Experimenter Effects in Behavioral Research* (Appleton-Century-Crofts, New York, 1966), pp. 158–179.

3. *Ibid.*, pp. 411–413.

4. Jean Umiker-Sebeok and Thomas A. Sebeok, "Clever Hans and Smart Simians," *Anthropos*, 76, 89–166, 1981.

5. Nicholas Wade, "Does Man Alone Have Language? Apes Reply in Riddles, and a Horse Says Neigh," *Science*, 208, 1349–1351, 1980.

6. Mary Jo Nye, "N-rays: An Episode in the History and Psychology of Science," *Historical Studies in the Physical Sciences*, 11:1, 125–156, 1980.

7. Jean Rostand, *Error and Deception in Science* (Basic Books, New York, 1960), p. 28.

8. Nye, *op. cit.*, p. 155.

9. Rosenthal, *op. cit.*, pp. 3–26.

10. Theodore Xenophon Barber, *Pitfalls in Human Research* (Pergamon Press, New York, 1973), p. 88.

11. Richard Berendzen and Carol Shamieh, "Maanen, Adriann van," *Dictionary of Scientific Biography* (Charles Scribner's Sons, New York, 1973), pp. 582–583.

12. Norriss S. Hetherington, "Questions About the Purported Objectivity of Science," unpublished MS.

13. Melvin E. Jahn and Daniel J. Woolf, *The Lying Stones of Dr. Johann Bartholomew Adam Beringer* (University of California Press, Berkeley, 1963).

14. *Ibid.*

15. Charles Babbage, *Reflections on the Decline of Science in England* (Augustus M. Kelley, New York, 1970).

16. Edward Anders *et al.*, "Contaminated Meteorite," *Science*, 146, 1157–1161, 1964.

17. J. S. Weiner, *The Piltdown Forgery* (Oxford University Press, London, 1955).

18. Charles Dawson and Arthur Smith Woodward, "On a Bone Implement from Piltdown," *Quarterly Journal of the Geological Society*, 71, 144–149, 1915.

19. L. Harrison Matthews, "Piltdown Man: The Missing Links," *New Scientist*, a ten-part series, beginning April 30, 1981, pp. 280–282.

20. Quoted in Stephen J. Gould, *The Panda's Thumb* (W. W. Norton, New York, 1980), p. 112.

21. J. B. Rhine, "Security Versus Deception in Parapsychology," *Journal of Parapyschology*, 38, 99–121, 1974.
22. J. B. Rhine, "A New Case of Experimenter Unreliability," *Journal of Parapsychology*, 38, 215–225, 1974.
23. Russell Targ and Harold Puthoff, "Information Transmission Under Conditions of Sensory Shielding," *Nature*, 251, 602–607, 1974.
24. Martin Gardner, "Magic and Paraphysics," *Technology Review*, June 1976, pp. 43–51.
25. Umiker-Sebeok and Sebeok, *op. cit.*
26. Cullen Murphy, "Shreds of Evidence," *Harper's*, November 1981, pp. 42–65.
27. Walter C. McCrone, "Microscopical Study of the Turin 'Shroud,' " *The Microscope*, 29, 1, 1981.

CHAPTER 7
THE MYTH OF LOGIC

1. Thomas S. Kuhn, *The Structure of Scientific Revolutions*, 2nd ed. (University of Chicago Press, 1970).
2. *Ibid.* Parts of this account of Kuhn's work are taken from Nicholas Wade, "Thomas S. Kuhn: Revolutionary Theorist of Science," *Science*, 197, 143–45, © 1977, American Association for the Advancement of Science.
3. Paul Feyerabend, *Against Method* (Verso, London, 1975; distributed in U.S. by Schocken Books, New York).
4. Bernard Barber, "Resistance by Scientists to Scientific Discovery," *Science*, 134, 596–602, 1961.
5. Quoted in Barber, *ibid.*
6. Max Planck, *The Philosophy of Physics* (George Allen & Unwin, London, 1936), p. 90.
7. Frank G. Slaughter, *Immortal Magyar* (Collier, New York, 1950).
8. Michael Polanyi, *Personal Knowledge* (University of Chicago Press, 1958), p. 13.
9. Stephen G. Brush, "Should the History of Science Be Rated X?" *Science*, 183, 1164–1172, 1974.

CHAPTER 8
MASTERS AND APPRENTICES

1. Parts of this episode originally appeared in Nicholas Wade, "Discovery of Pulsars: A Graduate Student's Story," *Science*, 189,

358–364, © 1975, American Association for the Advancement of Science.

Although the breakdown of the relationship between master and apprentice has recently accelerated, the roots of the problem are old. The case of Robert A. Millikan, recounted in Chapter 2 as an example of data selection, also illustrates the rush for credit by a superior. Millikan was assisted by a graduate student named Harvey Fletcher, who suggested to Millikan the idea of using oil drops instead of the fast-evaporating water drops. He also built equipment to help perform many of the critical experiments. Fletcher wrote the majority of the pivotal paper of 1910 which helped Millikan win the Nobel prize, and he fully expected to be a coauthor. But Millikan took all the credit for himself. For an account of the appropriation, see Harvey Fletcher, "My Work with Millikan on the Oil-Drop Experiment," *Physics Today,* 35, 43–47, 1982.

2. Julius A. Roth, "Hired Hand Research," *The American Sociologist,* August 1966, pp. 190–196.

3. Mike Muller, "Why Scientists Don't Cheat," *New Scientist,* June 2, 1977, pp. 522–523.

4. Robert J. Gullis, "Statement," *Nature,* 265, 764, 1977.

5. *Ibid.* Also see Charles E. Rowe, "Net Activity of Phospholipase A2 in Brain and the Lack of Stimulation of the Phospholipase A2-Acylation System," *Biochemical Journal,* 164, 287–288, 1977.

6. Eugene Garfield, "The 1000 Contemporary Scientists Most-Cited 1965–1978," *Current Contents,* No. 41, October 12, 1981, pp. 5–14.

7. Barbara J. Culliton, "The Sloan-Kettering Affair: A Story Without a Hero," *Science,* 184, 644–650, 1974; and "The Sloan-Kettering Affair (II): An Uneasy Resolution," *Science,* 184, 1154–1157, 1974.

8. Peter B. Medawar, "The Strange Case of the Spotted Mice," *The New York Review of Books,* April 15, 1976, p. 8. For an overview of the Summerlin case, see also Joseph Hixson, *The Patchwork Mouse* (New York: Doubleday, 1976).

9. Lois Wingerson, "William Summerlin: Was He Right All Along?" *New Scientist,* February 26, 1981, pp. 527–529.

10. This particular passage can be found in June Goodfield, *Cancer Under Siege* (Hutchinson, London, 1975), p. 232.

11. Culliton, *op. cit.,* p. 1155.

12. William J. Broad, "Harvard Delays in Reporting Fraud," *Science,* 215, 478–482, 1982.

13. William J. Broad, "Report Absolves Harvard in Case of Fakery," *Science*, 215, 874–876, 1982.
14. Nils J. Bruzelius and Stephen A. Kurkjian, "Cancer Research Data Falsified; Boston Project Collapses," *Boston Globe*, five-part series starting June 29, 1980, p. 1.
15. For an overall view of Straus's first public defense see William J. Broad, ". . . But Straus Defends Himself in Boston," *Science*, 212, 1367–1369, 1981. For this particular quote see "Team Research: Responsibility at the Top," *Science*, 213, 114–115, 1981.

CHAPTER 9
IMMUNITY FROM SCRUTINY

1. Parts of this account are taken from William J. Broad, "Imbroglio at Yale (I): Emergence of a Fraud," *Science*, 210, 38–41, 1980; "Imbroglio at Yale (II): A Top Job Lost," *Science*, 210, 171–173, © 1980, American Association for the Advancement of Science.
2. Helena Wachslicht-Rodbard *et al.*, "Increased Insulin Binding to Erythrocytes in Anorexia Nervosa," *New England Journal of Medicine*, 300, 882–887, 1979.
3. Helena Wachslicht-Rodbard, letter to Robert W. Berliner, Dean, Yale University School of Medicine, March 27, 1979, p. 2.
4. *Fraud in Biomedical Research.* Hearings before the Subcommittee on Investigations and Oversight of the Committee on Science and Technology, U.S. House of Representatives, Ninety-Seventh Congress, March 31–April 1, 1981 (U.S. Government Printing Office, No. 77-661, Washington, 1981), p. 103.
5. Philip Felig, handwritten memo to Robert W. Berliner, Dean, Yale University School of Medicine, April 9, 1979.
6. Vijay R. Soman and Philip Felig, "Insulin Binding to Monocytes and Insulin Sensitivity in Anorexia Nervosa," *American Journal of Medicine*, 68, 66–72, 1980.
7. For these extended quotes see Morton Hunt, "A Fraud That Shook the World of Science," *The New York Times Magazine*, November 1, 1981, pp. 42–75, © 1981, The New York Times Company.
8. *Ibid.*, p. 58.

CHAPTER 10
RETREAT UNDER PRESSURE

1. I. P. Pavlov, "New Researches on Conditioned Reflexes," *Science*, 58, 359–361, 1923.
2. Gregory Razran, "Pavlov the Empiricist," *Science*, 130, 916–917, 1959.
3. G. K. Noble, "Kammerer's *Alytes*," *Nature*, 118, 209–210, 1926.
4. Paul Kammerer, "Paul Kammerer's Letter to the Moscow Academy," *Science*, 64, 493–494, 1926.
5. Arthur Koestler, *The Case of the Midwife Toad* (Hutchinson, London, 1971).
6. Lester R. Aronson, "The Case of *The Case of the Midwife Toad*," *Behavior Genetics*, 5, 115–125, 1975.
7. Alma Mahler Werfel, *And the Bridge Is Love* (Harcourt Brace, New York, 1958).
8. Richard B. Goldschmidt, "Research and Politics," *Science*, 109, 219–227, 1949.
9. Zhores A. Medvedev, *The Rise and Fall of T. D. Lysenko* (Columbia University Press, New York, 1969).
10. David Joravsky, *The Lysenko Affair* (Harvard University Press, Cambridge, 1970).
11. J. M. Ziman, "Some Pathologies of the Scientific Life," *Nature*, 227, 996–997, 1970.

CHAPTER 11
THE FAILURE OF OBJECTIVITY

1. Stephen J. Gould, "Morton's Ranking of Races by Cranial Capacity," *Science*, 200, 503–509, 1978.
2. Stephen J. Gould, *The Mismeasure of Man* (Norton, New York, 1981).
3. Allan Chase, *The Legacy of Malthus* (Knopf, New York, 1976).
4. Gould, *The Mismeasure of Man*.
5. Franz Samelson, "Putting Psychology on the Map," in *Psychology in Social Context*, Allan R. Buss, ed. (Irvington Publishers, New York, 1979), pp. 103–165.
6. Arthur R. Jensen, "Sir Cyril Burt," *Psychometrika*, 37, 115–117, 1972.

7. L. S. Hearnshaw, *Cyril Burt, Psychologist* (Hodder and Stoughton, London, 1979).
8. Cyril L. Burt, "Intelligence and Heredity: Some Common Misconceptions," *Irish Journal of Education*, 3, 75–94, 1969.
9. Arthur R. Jensen, "How Much Can We Boost IQ and Scholastic Achievement?" *Harvard Educational Review*, 39, 1–123, 1969.
10. Richard Herrnstein, "I.Q.," *The Atlantic*, September 1971, pp. 43–64.
11. Nicholas Wade, "IQ and Heredity: Suspicion of Fraud Beclouds Classic Experiment," *Science*, 194, 916–919, 1976.
12. Cyril L. Burt, "The Evidence of the Concept of Intelligence," *British Journal of Educational Psychology*, 25, 158–177, 1955.
13. Cyril L. Burt, "The Inheritance of Mental Ability," *American Psychologist*, 13, 1–15, 1958.
14. Cyril L. Burt, "The Genetic Determination of Differences in Intelligence: A Study of Monozygotic Twins Reared Together and Apart," *British Journal of Psychology*, 57, 137–153, 1966.
15. Leon J. Kamin, *The Science and Politics of I.Q.* (Lawrence Erlbaum, Potomac, Md., 1974).
16. Arthur R. Jensen, "Kinship Correlations Reported by Sir Cyril Burt," *Behavior Genetics*, 4, 1–28, 1974.
17. Oliver Gillie, "Crucial Data Was Faked by Eminent Psychologist," *Sunday Times* (London), October 24, 1976.
18. Wade, *op. cit.*
19. Hearnshaw, *Cyril Burt, Psychologist*.
20. Leslie S. Hearnshaw, "Balance Sheet on Burt," Supplement to the *Bulletin of the British Psychological Society*, 33, 1–8, 1980.
21. Hearnshaw, *Cyril Burt, Psychologist*.
22. Wade, *op. cit.*
23. Wade, *op. cit.*
24. Wade, *op. cit.*

INDEX